Run Your Own Mail Server

Michael W Lucas

Tilted Windmill Press

Copyright Information

Run Your Own
Mail Server

Michael W Lucas

Brief Contents

Complete Contents

Acknowledgements

Tech review and related commentary was kindly provided by Dale Carstensen, Tim Chase, Andrew Cornwall, Jonathon Fletcher, Scott Horton, Tom Hukins, Maurice Kaag, Georg Kilzer, Marek Krzywdziński, Ganael Laplanche, Greg "groggy" Lehey, John W. O'Brien, Mike O'Connor, Neil Roza, Paul Anthony Stanton, Grant Taylor, Arrigo Triulzi, and Mikaël Urankar. I thank you all for your support.

I must also thank Wietse Venema, author of Postfix, for kindly offering new information and correcting my misconceptions, daft mistakes, and notably boneheaded typos. (My brain knows the difference between DKIM and DMARC even if my fingers sometimes don't, I promise!)

A bunch of folks wanted this book to exist so much that they paid extra before the book even existed. You'll find a complete list of my sponsors at the end of the book.

My Patronizers support my work every month, even though I don't release a new book every month. Kate Ebneter, Stefan Johnson, Jeff Marracini, Maximilian Paul, and Phillip Vuchetich Patronize me so much, I must thank them in the print versions of everything I write. If you'd like to join them, check out https://patronizeMWL.com.

Finally, I want to thank this book's Kickstarter backers. You were amazing, and I hope you'll consider returning for the next book.

Thank you, everyone.

In memory of Craig Maloney.

For Liz

Chapter 0: Introduction

Email is the heart of the Internet. Online forums and social media and chat systems have blossomed and thrived with the web, but like dedicated Star Wars fans we keep returning to the classics. Email works everywhere with an Internet connection, and in many places without. Unlike chats, where the other people involved see that you've received their message and are choosing to ignore them, you answer email when you feel like it. Your correspondents don't get a notification that you're typing a reply and watch the screen until you compose words. Email is one of the few surviving asynchronous communication tools available on every platform.

The first email-like message was sent in 1965 at MIT, when the Internet was only a drunken dream of comp sci grad students. When those students finally connected two mainframes, they developed the primordial Internet protocols so the machines could communicate and a program called MAILBOX. Today's email looks nothing like theirs—for one, email addresses have those esoteric @ symbols in them rather than nice simple exclamation points. Modern email is built on the lessons learned from those early protocols, however. That's not bad—all broadly used protocols evolved the same way. Today, a handful of providers dominate email services. Companies like Google and Microsoft control most email addresses. They're an Email Empire, while those of us who run our own email systems are a ragtag gang struggling for independence.

It *can* be done. The protocols are comprehensible, the software freely available, the debugging tools adequate, and the hardware affordable.

The problem with running email has nothing to do with the technology. Once you know how, you can set up an email server by hand in minutes—or in seconds with automation. The problem is that the email server is only one part of running an email server.

Consider setting up your first web site from scratch. You install the software, start the daemon, and point your web browser at the host's IP address. You get the default page and a warm thrill of victory. You have a web server! If you put content on it, you can tell your colleagues "Hey, browse to 203.0.113.99 and you'll find my new web site!" You have made a Thing. Add an entry in the Domain Name Service (DNS) and you can offer folks a link like `http://mwl.io`. More testing and you add TLS, granting you the precious *S* in https. Step by step, you build a web site that complies with modern standards.[1]

Email isn't like that.

Running email in the real world is not a configuration problem. It is about citizenship. Once the Email Empire declares your server inadequate or untrustworthy, it's very hard to get them to change their mind. A spammer's mark is not an easy thing to live with. You must prepare to solidly participate in email society before sending your first message to the outside world. Sure, you can set up a couple of throwaway hosts on expendable domains and fling email exclusively between them to see how the software works, but if you want to run a real email server and you want other organizations to accept your email, you must quickly establish a good reputation. You can't get basic SMTP up and immediately start sending messages to accounts in the Email Empire; they'll declare you untrustworthy. It's only safe to send mail to those accounts once you have fully configured SPF, DKIM, and DMARC. While the Empire often claims it needs less than that, they also reject messages because "they feel like it."

Once you establish your system as a good citizen that follows standard practices, operating a mail server is comparatively low maintenance. Most of the time I spend on my email is spent applying security patches, same as any other Internet-facing application. Running a mail server for a large corporation is a full-time job, yes, but most of that is spent explaining to users that an error message

---

1   Hopefully you stop before you install WordPress and join the dark side. Unlike me.

of "The recipient's email account is over quota" means that the email bounced because the recipient hasn't cleaned out their inbox.

Run Your Own Mail Server uses common freely available software to illustrate the mechanics of email, but the book's main focus is on establishing that citizenship. You can use any software you like that fulfills the necessary roles. This book does not cover every possible use case across every platform. It focuses on what *everyone* must do to support a mail system that can function on the modern Internet. You will learn how the components work together, and be able to research and add less common features that you need.

Who Should Read This Book

Read this book if you want to run an email server for a small organization, for yourself and your friends, or just you. This book will not prepare you to run email for a global enterprise or a large mailing list, but it will provide a foundation for you to study those advanced cases.

Most people with the background necessary for running their own mail system have several domain names, one or two organizations that they'd like to help, and perhaps even a friend. This book is designed to let you support those folks in a scalable manner. The common sysadmin tendency to offer too much help, become overloaded, and implode is left for you to cope with.

Ethics of System Administration

I have firm memories of the first time I got root on a mail server, back when the 1.544Mb T1 was the pinnacle of connectivity and my 33.6K modem thrilled me. I thought, "I can't possibly view everybody's mail." I ran `more /var/mail/boss` and immediately recoiled, guts churning in horror of my appalling power.

Whoever controls a server can see all the information stored on that server. Every system administrator knows this, but in most cases extracting the information is too much trouble to bother. Maybe you're the database administrator for your organization's ecommerce system, but you're probably far more interested in how much space the database uses than who bought what.

Until you're not.

Unlike a database, examining email stored as text files is trivial. You don't even need SQL, only privilege and a pager.

When you run a service, the people who use that service are trusting you. System administrators have no formal professional code of ethics, but organizations and society have privacy standards. I am not a professional ethicist, nor do I have a degree in philosophy, but society's overwhelming consensus is that snooping is wrong. Most organizations consider privacy violations to be against their policies and will terminate you for it. Your spouse might terminate your relationship for it. Just as the folks in HR shouldn't dig into your personnel file to satisfy their puerile curiosity, you shouldn't dig into someone's email except in response to an actual issue.

Sometimes you must examine a user's email. A long time ago, at an employer far far away, I had to troubleshoot a corrupt mailbox. A sender had innocently attached a word processor document to a message, and something in that document confused the POP3 server. I had to examine the individual characters in the mailbox file to identify the problem, which meant reading the user's email. I asked the user for permission to examine their mail. They granted it. I saw parts of a legal document I had no business seeing, identified the issue, extracted the problem document from the mailbox, and restored service.[2]

Why is that different? Consent. If the user had refused permission I would have had to escalate to our boss and let him sort through the personnel and privacy issues.

While most of email's rough edges have been burnished off since, violating privacy during troubleshooting remains a real possibility. Test users, full-on testing environments, and program analyzers like dtrace(1) are inexpensive. Use them.

---

2   And, as a result of seeing that document, sent my resume to everyone I knew before the buyout was announced.

Why Bother?

If email is such a pain, why run it yourself?

Privacy, control, and education.

Service providers often scan email for advertising keywords or saleable personal data. While ad blockers keep the ads out of your eyeballs, they solve the problem at the wrong end. Yes, if you email someone with an Email Empire address the Empire adds your content to their records, but when you correspond with other outsiders they learn nothing. Email can be maliciously intercepted, but that interception takes work and, for the most part, service providers don't bother.

Privacy is especially important in business. A service provider might promise not to mine your company emails, but one of their sysadmins trying to fix your issues might have to examine your email. If your organization's privacy needs violating, it's better someone in your organization does it.

You control your own email. Many service providers offer fancy dashboards that let you add and delete users or set quotas, but when something goes sideways you're stuck working with their support department. Waiting for a tech to claim your trouble ticket is infuriating, especially when you want them to do something trivial like check the log. When you run your own email, you control the problem.

Perhaps the least valid but most important reason for many is pure "geek cred." We want to know how things work. Just as building your own firewall is a great way to learn about networking, running your own mail server is the best way to understand this ecosystem. You run your own web server, DNS, cloud storage and home automation, why not run your own email?

Prerequisites

This is a book for beginning email operators, but it's not a book for a beginner sysadmin. You must have certain skills before you can hope to run an email server. Experienced mail administrators can probably work around many of the requirements below, but beginners shouldn't make their education any more difficult than necessary.

You must have used email. I will not explain what email addresses and attachments are.

You must know how to manage your operating system. You need to back up your hosts, apply security updates, know the difference between network and local sockets, and in general make your hosts fit to sit on the naked Internet. This book assumes and recommends open-source software. I demonstrate everything with Postfix running on FreeBSD or Debian Linux. I list all my configuration files and directories under `/etc`. That might not reflect your operating system's defaults. If I say `/etc/redis.conf`, you need to figure out that your operating system uses `/etc/redis/redis.conf` or `/usr/local/etc/redis.conf` or whatever. I provide the context for all my configuration choices so you can make your own decisions on any Unix-like platform or even your preferred mail server.

A mail system is not a single application. It is a system of interlocking applications. Every time you change anything, you must verify that the new part works and that you didn't break the rest of the system. If you're not comfortable double-checking your work and testing each stage of a deployment, become comfortable.

You need at least two test hosts attached to the Internet. Yes, hosts can often send mail to accounts on the local host, but that's worked fine for decades without trouble. These could be virtual machines out in the cloud, hosts in your lab, or whatever. Tests inflict negligible hardware load. These hosts need different static IP addresses. You must also control the world's access to those addresses, as email requires opening several TCP/IP ports to and from the hosts. Most home Internet providers specifically block these ports.

Those hosts should be in different domains. Yes, you could send email between `newyork.solveamurder.org` and `detroit.solveamurder.org`, but your brain absorbs better patterns if you test between wholly unrelated domains like `solveamurder.org` and `ratoperatedvehicle.com`. Domains are inexpensive these days. Get two—or set up private DNS and test between `example.org` and `private.test`.[3]

You must understand basic DNS, and control the forward *and reverse* DNS for your test hosts. Supporting email for a domain requires creating and maintaining several DNS entries in that domain. Similarly, the reverse DNS must match the hostname and the forward DNS. If your host advertises its name as `mail.solveamurder.org`, but reverse DNS identifies your host as `customer87.chicago.bighosting.com`, your email will go nowhere. When a client looks up the hostname for your IP address, they'll then check that the forward DNS points to that IP. Any extra hostnames tied to that address are ignored. Yes, a hostname can resolve to several IP addresses, but those IPs must all have reverse DNS that matches the mail server's hostname.

Be leery of hosting providers that offer limited web interfaces for DNS management. Many of these interfaces limit what sorts of records you can create, or do not permit enough characters for SPF or DKIM records. Before attempting to deploy email, verify that nobody else has trouble entering DKIM or SPF records into your provider's systems.

Follow best practices and have separate authoritative and recursive nameservers. The recursive nameservers should validate DNSSEC.

For testing you will need an email account from a provider that validates and provides SPF, DKIM, and DMARC. An account from Google or Microsoft works, as do those from many other providers.

---

3   It is the third decade of the twenty-first century, and petrified pettiness means we *still* have no standards defining specific domains for internal-only use.

Be familiar with CIDR (slash) notation for IP networks. Software increasingly expects to see `192.0.2.128/25` rather than `192.0.2.128 255.255.255.128`.

Familiarity with basic public key cryptography is also essential. You don't need to grind through Diffie-Hellman calculations on your abacus, but you must know the difference between public and private keys. You must routinely protect private keys. Similarly, you need a basic understanding of TLS. Many programs still use the acronym SSL, but you should know that the last version of SSL was deprecated in 2015. Transport Layer Security (TLS) has been the standard for a quarter century. Users must authenticate to check their email, and sending usernames and passwords across the Internet without TLS is unwise. If you still confuse SSL and TLS, don't feel too bad. Much of the software we'll use does the same.

You must be comfortable managing TLS and the associated X.509 certificates. Email did not always require TLS, but certificate prices have plunged to zero so TLS is fairly standard. This book uses Let's Encrypt certificates maintained by ACME, and presumes you can do the same. If your organization insists on purchasing expensive certificates and maintaining them by hand, you are welcome to do so.

We will also use outside services to support email troubleshooting. These are all services that can be replaced if you write custom code, a skill set that does not overlap with running mail servers. I'm certain that immediately after this book escapes someone will release a package that lets us easily handle said debugging.

If you lack any of these skills, permit me to recommend my books *Absolute FreeBSD, 3rd Edition* (No Starch Press, 2018), *Networking for System Administrators* (Tilted Windmill Press, 2015), and *TLS Mastery* (Tilted Windmill Press, 2021). I also recommend

Cricket Liu's *DNS and BIND* (O'Reilly, 2006)[4] and, once you've finished that, my own *DNSSEC Mastery, 2nd Edition* (2022).

From now on, I will toss around terms like *network port* and *X.509 certificate* and *floccinaucinihilipilification* and expect you to either know what they mean or how to look them up. You cannot suffer from hippopotomonstrosesquippedaliophobia and run an email server.

Email Tools In This Book

Email isn't a server, it's a system with several components. The most obvious is a "mail server." The mail server is a host that accepts email from users and exchanges mail with other servers. Most of the system speaks the *Simple Mail Transport Protocol* (SMTP). This book uses Postfix (https://www.postfix.org) as a reference platform.

Your users would probably like an option to check their email from their desktop. This might use a mail client like Thunderbird, using a protocol like IMAP. We'll use Dovecot (`https://www.dovecot.org/`) for clients and IMAP. Other users prefer a web interface, so we'll discuss Roundcube (`https://roundcube.net/`). We'll debug with mutt (`https://www.mutt.org`).

Once you have the core system working and can send email locally, you'll need basic antispam protections. We'll discuss greylisting, nolisting, DNSBLs, and rspamd (`https://rspamd.com/`).

With these in place, you can risk telling the world about your mail system via DNS. This routes us into topics like MX records, Sender Policy Framework (SPF), and DomainKeys Identified Mail (DKIM). With those basics you can consider acronyms like DMARC, MTA-STS, and TLS-RPT. The main goal of this book is to teach you about these tools and protocols so that you can improve deliverability of your email.

---

4   While I have written books on TLS, DNSSEC, and OpenPGP, as well as the infamous *Networknomicon*, I retain enough sanity and self-respect to *not* write a core DNS book.

We will focus on modern email. While some networks still rely on UUCP and bangpaths and POP3, those are vanishingly rare. Don't deploy them on the modern Internet.[5] Some users still like POP3, but even in the 1990s we knew it needed replacing and development on POP4 stopped in 2004 when the superior IMAP took over so don't permit anyone to persuade you to deploy it no matter how many e's they stick in *neeeed*. We will also ignore proprietary replacements for these protocols. Many mail service providers offer a convenient API that replaces SMTP or IMAP. There's nothing wrong with these if you're willing to accept complete vendor lock-in.

Today, we use the term *allow list* for entities that are permitted to skip a layer of protections, and *block list* for entities that are categorically refused. Many older programs, and some software developed by non-native English speakers, still use the older *black list* and *white list*. This book uses modern language except when configuring those programs. Do please encourage your favorite developers to update their language to the 21ˢᵗ century.

Spam

Unsolicited advertising is the scourge of email. While you'll hear it called things like *unsolicited commercial email* (UCE) or *junk*, the most common technical term is "spam" because the Internet was built to a Monty Python soundtrack. It's so pervasive that legitimate mail is called "ham."

For about thirty years, people considered email a miracle. You could write a message at your desk and hours or even minutes later it would reach the other side of the planet. The early Internet was populated by computer science university students, select computer-related companies, and the US military. Blissfully free of broader commercial interests, SMTP was designed for that open network. Sysadmins ran *open relays* that allowed anyone to send mail through

---

5   Unless your network involves phrases like "UDP over carrier pachyderm," "we get phone service every two-and-a-half Sundays," or "Callisto Colony One." Then you do what you must.

them, for the convenience of other sysadmins who suffered outages. Everyone worked together to sustain the miracle, with little concern about abuse.

In 1978 Gary Thuerk, a salesman for the Digital Equipment Corporation, emailed several hundred people he didn't know an invitation to a demonstration of the new DEC packet-switching systems. Nobody had ever tried commercial advertising over email. Reactions were overwhelmingly negative, but reasoned. The broader community agreed that commercial advertisements were unacceptable. Five days after the message went out the chief of the US Air Force's ARPAnet Management Branch, Major Raymond Czahor, called Thuerk's boss to tell them to *never* do it again on pain of disconnection.

This first advertising email also sold twelve million dollars of computers.

Thuerk's email established the "do not advertise in email" precedent. It also established the "random email marketing is highly profitable" precedent. Going forward, the network relied on the social contract and fierce Air Force Majors to prevent junk mail. Email protocols remained unchanged.

In 1990, UUnet started building its own commercial IP network. UUnet's AlterNet could communicate with the Internet, but was not bound by government rules. While individuals that run businesses might be fine, most corporations are indifferent to feeble social contracts and do not answer to the military.

The first spam soiled Usenet in April 1994, and spam email followed immediately afterwards. It hit like an unexpected toxic spill at the kindergarten playground. Mail administrators panicked, implemented short-term fixes, and quickly learned that a protocol optimized for deliverability was unable to stop delivering. Sysadmins blocked junk mail domains, so mailers forged their originating domain. Blocking spammers' networks led the spammers to relay their junk through well-meaning third parties or hacking into unrelated but unpatched mail servers. Despite spending time and money abusing the protocol, spammers profited. Today, viruses and worms compromise machines to transform them into *spambots* that spew junk mail as fast as they can.

Unchecked spam makes email useless. Almost every change in SMTP in the last thirty years has been propelled by the need to eliminate spam while retaining broad interoperability.

Opt-in email marketing is fine. If you want your favorite creator to tell you when their next big thing escapes, great! You should get those emails until you opt out. I run a mailing list for exactly that. I live and work in Detroit, though, and the dude that keeps trying to sell me courses on South African taxation law can take a long walk out of a short airlock.

Some mail is definitely spam: some is definitely legit: but some is fuzzy. Many spam detection systems work by building a spam *score*, indicating the likelihood that a piece of email is spam. Higher scores are bad. We'll consider this in Chapter 14, but for now just know that software can increase or decrease a message's spam score.

Spam evolves, and the spam you receive will be different than what your neighbor gets. One of the advantasges of running your own mail system is that you can train your spam identification system to recognize the precise flavor of spam you receive. The disadvantage is that training your spam system requires a collection of the precise flavor of spam you receive. You probably delete your spam unread after a few days. Stop doing that. Curate a collection of your personal trash. According to rspamd's documentation, training the spam parser takes at least two hundred spam messages.

If you wonder why email-related software works as it does, or why we have all these add-on protocols, the answer is almost certainly "spam."

While spam is bad, some responses to spam are worse. Do not generate automated responses to spam; such *backscatter* is mostly undeliverable and creates more work for other mail operators. Creating work for other mail operators is a great way to get your host on block lists.

Today, messages that are clearly spam or ham are not the problem. We know to block emails from ice planet princes trying to move millions of Imperial credits off-planet. We know medical appointment confirmation messages must go to our users. People have their own opinions on what they want to receive, though. Many messages fall into a gap where some users declare them legitimate, but others insist they are spam. No matter how your system flags them, someone will complain. Every user you add to your system accentuates this problem.

There is a difference between "unsolicited but legitimate" messages and spam, but many people believe that all unwanted email should go into the spam folder. The user interface on big mail systems encourages this—yes, there's a block button, and an unsubscribe link, but the prominent *Spam* button means most folks look no further. Some of these systems even walk you through unsubscribing, then offer to file the offending message as spam. If enough Gmail or Microsoft users flag your legitimate messages as "spam," their algorithms decide that your domain sends low quality messages that should always go straight into the spam bucket. Some people who signed up for mailing lists and later want to unsubscribe do so by routing the messages to the spam folder. Bloggers cold-mailing possible sources often suffer from this, as do legitimate debt collectors.

I find myself wanting to do the same. I need the business notices Stripe and PayPal send me, but they use our business relationship to legally stuff advertisements for their loans into my inbox. Before approaching PayPal for a business loan, I would go to the alley by the lead paint factory's toxic waste heap and apply at Larry Leg-Breaker's Betting Parlor and Emergency Financial Services. As much as I loathe those announcements, if I start teaching my spam filter that messages from PayPal and Stripe are spam, it will probably misfile critical emails. I must write more selective filter rules.

Someone else would consider those offers not spam.

Deliverability

Your users expect their email to reach the intended recipient. *Deliverability* is how well mail to and from your system fulfills this expectation. Before spam, deliverability wasn't a huge issue. In the 1970s and early 1980s you might have to route your email through U of C Berkeley to MIT to the Imperial College of London to TAMK via overloaded phone lines, but it was a well-understood problem. The decade of 1983 to 1993, after the standardization of the Simple Mail Transfer Protocol but before spam, was a golden age of email connectivity.

If mail from your server resembles spam, the destination server will discard it. Your email is not *deliverable.* As all mail systems have different spam-identification systems configured in different ways, deliverability varies by destination. The goal of this book is to help you make your email as deliverable as possible by configuring protocols that allow recipients to verify your mail's authenticity.

In some ways, high deliverability is easier when you're running a small mail server. Google has requirements for sending them mail, but those requirements become more stringent with the amount of mail you send. In 2024 they imposed additional requirements on hosts that send them over 5,000 emails per day. That was my warning to start looking at those requirements, because over the next few years they will push those requirements down to smaller and smaller servers. People will spend those years developing compliance tools. You can contribute to developing those solutions or, worst case, benefit from them. Running a medium-sized server that supports hundreds or thousands of users will trip those limits far sooner, and you will have fewer tools available.

The greatest risk to deliverability is your users. You can configure DKIM, SPF, and DMARC. You can send strictly non-commercial messages only to contacts expecting to hear from you. You can achieve technological perfection in antispam deployment, and you will not overcome the human problem.

The spam folder is not like any other folder: it is an algorithmic pit. Once a message is flung down the pit, climbing out is hard. If enough recipients toss your messages into the pit, they will drag your domain with it. The best way to keep people from flinging your messages into the spam pit is to send messages that people want to read. If enough people haul your messages out of the spam pit, the algorithm can be reversed—but that's much harder than not falling into the pit.

The algorithms also watch how you behave. If a host normally emits a roughly consistent amount of email over months and months, but suddenly launches a flood of emails, everyone gets suspicious. I have outsourced my new book announcement list for that reason. If my quiet server that only sends a few dozen emails a day suddenly spews thousands of emails, big provider algorithms will declare those messages suspect. Deliverability will be better if those messages come from a server that is known to host legitimately managed mailing lists.

Sending *only* mail that people want to receive is a key component of avoiding the spam pit.

Even with every defensive and authenticity protocol configured properly, you can still trash your deliverability by sending spam. Worse, other spam senders can trash your deliverability before you start.

IP Addresses and Email

"I need full control of a test machine on the public Internet? I'll go to my favorite provider and spin up a VM!"

Not so fast.

In the email ecosystem, IP addresses have reputations. Anyone with an email address and a credit card can create a virtual machine in moments. Spammers have no problem setting up a cheap VM and spewing garbage into everyone's inbox, incidentally soiling the reputation of their rented IP address. Hosting companies that provide easy automation of fully configured servers are especially vulnerable. While spewing spam violates every hosting company's Terms of Service, spammers don't care.

One of the tools mail administrators use to block spam is filtering network addresses of known spammers. Hosting provider IP addresses have almost certainly been used before. If a spammer previously soiled your address, it's probably on one or more *block lists* of known bad addresses (Chapter 8). Almost every mail system uses at least one block list to stop attacks. Emails from soiled IP addresses are broadly undeliverable before you start.

With automation, a spammer can send millions of emails before the provider's Network Operations Center can shut them down. The provider will receive dozens or hundreds of complaints within minutes of this flood beginning and will quickly shut down spammers. Many providers send their customer IP addresses to block list maintainers, steering their customers to their mail exchanger or to commercial mail servers instead. You cannot successfully host mail servers on these providers. Large hosting providers like Amazon, Microsoft, and Oracle often impose restrictions on mail servers.

Other providers have terms of service that declare that spam is not allowed, but do not enforce them. Block list maintainers quickly identify the entire range of IP addresses assigned to these providers and add them to their lists. No matter how much you intend to be a good citizen, any email server on these providers will have poor deliverability.

The best hosting providers for mail servers block email's network ports by default, and only open those ports by request. They might require you to have an account for 30 days before they will open the port. Spammers have no patience. You must.

Before choosing a hosting provider for your email systems, ask around to see if other people run email servers on that provider and if that email is broadly deliverable. If you have no contacts who run mail servers, go ahead and try on your favorite provider—but be prepared to move. I will not offer recommendations, as every time I recommend a company they implode, explode, or get bought immediately after publication.[6]

---

6   Correlation is not causation, but after all these books I can't help noticing the pattern.

Perhaps your organization has IP addresses issued by an ISP, or owns its own addresses. A previous owner could have soiled those addresses. Also, some Internet Service Providers block outgoing email at their network border. Check these before starting.

If your addresses have never been used for email, they have no reputation. "No reputation" does not mean that they are trusted, merely that they are not untrusted. You get to make your own reputation. This book will help you do it well. No matter what, some sites will not accept mail from domains less than 30 days old.

If you have no control over your test system's IP address, you can still educate yourself but remember that your tests will be limited in scope. Check your IPv4 and IPv6 addresses against one of the many anti-spam block list testers. Commercial sites like `mxtoolbox.com` offer free block list testers as part of their efforts to persuade you to outsource your email. Chapter 9 discusses attempting to get your address off block lists.

Email Components

If you're accustomed to web-based email, you've probably picked up a sense of how mail works. When you send an email your web browser talks to the mail server. That mail server talks to the recipient's mail server. When the human wants to read the email, they open their browser and see it.

If you use a desktop email client you know it's a little more complex. You compose a message on the client and send it to your mail server. Your mail server sends the message to the recipient's server. When the recipient opens their email client, the client downloads the email.

That's a shallow view. Actual computer scientists designed email, and email systems have an actual architecture as documented in RFC 5598. Every email you send flows through the system. Here's a slightly less shallow view. Any given system might have special configuration to override any part of this.

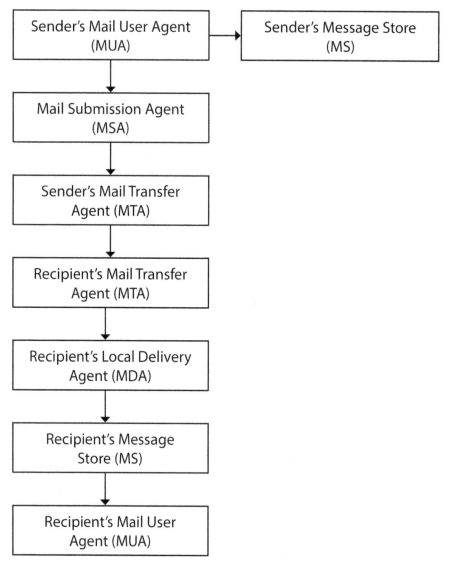

Figure 1-1: message flow through email

Any email user interface is called the *Mail User Agent* (MUA). The MUA is most often called the *mail client*. It might be Thunderbird, a web page, or part of an office suite. You can even use a program like netcat to manually send mail to the server. (There are also command-line clients that you can run on the mail server itself, like mutt. They unfairly leverage their location to skip the next step, so let's ignore them for now.) When you send the email, the MUA transmits it to the Mail Submission Agent. This is usually done via SMTP, but Microsoft uses *Messaging Application Programming Interface* (MAPI) and other vendors might have their own special tools. Usually, but not always, the client copies the message to the Message Store.

The *Message Store* (MS) is the server's copy of the user's emails. Most Message Stores retain a copy of both the incoming and outgoing messages until the user deletes them. Most mail clients use the *Internet Message Access Protocol* (IMAP) or the older *Post Office Protocol* (POP3) to synchronize their messages with the server. Microsoft uses MAPI and ActiveSync instead. On Unix systems the Message Store is often in the user's home directory, something like `/home/mwl/Mail` or `/home/mwl/Maildir/`.

The *Mail Submission Agent* (MSA) runs on a server. It accepts mail from mail clients and sends it to the Mail Transfer Agent. The MSA communicates with SMTP.

The *Mail Transfer Agent* (MTA) receives emails from the Mail Submission Agent and other Mail Transfer Agents. You might hear the MTA called a *mail exchanger* or an *MX*. If the MTA can immediately deliver the message, such as for a local account, it does so. Otherwise, the MTA stores new messages in a *mail spool* or *mail queue*. The MTA works through the queue, attempting to identify the recipient of each message.

If the message is addressed to a foreign network, the MTA checks DNS to identify the remote network's MTA and contacts it. The two servers have a dialog over SMTP that boils down to "Hi, I have an email for one of your users." "Yes, that's my user, please send the mail." You might have email service providers, antispam or antivirus vendors, or other third parties inserted here.

If the MTA determines that a message is addressed to a local user it forwards the message to the *Local Delivery Agent* (LDA). The standards call this the *Message Delivery Agent* (MDA), but LDA has become the accepted term. The LDA accepts the message and stores it in the user's mailbox. The LDA also handles tasks like server-side email forwarding, automated out-of-office messages, and filtering email into folders.

When the recipient's MUA checks for new email and downloads it, it usually moves messages into the recipient's Message Store. The recipient's MUA might further sort the messages, delete certain messages, or any other sort of processing configured by the user.

Finally, the user's mail client downloads a copy of the mail. The email's journey is complete.

Out of all these components, which is the "mail server?" None of them, and all. Each component might be on a separate machine, or any of them could be combined with their peers. A single organization might have different MTAs for receiving and sending email. It depends entirely on the system load, the number of users, and which headaches each organization prefers. A user might call the Message Store or the MSA the mail server. Outside organizations might think that your MTAs that receive email from the outside world are your mail servers, unless they're having trouble receiving your emails and realize that you have entirely different MTAs for outbound mail. Even if you have only one server that controls all of these roles, stop using the phrase "mail server." Look more deeply.

Email Security

Before spam, email clients authenticated only when connecting to the message store. Clients did not authenticate to send mail to the mail submission agent. Mail submission agents could dump email straight into the MTA. MTAs did not verify each others' identity, and often flung messages at any server that looked vaguely suitable. An unprivileged user could trivially forge emails from federal tax agencies. Everybody knew that email was public and that someone with a carefully placed packet sniffer could capture messages.

The appearance of spam made everyone say, "Maybe we should lock down these other connections?"

The server-to-server protocol is still called Simple Mail Transfer Protocol. People scorn that SMTP is not simple, but even with all the modern extensions it's simpler than what it replaced. SMTP uses different TCP/IP ports depending on which piece of the system you're talking to. The protocol commands are still pure text, and can be replicated by a sysadmin with netcat and knowledge. Client protocols like IMAP do the same. Even wrapping the connections in TLS only prevents eavesdropping in transit.

As with everything in computing, these protections are not perfect. TLS can be broken through rogue Certificate Authorities and misconfiguration and good old-fashioned theft of private keys. Clever people can figure out tricky ways to violate the underlying protocols. You must keep up with routine system maintenance. A public facing email server is valuable to spammers. Intruders *will* probe your security. If you leave any gap, they will hijack your host and start spewing spam.

On a related note, Unix sockets are faster, more efficient, and more secure than network sockets—even a network socket listening only on `localhost`. Any time a daemon accepts connections only from the local host, we'll configure it to offer only a Unix socket rather than a network port. If your mail system grows to a point where you need separate beefy hosts for Postfix and Dovecot and rspamd, configuring the software to work over the network will be the least of your problems.

Queues and Asynchronicity

Today we have clusters and virtual IPs and load balancers and geographic distribution for a few dollars a month, perhaps not guaranteeing availability but at least providing a higher class of outage. Email was developed before any of that. Back then, cheap servers cost tens of thousands of dollars. Only the biggest organizations could afford a backup mail server, and an upgrade might demand hours of painstakingly planned labor. The sysadmins couldn't post a notice on the company web site, because web sites did not exist. The connections between sites were also fragile. Your home today might have gigabit Ethernet, but back then a well-connected university with tens of thousands of students might have a massive one megabit per second connection that failed only every third day. Messages might be sent via overloaded phone lines and pass through multiple systems, each subject to all the same failures.

If someone at another organization was so inconsiderate as to send an email while the recipient's system was unreachable, the message would be *undeliverable*. If the email system immediately informed the sender it couldn't deliver a message, the sender would probably call the helpdesk to find out what was broken and what the helpdesk was going to do about it. The answers were, of course, "I don't know" and "nothing."

Rather than make more work for the helpdesk, email was designed to be asynchronous and queueable. If an email could not be immediately handed off to the next stage of its journey, it sat in a queue of outbound mail. Every so often, the email system tried to deliver those messages again. When the recipient system became reachable, the message would be delivered.

Today email is most often delivered in moments, but servers still have a mail queue to cope with transient connection problems. The queue might swell during an outage, or if the system can't cope with the volume of email. I've worked for more than one company that closed its offices at five PM each night, but the mail server chugged away until midnight or later every day catching up with the queue. Management might insist that email always appears instantly, but that's not so. Mail can remain in queue for up to five days, although many MTAs quit after one day.

"Urgent email" is as oxymoronic as "jumbo shrimp," "peace offensive," or "scented deodorant." It might exist at the personal level, but not at the protocol level. Your phone's text messages can also take days to deliver, and are less certain to arrive. If you want synchronous real-time communication, make a voice call.

TLS and Email

You've probably seen all sorts of recommendations for TLS configurations: disabling weak ciphers, disabling TLS 1.0, 1.1, and all versions of SSL, and so on. Those recommendations are great for web sites, but irrelevant for server-to-server SMTP on the public Internet.

Primordial SMTP did not use any encryption. Once the Internet was turned over to commercial interests, however, law enforcement became interested in email. In 1997, the FBI's Carnivore large-scale packet capture system sparked an interest in SMTP encryption. That led to the creation of STARTTLS, which lets unencrypted connections convert to TLS without creating a new TCP connection or using a different TCP port. When a client connects to an SMTP server, the server declares what features it supports. If STARTTLS is among them, the client can say "Before we do anything let's switch to TLS," or it can proceed without TLS. This is often called *opportunistic TLS*. STARTTLS became a standard in 1999. Not changing SMTP's port numbers permitted a gradual rollout of TLS across the Internet.

X.509 certificates for TLS were still expensive. While self-signed certificates offered no protection against man-in-the-middle attacks, they sufficed for evading large-scale passive packet capture. Many organizations had dozens of mail servers and had no interest in spending hundreds of dollars for certificates that users would never see. While self-signed certificates make a web browser screech warnings, SMTP has no human component and servers will merrily ignore warnings if told to do so. We promptly told them to do so. While certificate prices have plunged over the decades, many mail operators still use self-signed certificates.

Today, very few mail systems verify certificate authenticity during server-to-server communication. You can tell your server to require TLS on all incoming connections, but the SMTP protocol doesn't let you force external MTAs to validate *your* certificate. You could tell your server to validate the certificate on external servers, but you'll discover a whole bunch of sites still use self-signed certificates.

Client-facing services like IMAP and submission (Chapter 5) need globally valid X.509 certificates, because users see them. You might as well use that certificate for server-to-server SMTP. Some of those services offer dedicated TLS ports, others support only STARTTLS. This book prefers dedicated ports, as they resist certain classes of attack STARTTLS is vulnerable to.

DNS-based Authentication of Named Entities (DANE)

One of the big objections to common X.509 certificates is the existence of Certificate Authorities (CA). Not that they're expensive, or difficult to work with: that they *exist*. Bringing this up at the right conference is a great way to start a fight. The argument is beyond the scope of this book, but as a steady consumer of self-signed certificates, SMTP welcomed an alternative.

DNS-based Authentication of Named Entities (DANE) is a way for organizations to publish X.509 certificate fingerprints via TLSA DNS records, as documented in RFC 7671. It allows a domain owner to self-authenticate both self-signed and CA certificates. DANE is arguably stronger than standard CA-based TLS, and enforces transport encryption and host authentication.

DANE is also contentious. Arguments about it are almost an inversion of the arguments about certificate authorities. It requires DNSSEC, which starts another chain of parallel-but-different arguments. These battles will not be settled by myself or anyone likely to read this book. Different people have different priorities about different risks and their unique pain points, that's all.[7]

Email is the single largest user of DANE. If someone has gone to the trouble of publishing DANE information for their MTAs, we should respect them.

Can you implement DANE for your own email system? Certainly! Signing your zones with DNSSEC is a prerequisite, however, so I discuss it in my book *DNSSEC Mastery* (Tilted Windmill Press, 2022).

---

[7]   Rule of System Administration #3 applies here. "Nothing is secure. Everything is terrible."

MTA-STS (Chapter 15) is a newer standard for requesting people actually validate your certificate. As much as I philosophically prefer DANE, the Email Empire prefers MTA-STS and I expect it to eventually be a requirement.

TLS Strength

Ignoring certificate validity is one example of how opportunistic TLS differs from client-visible SMTP. You might get prompted to update your web browser every week, but months or years might pass between MTA upgrades.

Many readers of this book ensure that their systems have the latest cryptography libraries and security fixes and carry that practice all the way down to patching `cat`. The rest of the world doesn't do that. Postfix *can* support every version of TLS offered by the underlying OpenSSL cryptography library, but by default offers TLS 1.0 and newer. TLS versions 1.0 and 1.1 were officially deprecated in the protocol standard in March of 2021. While TLS 1.2 came out way back in 2008, certain high-traffic sites still use deprecated TLS versions. Disabling them will cut you off.

Similarly, you'll find recommendation sites like Mozilla's *SSL Configuration Generator* that disable low-quality ciphers and algorithms. Their recommendations are applicable to client-facing systems, but if you apply them to SMTP you will become unable to communicate with ceain sites.

Opportunistic TLSnegotiates the best encryption that both sides support. Yes, TLS 1.0 and 1.1 are considered insecure. If you disable those protocols, thou the connection falls back to using plain text, which is even more insecure. You could set your system to require TLS, but then you lose connectivity with sites that don't support it. Remember, we're talking about a protocol that doesn't require validating certificate authenticity. The standards for TLS in email are low, no matter how much we might wish otherwise.

So, what do we do?

One group of mail operators prioritizes broad compatibility. They still allow deprecated TLS and weak ciphers because they're better than plain text. Postfix ships with this configuration, because otherwise people complain. Another group prioritizes transport integrity. They encourage DANE (or more recently, MTA-STS) and reject both plain text and any version of TLS other than 1.2 and 1.3. A third group keeps reminding everyone that email is not secure, has never been secure, and if you want privacy you should send physical postcards. You must understand which group you fall into, and recognize that other groups have different requirements.

Email Infrastructure

SMTP itself is not enough to successfully exchange mail with another network, however. Email has added protocols that help secure, restrict, and authenticate email. Most of this book discusses those ancillary protocols. We'll cover them briefly here to orient you, then delve deep into each.

DNS

The Domain Name Service maps hostnames and IP addresses to one another. You must have solid control of your DNS to successfully run email, and you must already understand the basics of zones and SOAs and common record types like AAAA and PTR. Domains declare their mail information in DNS. Most of email's ancillary protocols provide their information in DNS. Email is built on the assumption that whatever entity controls the DNS controls the domain.

Ideally, each MTA should have its recursive DNS server installed on the local host. Less ideally, they can use your organization's local recursive DNS servers. Using any of the large DNS providers, such as Google or Cloudflare, breaks DNS-based block lists, one of the most essential anti-spam protections.

Like email, DNS was created when the Internet was largely a private network. Also like email, security was integrated afterwards. DNS Security Extensions (DNSSEC) are today's standard for maintaining the integrity and authenticity of DNS information, and are more widely deployed each year. Your recursive servers should validate DNSSEC.

Media Types and MIME

Primordial email was not merely plain text, but limited to ASCII. People wanted more. The first person to glue a colon to an open parenthesis and call it a smiling face was hailed as an annoying hero. Eventually the Internet acquired enough computing power and bandwidth to spend a bit on more complicated mail formatting, permitting email in HTML and attaching viruses or, worse, price quotes.

Multipurpose Internet Mail Extensions, or MIME, is a standard for encoding non-ASCII characters in ASCII. It divides messages into clearly labeled chunks, so that the recipient can identify the plain text version of an email, the HTML version, and any attachments. It uses a *MIME type* to identify the format of each piece. In 1996, RFC 2046 attempted to rename MIME types as *media types*, but the attempt failed. "Media types" is more correct but, like "server," is ambiguous and you'll see it used interchangeably with "MIME type."[8]

MIME problems are user-visible, so developers have been pressured to get MIME encoding correct. I haven't needed to fix a MIME problem in decades. You should be aware of what MIME is, however.

Note that any email you send should include a plain text version. The screen readers used by people with vision problems rely on that plain text version.

Sender Policy Framework (SPF)

Whereas the MX record tells the world which hosts receive a domain's email, the Sender Policy Framework (SPF) tells the world which hosts are authorized to transmit mail for a domain. SPF declares the hostnames and networks of outbound MTAs, not clients or mail submission agents. Modern SPF is distributed via DNS TXT records.

SPF syntax lets you declare who can send mail from your domain. You can make rules like "only these addresses," "any of the MTAs for this other domain," or even "this domain does not send mail." For

---

8   You must infer from context if "media type" refers to a MIME section, Ethernet, or disk drive architecture.

43

example, the SPF record for my domain `mw1.io` contains a few IP addresses and a hostname.

When an MTA receives a connection claiming to have mail from a particular domain, the MTA is supposed to check the SPF against the incoming machine's IP address. If they don't match, the connection is dubious and probably should be rejected. If someone sends email from `mw1.io` to a Gmail user, Gmail's server checks the SPF record for `mw1.io`. If the forger's IP address is not in my domain's SPF record, Gmail drops the connection and records that the forger's IP is untrustworthy.[9]

SPF is considered the lowest level of authenticity, and is easy to implement. New domains should implement SPF immediately. It requires zero maintenance until you add a new outbound MTA.

DomainKeys Identified Mail (DKIM)

While SPF declares where email comes from, *DomainKeys Identified Mail* (DKIM) authenticates the email's sender. DKIM information is published in DNS TXT records via a `_domainkey` entry.

DKIM is more difficult to implement than SPF, but less terrible than having your domain spoofed by a spammer. Best practice declares that you should rotate your keys regularly, so it does require more maintenance.

Domain-based Message Authentication, Reporting, and Conformance (DMARC)

SPF and then DKIM improved mail authentication. Domain-based Message Authentication, Reporting, and Conformance (DMARC) is the next evolution. It uses SPF to identify legitimate mail sources. It uses DKIM to authenticate email. Its robust policy language lets organizations define how recipients can identify legitimate mail and report failures in those two protocols.

DMARC records are distributed via TXT records, tied to a `_dmarc` record.

---

9   If the forger's address *is* in my SPF record, I am having a very bad day.

Brand Indicators for Message Identification (BIMI)

If your organization uses a trademark for marketing, you might have an interest in Brand Indicators for Message Identification (BIMI). If the end user has a BIMI-aware email client, it will check for BIMI DNS records and use them to display a digitally signed corporate logo next to the email. BIMI is built on DMARC, so it is cryptographically verified.

Deploying BIMI starts with "register an expensive trademark," "purchase an artificially expensive certificate," and "hire an expensive trademark attorney to advise you on international trademark law interactions," so these two paragraphs are this book's only coverage of the topic.

Mail Transfer Agent Strict Transport Security (MTA-STS)

Originally, email was transmitted unencrypted. Anyone with a properly placed packet sniffer could eavesdrop on all email transactions. We eventually added encryption to user authentication, securing usernames and passwords, but using TLS between MTAs was optional. Most mail operators who deployed TLS considered large-scale capture programs like Carnivore their primary risk, so self-signed certificates became acceptable even though they do not prevent other attacks.

Mail Transfer Agent Strict Transport Security (MTA-STS) is a declaration that your MTA only accepts SMTP over TLS. You must offer a policy statement on a web site. MTA-STS is activated via a DNS record, using the `_mta_sts` identifier.

TLS Reporting (TLS-RPT)

Every sysadmin has seen email bounce messages, declaring that the recipient has no account or that a server is misconfigured or that the receiving MTA is on an unscheduled vacation. These messages go between MTAs via SMTP.

If your MTA uses MTA-STS to declare it only accepts connections over TLS, and it has a TLS problem, those SMTP messages will not go through. Your MTA will continue merrily rejecting connections, leaving you ignorant of the problems. *TLS reporting*, or *TLS-RPT*, is how MTAs exchange reports of TLS problems. If you deploy MTA-STS, you also need TLS reporting.

Like everything else in email, TLS-RPT information is distributed via DNS.

Sieve

Anyone who receives large amounts of email absolutely needs filtering. While clients can filter messages, server-side filtering is much more efficient and helps maintain consistency between clients. Sieve is the industry-standard platform-independent language for writing mail filters. The ManageSieve protocol allows clients to configure their filtering rules.

Simple Authentication and Security Layer (SASL)

X.509 certificates were priced unreasonably for decades, driving people to develop alternatives for securely exchanging data that did not depend on SSL or, later, TLS. The alternative adopted by email systems was the *Simple Authentication and Security Layer, SASL*. SASL allowed clients to securely identify themselves across the public Internet. Certificates are no longer so expensive, but protocols change slowly. While certain protocols can easily insist on wrapping all authentication requests in TLS, others cannot.

SASL also allows applications to pass authentication requests to other applications. We'll use this feature to configure our services.

Which Do You Need?

These protocols were developed years apart. Some of their functions overlap. Which do you need, and which can you ignore?

Many people deployed the protocols available when they set up their server and never circled back to add new ones. You'll see servers with only SPF, or only SPF and DKIM. Which you need isn't just a question of what you want to offer the world. It's about what other servers can validate. If an MTA can only validate SPF, but you only offer DKIM, the recipient might consider your mails suspicious.

To maximize deliverability and to become aware of any problems, implement SPF, DKIM, and DMARC for your outbound mail. To minimize junk mail, verify any SPF and DKIM for your inbound mail.

Do you need MTA-TLS and TLS-RPT? That depends on your threat model. Maybe you don't care if incoming connections are encrypted or not. It's fairly new, so perhaps your MTA doesn't yet support it. If you're deploying a new mail system or taking the time to polish your existing system, however, you might as well experiment with it. Use a very low timeout when testing, so remote servers won't cache your mistakes for months or years.

Spammers can deploy these protocols as easily as the rest of us—more easily, if they invest in automation. Supporting them is not sufficient to deliver your emails, but it's a start.

What's In This Book?

Chapter 0 is this introduction.

Chapter 1, *Unix and Email*, discusses our test environment for learning email and how email works on Unix systems.

Chapter 2, *The Simple Mail Transfer Protocol*, covers the core of server-to-server email transmission and the essential concepts.

Chapter 3, *Postfix and Dovecot*, covers the basics of the Postfix mail transfer agent and the Dovecot IMAP server.

Chapter 4, *Virtual Domains*, covers supporting multiple domains on one system.

Chapter 5, *IMAP and Submission*, guides you through providing client-facing services.

Chapter 6, *Database Back Ends*, moves parts of the system configuration from static text files to more user-friendly databases.

Chapter 7, *Rspamd Essentials*, introduces the rspamd message management engine.

Chapter 8, *MX and SPF Records*, lets you introduce your mail system to the wider world.

Chapter 9, *Protocol Checks and Block Lists*, covers essential anti-spam protections.

Chapter 10, *DomainKeys Identified Mail*, discusses the DKIM standard needed to send mail to the outside world.

Chapter 11, *DMARC*, guides you through setting up Domain-based Message Authentication, Reporting, and Conformance.

Chapter 12, *Webmail*, covers the Roundcube web-based email agent.

Chapter 13, *Filtering with Sieve*, discusses sorting mail into folders on the server side rather than in your client.

Chapter 14, *Managing Rspamd*, takes you through less basic usage of rspamd and tuning it to fit your needs.

Chapter 15, *Technical Edges*, discusses less essential pieces like MTA-STS, throttling outbound mail, and nolisting.

That's a lot to cover, but if you follow along you'll learn it all. Onward!

Chapter 1: Unix and Email

Setting up a public mail server means fully participating in email standards, but you can neither learn nor configure everything simultaneously. Learning means studying one piece at a time without informing the whole world that we're amateurs. The simplest way to do this is to configure two test hosts in different domains and have them exchange email *only* with one another. You control what these hosts accept. You see the error logs on both sides. By not declaring to the rest of the world that they exist, you don't have to worry about spam. You can even use packet filters to block outsiders.

Once you have a full-featured email configuration, you can tell the world and see what happens next. If it works as you hope, set up your production server on your real domain the same way.

Your test servers don't need to be large. Mine are virtual machines with 1GB of RAM, 20GB of disk, and a single CPU core, running FreeBSD or Debian. The email software did not challenge system resources.

Once you have test servers, you must understand the basics of how email works with Unix. We'll consider sending, receiving, and viewing email. You'll learn about mail headers, the types of mail directories, sending mail at the command line, and more.

Server Configuration

Install your operating system as usual. Patch it and enable automatic security updates. This will be an Internet-facing server, people *will* try to break in. Constantly.

Your server needs a public hostname. Don't use the bare domain name, like `solveamurder.org`—you'll want that hostname to resolve to your web server. If you don't have a hostname scheme, try something dull like `mail`, `mta`, or `mx`. That will help outside people understand that yes, this host is involved in email. Configure that name on the host and in forward and reverse DNS. Set it up to work with your network management tools. Bad time will break many things, so automate clock synchronization with ntpd(8).

Servers do not need any sort of GUI. Don't bother installing X or Wayland.

Do not use NFS to store any part of your mail infrastructure or files. Mail systems rely *heavily* on file locking. NFS provides something that resembles file locking if you don't peer at it too closely, but it will only extend your counseling sessions. SAN disks are fine, and iSCSI is merely slow and finicky, not malicious.

You personally need an unprivileged user account. Not only is logging in directly as `root` poor systems administration practice, as you build your system you'll send email to ordinary users. You must share the ordinary user experience.

Most of the mail will end up on a `/vhosts` partition. Use a different name if you wish, but whatever you call it, create the filesystem or dataset and give it lots of room. Do not put your email on the root partition unless you want to discover that incoming mail has filled your disk overnight.

After that, you'll require an assortment of other services and accounts.

Service Accounts and Groups

Many of the programs we'll use need their own users. Never log in as any of these accounts, and block them from logging in via SSH or even the console. Your Unix might create these service accounts when it installs the software we'll use, and it'll use its own names for those accounts. This book uses the `postfix` account for Postfix, the `dovecot` and `dovenull` users for Dovecot, and the `rspamd` user for rspamd. Your package might add them for you, or not.

We'll also use the account `vmail`, with UID and GID 5000, to support virtual hosts. There's no particular reason for using this account name, but after being repeated in thousands of tutorials it's become a *de facto* standard, so we'll surrender to the crowd. It's not part of any package, so you must create it by hand.

On FreeBSD systems you'll use pw(8).

```
# pw groupadd -n vmail -g 5000
# pw useradd -n vmail -u 5000 -g 5000 -d /home/vmail \
  -w no -s /sbin/nologin
```

Linux systems use groupadd(8) and useradd(8).

```
# groupadd -g 5000 vmail
# useradd -u 5000 -g 5000 -d /home/vmail \
  -s /sbin/nologin vmail
```

Once you have that account, let it own your virtual mailboxes.

```
# chown vmail:vmail /vhosts/
```

We'll also use groups to give multiple daemons access to shared resources. Groups are a neglected aspect of Unix permissions. Any time you find yourself thinking you want to make something world-readable or (ick) world-*writable*, you probably need to create a group instead.

If your organization or operating system has different standards, follow them.

Backups

Why back up test servers? Because you will make mistakes and be forced to revert changes. After decades of watching people plan to configure backups during the last stage of deployment and then failing to do so, I recommend configuring, automating, and verifying routine backups before doing anything else.

If you don't have a backup system for your Unix hosts, permit me to suggest Tarsnap.

DNS Resolver

Mail systems make many DNS queries to find foreign mail exchangers. SPF, DKIM, and DMARC are all distributed via DNS. Block lists run over DNS, and most restrict access based on the number of queries a host makes. Do not forward these queries to a provider like Google or Cloudflare; you shouldn't even forward them to your ISP. Each MTA should perform its own recursive DNS searches.

Why? Suppose a block list provider allows 100 queries per hour per host, and your two mail hosts query them about 80 times an hour—sometimes more, sometimes less. Standing on their own, each host falls comfortably under that limit. If the mail hosts forward all their queries to the organization's recursive server, yes, they'll benefit from that server's cache. All queries to the block list server will come from your recursive nameserver's single IP, however. You will overflow the rate limit and, depending on your configuration, either reject good email or accept spam. How many people use 8.8.8.8 as a recursive DNS server, and how quickly do you think Google's nameservers exhaust their 100 queries?

Run your own recursive, non-authoritative, non-forwarding, DNSSEC-validating DNS server on each and every mail host. Almost every Unix-like system has an install-time option to enable a resolver like BIND or Unbound with a single command.

Packet Filtering

Email hosts run many services. Some of those must be available to the world. Others should not. Some services ship with default configurations open to the entire world, even though those services don't need to be public or even activated. If a network service doesn't need to be publicly accessible, don't let the public access it. The simplest way to prevent nasty surprises is to use a host-based packet filter.

What access is necessary? During testing, you might block new connections to your hosts from everywhere except your test network and your desktop. In production, however, you need select ports open to the outside world. Allow the public to connect to these TCP ports:

- 25 (SMTP)
- 80 (HTTP, for web services and ACME)
- 443 (HTTPS, for webmail)
- 465 (Client email submissions)
- 993 (IMAP over TLS).
- 4190 (ManageSieve)

You'll also need a TCP port for SSH, but you might restrict that to connections from your management network. Use keys or another non-password authentication for SSH.

You might see references to port 587 or 143. Originally, email used port 465 for TLS-protected client submissions. IANA declared that people should not use a dedicated TLS port, instead using STARTTLS on port 587. They recently rechanged their mind, and made dedicated TLS on port 465 the standard.[10] Similarly, port 143 is for unencrypted IMAP.

Allowing your mail host to only send email is trivial. Email needs TCP port 25 for SMTP, and both TCP and UDP port 53 for DNS. Identifying the connectivity your host needs for management and operating system updates is highly OS-dependent and far from trivial.

TLS and X.509 Certificate

You must encrypt connections between clients and your Message Store, which usually means TLS. TLS requires an X.509 certificate. Years ago self-signed certificates sufficed, but that's no longer true. Any globally valid X.509 certificate will do.

Some organizations have a policy requiring that all X.509 certificates be purchased from a specific CA. If they have no such policy, however, I encourage using a free certificate from an organization like Let's Encrypt. An ACME client will both get you free certificates and will automate renewal, so that X.509 certificates become a non-problem. If you're not familiar with ACME, permit me to suggest the `dehydrated` client (`https://dehydrated.io`) and my book *TLS Mastery* (Tilted Windmill Press, 2022).

The simplest way to configure ACME requires your host to run a web server.

---

10   After all these decades, my capacity to be annoyed by standards ping-pong sincerely surprises me.

Web Server

Many users will expect you to provide a web-based email client. We'll look at that in Chapter 12, but in any event it will need a web server beneath it. Also, the easiest way to get free X.509 certificates uses one. This book uses Apache, but any modern web server with PHP support should work.

If you do not intend to provide webmail, and your organization's policies require you to use expensive commercial certificates, and you don't want to use any web-based configuration tools, skip the web server.

Database

Postfix and Dovecot can use a database for virtual user management, and you'll need a database to store aggregated DMARC reports. MariaDB[11] is the most commonly supported database among these applications.

Secure your database, create administrative accounts, and perform any optimizations you want before proceeding. The database should allow connections only from the local host, either via the network or a Unix socket. It should not listen to the external network.

The antispam engine rspamd requires Redis. Redis isn't exactly a database, but it's close enough that I'll cram it into this section.

Postfix

Postfix is an incredibly flexible mail system that can support almost anything on the modern Internet. Install the package that supports your preferred database.

Postfix includes the core features that every mail system needs, and many add-on features required by only a handful of environments. We will focus on the tools needed to get a standard mail system running and working. If you discover that your environment requires something special, there's a good chance that Postfix supports it. Get your core system running first, then add to it.

---

11   Yes, MySQL is also an option. But why resist the Email Empire if you're just going to capitulate to Oracle's Database Empire?

This book discusses Postfix 3.8. If you have inherited an older (or newer!) Postfix system this book might help orient you, but you must double-check everything against the documentation for your version. The documentation at `www.postfix.org` retains extensive information on historical releases.

Dovecot

The Dovecot suite is best known as an IMAP server, but it includes several smaller programs useful to Postfix. Yes, Postfix includes its own versions of those programs, but Dovecot's provides useful features like mailbox filtering and indexing. By installing Dovecot before configuring Postfix, you can optimally configure Postfix. Dovecot also provides vital features such as a user database for email accounts not tied to Unix accounts.

Dovecot is an incredibly powerful program, created by service providers for service providers decades ago. Dovecot developed features to support the ever-expanding population of email users. This book documents a tiny portion of Dovecot's features, much like it does with Postfix.

If your operating system provides a separate package for Dovecot's Pigeonhole, install it. Pigeonhole provides the Sieve mail filtering language. You also need Pigeonhole's IMAPSieve and Extprograms extensions, which might be additional packages or options.

Netcat and OpenSSL

Netcat is a flexible network tool that, among other things, allows you to connect to arbitrary TCP/IP ports. We'll use it for testing services. Over the decades netcat has been forked, reimplemented, and served as inspiration for other programs that also call themselves `netcat`. These variants made no effort to make their added features compatible with other variants. Your Unix might provide a netcat-alike such as `ncat` or `socat`. Long commands are not very Unixy so `netcat`, `ncat`, and others often get installed as `nc`. If you have a problem using netcat check the manual for your exact variant.

With all these issues, why use netcat and not telnet? If you think netcat has been forked, wait until you get a look at telnet. Telnet mingles standard output with standard error, and silently modifies text for compatibility with interactive shells. Netcat is also scriptable, supporting automation. The examples in this book work on BSD variants and Debian.

If your netcat supports TLS with an option or two, feel free to use it for testing TLS-wrapped services. This book uses OpenSSL. Most operating systems ship with OpenSSL-compatible command-line tools. OpenSSL's main advantage is that it is consistent across operating systems, so we'll use it to test TLS-wrapped services.

Mailx

The mailx(1) program is the Unix standard for sending and reading email, in the same way that ed(1) is the standard text editor. It's often linked to the `mail` and `Mail` commands. We will use `mailx` to send mail in a terminal.

Every version of Unix has its own, slightly incompatible, version of `mailx`. Some versions contain everything required to send, debug, and read modern email. Others do not. If you have a full-featured version, feel free to use it. Otherwise, you'll need a more modern mail client. The mailx program does not deliver directly to Maildir.

Email Client

You need an email client that works in a terminal, so that you can bypass IMAP while troubleshooting. It must support modifying headers while composing emails. If you have a preferred console client that fits, use it. If not, I recommend mutt (`https://mutt.org`).

When reading documentation you might see references to the `.mailrc` or a `.aliases` file. These files were intended for configuring mailx(1). While some modern clients still parse `.aliases` or offer an option to set an alias file, `.mailrc` is inapplicable to modern mail clients. When you see these references, immediately double-check if the document you're reading is relevant to your client.

Syslog

Email generates logs. Every Postfix, Dovecot, anti-spam, and client interaction spews lines into the logs. By default, all of these programs log to the system mail log. This quickly becomes unsustainable. You must be familiar with your operating system's logging system, and know how to steer log messages from different programs into their own dedicated log files. You don't have to implement finely separated logs immediately, but if debugging turns into a problem be prepared to change the logs.

Email and Unix

Email grew up with Unix, and most Unixes integrate email into its software. This integration evolved, but old documentation lingers. Set up your test email systems to reflect current best practices.

Virtual Hosts

Computers support virtual IP addresses, web servers support virtual sites, hosts support virtual servers, and email systems support *virtual hosts* or *virtual domains*. Just as with other computing uses of the word "virtual," a mail system's virtual hosts lets a host manage SMTP for hosts and domains other than the host itself.

One of my test hosts is `mail.solveamurder.org`. The MTA on that host is configured to handle mail for users at that host, such as `mwl@mail.solveamurder.org`. This is the server's real, or *primary*, domain. I want it to also handle mail for the whole domain, such as `mwl@solveamurder.org`. That's a virtual host. If I want to add support for mail for more domains, those are also virtual domains. Just as a web server might have a hostname like `www9.bighostingcompany.com` but host hundreds or thousands of web sites, a mail system can support as many domains as it has disk, memory, and CPU for.

Email addresses on virtual hosts have one decided advantage over the mail system's primary domain. Mail addressed to users at the server's primary domain must have a Unix account to receive that mail. It's not a problem if the sysadmin has that account, but giving every user in your organization a Unix account just to receive email opens many possible attack venues and complicates system management. You can create and manage virtual domain accounts separately from the operating system.

An MTA has one "primary" domain and can add-on other "virtual" domains. I strongly recommend keeping the hostname (e.g. `mail.solveamurder.org`) as the system's primary email domain and making everything else, including the domain you're actually interested in (e.g. `solveamurder.org`) virtual. Doing otherwise might make sense if you are running a one-person email system, but it limits your future flexibility.

Standard Email Addresses

By standard and tradition, folks expect certain email addresses to exist at every domain that uses email. The `postmaster@` address is expected to accept messages about email problems. The `hostmaster@` address is the contact for DNS matters. If someone has trouble with users from your network, they might contact `abuse@`. Finally, web-related matters get sent to `webmaster@`.

Must you have these? No.

Will knowledgeable people who try to contact you use these addresses? Yes.

If the addresses don't exist, will those knowledgeable people think you're incompetent? Also yes.

Create these addresses. Forward them to real people. Domains that don't send or accept email are exempt from this practice.

The sendmail Command

When the SMTP protocol first escaped, the standard MTA was Sendmail (`https://www.sendmail.org`). Sendmail was revolutionary for the 1980s. Its configuration file allowed sysadmins to make minor changes without recompiling the program. That configuration file used a unique syntax specifically developed for the challenges of processing and delivering email, but email administrators needed a deep understanding of SMTP so that was okay.

Sendmail was designed for a network without spam or malicious users, and was optimized for delivery. Unlike most other Unix programs it was a single monolithic binary that performed several different tasks. It received email from users and programs and the network, and sent messages across the network. It retried queued mail. It was all things email for all people.

Over the next decade, people learned that the sendmail(8) program was the interface to email. You'd use a mail client to read and send email interactively, but if a shell script needed compose and send email it probably called `sendmail`. Dang near every Unix system had Sendmail, even when configuration files became more common.

Exim arrived in 1995, and Postfix in 1998.[12] These new mail servers faced an overwhelming install base accustomed to Sendmail's peculiarities and hardened by years of fighting spam with makeshift tools. Folks also had over a decade of add-on programs written to work with Sendmail. To ease migrations, both Exim and Postfix were command-line compatible with Sendmail. They could read Sendmail-specific files like the aliases database. They even included a `sendmail` command, linked to the actual binary.

Innovations like "human-readable configuration files" and "break mail handling up into several small single-purpose programs" eventually won out. Today, Sendmail is a commercial product with an open-source version, mostly used by us geezers who have become inured to using a configuration file to generate our configuration files.

Finding a `sendmail` command on your Unix does not mean that you're running Sendmail. You might have Sendmail, or Exim, Postfix, OpenSMTPd, R2D2's Mail Thing, or some other mail handler. The world is full of legacy stuff that expects to find a `sendmail` command, and providing that command is easier than fixing them all. Always differentiate between the Sendmail program and the `sendmail` command, and remember that `sendmail` is not necessarily Sendmail.

---

12   Microsoft Exchange 4.0 added SMTP support in 1997, creating endless billable hours for freelance intrusion response consultants like myself.

Local Mail Systems

As a general rule, a host that wants to send email should have a mail program. This doesn't need to be a full-fledged mail system. Most of my hosts run simple mail agents that only forward mail to my actual MTA, where I decide what to do with it.

Local mail programs like mailx(1) or mutt(1) use the system's sendmail(8) command to drop outgoing mail into a queue directory. The location of the queue directory depends on what server software you're using. Postfix uses subdirectories beneath `/var/spool/postfix/`. The MTA regularly scans the queue directories and attempts to deliver the messages.

Installed but unconfigured mail software will probably be able to deliver messages to accounts on the local system. It *might* be able to forward email to your actual MTA. Your MTA might or might not accept those messages. You will not be able to reliably send those messages beyond the systems in your organization.

Aliases

Traditionally, every Unix account could receive and send email. This made sense when accounts were rare and human users outnumbered service accounts. Service accounts have proliferated while shell users have dwindled, however. While a service account emailing `root` to warn of a problem is sensible, you can't email `httpd` or `nobody` and expect an answer. Even then, if you manage hundreds of servers, how often will you log into an individual account on a specific server to check mail there?

That's where the `/etc/aliases` file comes in. It's originally from Sendmail, but all other mail software uses it. Depending on how your Unix packages Postfix, you might have a second aliases file in Postfix's configuration directory. You might find replacing one with a link to the other less confusing.

The aliases file redirects email sent on the system. Mail addressed to one account can be aimed at another. Each line is the aliases file is a single redirection.

```
user:   destination
```

All service accounts should have a redirection in `/etc/aliases`. The user `daemon` exists to own various system binaries, and is forbidden to log in. Nobody will ever check this user's email. Here, I forward email sent to the user `daemon` to the `root` account.

```
daemon:    root
```

If something sends email to the user `daemon`, the host sends that mail to the `root` account instead.

How often will you check the email for `root` on this host, though? Forward email for `root` to a human being. Here I redirect root's email to my account on this host.

```
root:    mwlucas
```

If I don't read email on this host, send it to a host where I do read email.

```
root:    mwl@mwl.io
```

Redirect mail to multiple accounts by separating them with a comma.

```
root:    mwl@mwl.io, vader@galacticempire.gov
```

Programs do not directly parse `/etc/aliases`. They consult `/etc/aliases.db`, a hash file created from `/etc/aliases`. Whenever you change the alias file, you must update the hash file. You'll see references to newalias(8), but that's a Sendmail program. Postfix provides postalias(1) for that.

We'll look at Postfix's handling of the aliases file in Chapter 3. It has the exact same format as the system aliases file. If you have both files, it's easy to get confused. I recommend replacing one with a link to the other.

Mailbox Format

A Unix system stores email in one of two formats, mbox and Maildir. While my books normally provide guidance so people can make their own mistakes, this time I categorically declare: always use Maildir, end of discussion.

But we'll discuss them anyway.

The *mbox* format was Unix's first mailbox format. Each mail folder is a single file containing all the messages in the folder, one after the other. It worked adequately when inodes were rare, email messages were small, and ASCII reigned—that is, before the working lifetime of most everyone in computing today. An mbox separated messages with a From keyword, which is straightforward until someone included a message using the word From at the beginning of a line. Deleting a message in the middle of the folder meant resectioning the file. A single corrupt message scrambled the whole folder. Mail arrived in `/var/mail/username` and got moved into the user's home directory when it was saved to a folder, so someone else's monstrously huge message could block your ability to receive email. Most software that involves email supports the mbox format, and it's the default on many Unix installs. Most Unix installs don't handle email locally, however, instead forwarding messages to select accounts on the mail system.

The *Maildir* format places each message in its own file. Folders are filesystem directories. Placing each message in its own file simplifies administration. Removing a message from the folder doesn't mean rewriting a file. A single corrupt message will not destroy the folder. If troubleshooting compels you to poke at the user's messages, each message having its own file simplifies troubleshooting.

The Maildir format creates a directory in the user's home directory, often but not necessarily called `Maildir`. A brand-new Maildir includes three subdirectories: `cur` (for messages in the user's inbox), `new` (for messages that have arrived since the last time the user checked their mail), and `tmp` (temporary space). Each new folder the user creates will be another directory. Each message file within the folder has a unique name that might or might not include the host that wrote the file, the size of the message, the date the message was received, or more.

Many default Unix installs use the mbox format, because most individual hosts are not expected to process mail locally and mbox is universal. Maildir is considered the modern standard, but some legacy software doesn't like it.

Sending Mail Interactively at the Command-Line

Scripts and programs use mailx(1) (aka mail(1)) to send mail, and you can do the same. While mailx's features vary between operating systems, they all contain the POSIX-mandated core functions. The `mailx` program has one required argument, the destination address. Here, I try to mail my account on the local system.

```
# mailx mwl
```

I am immediately prompted for a subject. I put something there. (If your mail isn't about something, why send it?)

```
Subject: interactive test 1
```
After that, the screen is blank. Enter the body of the mail.

```
Does this work?
```
End the message with a single period on a line of its own.

```
.
EOT
```

Mailx uses EOT, or End Of Text, to acknowledge that my message is complete. Depending on your mailx implementation you might get offered a few more fields to fill in, but you can hit ENTER to ignore them for this test.

When you finish the message, mailx hands it off to the local mail system. Postfix uses */var/spool/postfix/maildrop* to queue incoming mail that hasn't yet been accepted by the MTA. If your MTA is not running, your message will linger in that folder. If you have a running MTA, it will immediately pick up the message and deliver it to the local account.

The most common use for command-line email is non-interactive.

Sending Mail Non-Interactively at the Command Line

Also use mailx(1) to send mail non-interactively at the command line. Specify a subject with `-s`. Feed your message to `mailx` through a pipe.

```
# echo "message body" | mailx -s "subject" recipient
```

If you have a file containing your message, you can redirect it into `mailx`.

```
# mailx -s "subject" recipient < filename
```

Here I mail a line of text to root, just to see how it works.

```
# echo "test message 1" | mailx -s "test 1" root
```

The system logs the message and sends it to the recipient.

Message ID

When a mail system receives a brand new mail, it assigns it a unique message ID. You can use the message ID to track an individual email through the network. Different carriers and software use different formats. Postfix uses this.

timestamp.shortID@hostname

The timestamp is in ISO8601:2004 format. Each message is also assigned a random ten-character short identifier, to differentiate it from other messages sent during the same second. The hostname is the MTA's best understanding of its fully qualified domain name. The test message above gets this message ID:

`20230501183208.9E73A20116@mail.solveamurder.org`

This message was sent in on 1 May 2023, at 18:32:08 UTC according to the host's clock. The short identifier is *9E73A20116*, and the host is `mail.solveamurder.org`.

Where do we get this message ID? In the message.

An Email Message

You've almost certainly seen email messages, but most folks never look beyond what their email client presents. I sent the email in the last section on my host `mail.solveamurder.org`. Let's look the raw mail file in */var/mail/root*.

How did this three-word mail become eleven lines long? Headers. An *email header* is processing information added to the message by components of the email system. Here are some common headers in a minimal mail message. Not all headers appear in all messages.

```
Return-Path: <root@mail.solveamurder.org>
X-Original-To: root
Delivered-To: root@mail.solveamurder.org
```

I sent the email as `root`, to `root`. The `Return-Path` header, when present, tells the recipient where to send bounced messages. It's generally the `MAIL FROM` address. A *bounced* message is one where the destination server or some intermediary MTA could not deliver the message. (The word "bounced" also describes a forwarding method, which we'll discuss later.)

The `X-Original-To` header gives the original recipient address. This mail was addressed to `root`, and `X-Original-To` preserves that information. Any header beginning with `X-` is called an *X-header*. X-headers were originally used for "other information not included in the protocol," and were widely adopted in early text-based protocols. RFC6648 deprecated X-headers for newer protocols in 2012. While some X-headers became widely used and were even standardized, any mail software developer can add their own X-headers.[13] X-Original-To is one of the most common ones.

The `Delivered-To` header says who received the email, after any bouncing, forwarding, or alias expansion. This mail was received by `root` on the host `mail.solveamurder.org`.

---

13   Some vendors even verify that their invented X-headers are not already used by other software before deploying their product!

```
Received: by mail.solveamurder.org (Postfix, from userid
    0) id 9E73A20116; Mon, 1 May 2023 14:32:08 -0400 (EDT)
```

Here, the sending MTA logs that it received the message. It was sent via Postfix, by a user with UID zero. The *id* space gives the short message ID. In the next section, we'll see how message IDs can be used to track an email through the log. We also get the timestamp of when the sending MTA received this email.

```
To: root@mail.solveamurder.org
Subject: test 1
```

These two headers should be familiar to anyone who has used email. To is the person the message was addressed to. The Subject should be sufficiently enticing to make me not delete your email unread.

```
Message-Id: <20230501183208.9E73A20116@mail.solveamurder.org>
```

Here we have the complete Message-id assigned by the sending MTA.

```
Date: Mon,  1 May 2023 14:32:08 -0400 (EDT)
From: Charlie Root <root@mail.solveamurder.org>
```

The Date field records when the client sent the message. From identifies the person responsible for disturbing my peace.

We then have a blank line. Email uses a single blank line to separate the headers from the body of the message. And finally, there's our content.

```
test message 1
```

We'll expand on headers and related topics throughout this book. Debugging almost any mail problem means reading headers carefully.

The Mail Log

Email is so integral to Unix it has a dedicated logging facility, *mail*. Most Unixes log mail messages into one or more files in */var/log*, such as */var/log/maillog*, */var/log/mail.info* and */var/log/mail.log*, or something similar. If you can't find your mail log, check your system's logging configuration in */etc/syslog.conf*, */etc/rsyslog.conf*, or something like that. My examples use */var/log/maillog*.

One of the best ways to troubleshoot email problems is to watch the system log. Running `tail -f /var/log/maillog` shows you Postfix's actions in mostly-real time. Checking the log, I see five entries.

```
May  1 14:32:08 mail postfix/pickup[61207]: 9E73A20116:
   uid=0 from=<root>
```

The host's name is **mail**. Postfix's `pickup` program accepts your message.

```
May  1 14:32:08 mail postfix/cleanup[5708]: 9E73A20116:
   message-id=<20230501183208.9E73A20116
   @mail.solveamurder.org>
```

Here, postfix's `cleanup` program accepts the message and assigns it a message-id. Postfix knows the local hostname, so it uses that as part of the message-id. It also normalizes the recipient address from naked root to *root@mail.solveamurder.org*.

```
May  1 14:32:08 mail postfix/qmgr[30830]: 9E73A20116:
   from=<root@mail.solveamurder.org>, size=340, nrcpt=1
   (queue active)
```

The queue manager `qmgr` accepts the message from `cleanup`. The random part of the message ID gets logged, then the message sender.

```
May   1 14:32:08 mail postfix/local[6618]: 9E73A20116:
   to=<root@mail.solveamurder.org>, orig_to=<root>,
   relay=local, delay=0.02, delays=0.01/0.01/0/0,
   dsn=2.0.0, status=sent (delivered to maildir)
```

The queue manager sent our message to the `local` program, which sends it to root's inbox. When you're troubleshooting mail problems, look for `relay` and `status`. The relay is the host where the message was sent to. The status declares the result of sending that message to that host.

```
May   1 14:32:08 mail postfix/qmgr[30830]: 9E73A20116:
   removed
```

Once another program accepts responsibility for the message, the queue manager removes it from the queue.

This is a lot of activity, yes, but note the timestamps. In this message, handled entirely on `localhost`, everything happened within a single second. Messages to outside networks will probably take longer.

With these basics, let's look at configuring Postfix and Dovecot.

Chapter 2: The Simple Mail Transfer Protocol

Email uses several protocols, but only one will routinely give you fits. You control both ends of a Local Mail Transport Protocol (LMTP) connection. You can set up oddball clients to duplicate a user's IMAP configuration. DNS, TLS, these are well-understood headaches. But the Simple Mail Transfer Protocol (SMTP) underlies all of email, and you can't possibly build test systems that replicate every whackadoo environment you communicate with. The protocol's simplicity is a huge part of why it's so successful, and why it's so abused. To run your own email system you must understand SMTP's weaknesses all the way down to your marrow. We'll start by using the protocol, proceed to abusing the protocol, and discuss status messages, greylisting, block lists, and forwarding.

The "Protocol" Part of SMTP

Like many primordial protocols, SMTP is pure text. The client connects to TCP port 25 and exchanges ritualized text with the server. If the client and the message passes the server's integrity and validity testing, the server accepts the message and hands it off to the recipient.

We'll use netcat(1) to test email.

Sending Mail via Netcat

Netcat requires two arguments, the hostname to connect to and the port. It defaults to using TCP. Here I'm on my host `mail.ratoperatedvehicle.com` and connecting to port 25 on the local server to send mail to the host `mail.solveamurder.org`. While nc accepts hostnames, you must identify ports by number.

```
$ nc localhost 25
220 mail.ratoperatedvehicle.com ESMTP Postfix
```

I've connected to port 25, where Postfix is listening. Every response from an SMTP server starts with a *reply code*. Codes in the 200 range are for normal communication with the server. A 220 is the server declaring it is ready to begin a conversation. Postfix also introduces itself by hostname, the version of SMTP it supports, and the server software name. This server speaks Extended SMTP (ESMTP), the industry standard since 1995.

EHLO mail.ratoperatedvehicle.com

Postfix has introduced itself, so it's only fair I do the same using the EHLO command. Original SMTP used the HELO command, but EHLO is how the client declares that it also speaks modern ESMTP. I add the hostname I'm connecting from.

```
250-mail.ratoperatedvehicle.com
250-PIPELINING
250-SIZE 10240000
250-VRFY
250-ETRN
250-ENHANCEDSTATUSCODES
250-8BITMIME
250-DSN
250-SMTPUTF8
250 CHUNKING
```

The server responds with reply code 250, indicating that it's okay with what you've asked for. It gives an acknowledgement of my hostname, and follows that with a bunch of 250 reply codes to list the supported protocol features. What are all these features?

PIPELINING lets an SMTP client combine commands before asking the server to respond, and is especially valuable on loaded servers.

The *SIZE* feature informs the server of the largest message it will accept, in bytes.

VRFY, or *verify*, tells the client that the server is willing to confirm that addresses exist or not. Intruders can use VRFY to probe for legitimate accounts without attracting the notice of systems administrators, so many sites disable it.

Sites with intermittent connectivity use *ETRN* to ask a remote server to immediately retransmit all queued mail.

The *ENHANCEDSTATUSCODES* feature lets an SMTP server return more specific errors than those permitted by the common three-digit codes. Everything on the Internet today should support the enhanced status codes.

8BITMIME promises that the server preserves the 8th bit of each byte. Proper ASCII is a seven-bit character set, which was fine when bytes ranged from five to twelve bits depending on your hardware. In the 90s, people generally agreed that a byte would be eight bits. If a server doesn't declare 8BITMIME support, Postfix encodes text as quoted-printable.

Delivery Status Notifications, or DSN, is a protocol for how the destination server can inform the sender that there was a problem. It gets used if the destination server accepts the message but can't deliver it. We'll see examples later in this chapter.

UTF-8 is the modern character encoding standard. Everything we've done in this transaction has been old-fashioned ASCII. The SMTPUTF8 feature lets you perform SMTP operations involving non-ASCII text. It's involved if your email addresses and hostnames are in, say, Chinese or Cyrillic or Arabic.

Finally, old SMTP required messages be sent one line at a time. *CHUNKING* lets the sender send messages in larger or smaller lumps.

You'll see other features out in the wild, but most are even less useful than 8BITMIME.

Now that the server has told us what it can do for us, we declare exactly who we are, using the MAIL FROM command. According to the standards, SMTP will report any problems to this address.

```
MAIL FROM:<root@mail.ratoperatedvehicle.com>
250 2.1.0 Ok
```

Again, 250 indicates that the requested action is acceptable. The 2.1.0 is new, however. It's an *extended status code*, providing more information. 2.1.0 indicates that the sender is acceptable.

The information provided in the EHLO and MAIL FROM are called the *envelope*. If the receiving MTA has problems after accepting the message, it sends warnings to the envelope's MAIL FROM address. Envelope information is recorded in the message headers, but by default are not shown to the recipient. The MAIL FROM address usually appears in the `Return-Path` header, but some MTAs use a user-invisible `From` instead. You need to look at the headers to be sure what your system does. If a message is forwarded from one server to another, the message envelope changes.

This server accepts mail from my email address, so I can pick a recipient on the other server with the `RCPT TO` (receipt to) command.

```
RCPT TO:<mwlucas@mail.solveamurder.org>
250 2.1.5 Ok
```

250 says this action is acceptable, and the extended status code 2.1.5 declares that the recipient is acceptable. We can now send our message.

```
DATA
354 End data with <CR><LF>.<CR><LF>
```

The `DATA` command is where you send the meat of the message. We get reply code 354, which is reserved for accepting a message. Start your message with the user-visible headers. Leave a blank line to separate the headers from the body of the message. End the message with a single period on a line by itself.

```
From: <root@mail.ratoperatedvehicle.com>
To:   <mwlucas@mail.solveamurder.org>
Subject: manual email message

I sent this message via netcat, like a rebel!
.
```

The first three lines, `From`, To, and Subject, are what mail clients display. With that lone period, you are back in the main SMTP session. You could just kill the netcat session, but many mail programs log such abrupt disconnections as a hint of possible network issues. Be polite, say goodbye.

```
QUIT
250 2.0.0 Ok: queued as 899B210471
221 2.0.0 Bye
```

In a moment, my account on the destination machine will have an email.

Testing Trust

We've seen how to send mail from one host to another. But what happens if you involve a third host in this transaction? Here I'm still on my host `mail.ratoperatedvehicle.com`, and I've connected to `mail.solveamurder.org`. We've completed the initial exchange of greetings and are getting down to sending actual mail.

```
MAIL FROM:<mwlucas@ratoperatedvehicle.com>
250 2.1.0 Ok
```

My sender address is fine. But I'm going to ask this system to send mail to a host that has nothing to do with it.

```
RCPT TO:<mwl@mwl.io>
454 4.7.1 <mwl@mwl.io>: Relay access denied
```

Oooh, new status messages! Status messages in the 400s are temporary errors. You could try again later. The extended status code 4.7.1 is also new. The leading 4 also means this is a temporary failure, while the 7 indicates this is a security policy. The .1 indicates that this message is not authorized, and is refused. You could try again later. It probably won't change.

This is a result of the `mynetworks` and `mynetworks_style` options. We have said which IP addresses we trust. For our initial tests, our host trusts only itself. It will never relay mail for others.

What's Wrong With SMTP?

The SMTP language is highly formalized and you must use the correct terms in the right place, but it's a computer protocol. Why does it accumulate so much loathing?

Because it's easily fooled. Consider the following session.

```
$ nc localhost 25
220 mail.ratoperatedvehicle.com ESMTP Postfix
EHLO mail.ratoperatedvehicle.com
250-mail.ratoperatedvehicle.com
...
MAIL FROM:<mwlucas@mail.ratoperatedvehicle.com>
250 2.1.0 Ok
RCPT TO:<mwlucas@mail.solveamurder.org>
250 2.1.5 Ok
DATA
354 End data with <CR><LF>.<CR><LF>
From: Emperor Palpatine <ImmortalLord@galacticempire.gov>
To: Loyal Lackey <mwlucas@mail.solveamurder.org>
Subject: Promotion

Congratulations! You have been selected as Lord Vader's
new personal assistant. Please notify your next of kin
and report for duty.


.
250 2.0.0 Ok: queued as 5D7C5105CB
QUIT
221 2.0.0 Bye
```

The EHLO, MAIL FROM, RCPT TO, and DATA commands are all exactly
what we used before. It's what's inside DATA that makes everything
go wonky. Standard mail clients default to showing only the headers
within DATA, so most users will see that this message comes from
Emperor Palpatine. If the recipient happens to work for the Empire,
they might just show up for their new job.

In real life, should the MAIL FROM and the From headers match? Yes.
Do they usually? Also yes. Is it best if they do? Certainly! Matching
headers make an email more deliverable. But *must* they? No.

If we were designing a protocol today, it would not work like this.
But SMTP is a relic of an earlier Internet, when email was a miracle
and spammers received personalized threats from Air Force officers.
Many of SMTP's ancillary protocols mitigate or reduce these flaws.
That's why I tell you to not share your test servers with the world
yet. Certainly don't tell anyone they exist until you have some basic
protections in place.

Ongoing Testing

Testing raw SMTP by hand is part of a mail administrator's education and a better party trick than psychically hauling a spaceship out of a swamp. Many antispam systems, including rspamd, hate hand-forged email. If you routinely need to test email at the protocol level, investigate Swaks (`http://www.jetmore.org/john/code/swaks/`).

SMTP Response Codes and Error Messages

Every response from an SMTP server includes a three-digit *reply code* (sometimes called a *response code*). The reply code formally states how the server reacted to your command. It's often followed by a text interpretation of that response. Reply codes include things like 220 (service is ready), 250 (request is acceptable), and 550 (request is unacceptable, fling yourself into a sarlacc pit). Human beings exposed to SMTP tend to slowly absorb the meaning of the response codes from the text interpretations, but each code has a specific formal meaning. The text expands on that meaning, explaining exactly *why* you should throw yourself into a pit. These codes were intended to be flexible and easily interpreted by human operators. A dash after the reply code means that more lines of reply follow, while a space indicates that this line is the only reply.

It turns out that flexible codes lack precision and provide insufficient guidance for literal-minded software. Also, the design of response codes left no space for expansion. A newer system of *Enhanced Mail System Status Codes* was developed to provide precise errors. Enhanced codes are composed of three numbers, like 2.1.5 or 5.7.13, and appear immediately after the response code.

We'll look at each set of messages separately.

SMTP Reply Codes

Every time the client issues an SMTP command, the server issues a *reply code* declaring how it reacted to that code. The essential reply codes are documented in RFC 5321, although later standards define occasional add-ons. While replies like "I've done that" are generic, reply codes that indicate errors often use freeform text to define the precise error. The system administrator can change that text, but the numbers must remain unchanged.

Reply codes are three-digit numbers. Each digit can have a specific meaning, depending on the number in that space. These codes were chosen to resemble FTP reply codes, so some numbers are deliberately skipped.

The first digit indicates the general type of reply.

Codes 200 to 299 are *Positive Completion* replies. Whatever the client asked for, the server did it. Maybe you just connected, maybe you finished sending an email, maybe anything in between. In general, everything is fine.

Codes 300 to 399 are *Positive Intermediate* replies. The server accepted the command, but is waiting for more information before completing the transaction. The most common is the 354 used to tell clients to begin sending the text of their message.

Codes 400 through 499 are replies. The message failed, but the client can and should try again. Perhaps the recipient's mailbox is full, or the server is undergoing maintenance, or LDAP is broken and the server can't complete anything. The client should try to resend later, without altering the message or the protocol exchange.

Codes 500 through 599 are *Permanent Negative Completion* replies. These are hard failures. The server will not accept the message, ever.

The second digit gives clarity to the type of response. Combine the first and second digits to figure out what kind of reply this is.

A middle digit of *0* indicates the reply is about *syntax*. For example, a 50x error means that the client did not speak correct SMTP.

Informational replies use a middle digit of *1*. If the client asks the server for help, and the server is willing to provide it, you'd see a 21x response.

A *2* means the reply is about the connection itself. We've seen 220, which means that the base TCP session is open and the two sides can communicate. Theoretically you could put this together with the 400 errors to declare "420 – TCP session terminated," but we can't send that message without the TCP session.

The *3* and *4* codes are not specified. They get used, but they have no cross-category definition.

A *5* is a message about the mail system itself. That's why 250 means "all is fine," while 550 is "nope, go away."

The final digit has no cross-category meaning, and is used to more specifically define the reply. That's why a 221 can be a status report, while a 551 tells the client to go elsewhere.

Reply codes first appeared in RFC 822, back in 1982. Later standards preserved old reply codes while adding new ones. For the full list as of 2023 see RFC 5321 and its updates, but many of those codes appear rarely if ever. Here are some of the most common reply codes, their formal descriptions as per the standard, and their meanings.

220 *client-hostname* Service is ready
You may proceed.

250 *client-hostname* Requested action okay and completed
Whatever the client requested, happened.

354 Start mail input; end with <CRLF>.<CRLF>
The server will accept your message.

421 *client-hostname* Service not available
The server refuses to continue not just the SMTP command, but this entire SMTP session. You'll need to reconnect to try again.

450 Requested mail action not taken: mailbox unavailable
Some temporary error with the user's account prevents the server from completing the client's command.

451 Requested action aborted: local error in processing
Something is wrong on the server. Hopefully the system administrator will notice there is a problem.

452 Requested action not taken: insufficient storage space
The server is out of disk.

500 Syntax error, command unrecognized

Maybe you misspelled RCPT TO. Maybe a Wookie pounded on your keyboard.

502 Command not implemented

You requested an SMTP feature that the server does not support.

550 Requested action not taken: mailbox unavailable

You can't mail this person, and retrying won't help.

554 Transaction failed

Whatever you requested is not going to happen. This is not your day. Go away.

The server can change the text to something more appropriate for the error. My servers use greylisting (Chapter 2). If a new host contacts them, they'll get a 451 error and the message *Greylisting in action, please come back later.* Clients automatically retry when they get a 451, but any sysadmin viewing the log will understand what's happening.

It's common to refer to categories of errors by the first digit. When someone says "a 400 error," that doesn't mean the specific code 400. There is no specific code 400. They mean an error starting from 400-499. You will also see this written as 4xx.

Enhanced Status Codes

You can easily memorize this nice simple system of three-digit codes, or read the text and figure out what's happening. Each category supports up to ten general classes of errors.

Unfortunately, even when broken up by category, the real world provides far more than ten errors. That's where *Enhanced Status Codes* come in. Each enhanced code is rigidly defined by standards. Where you might add clarifying text to a reply code, if you need a new enhanced code you must work through the IETF and IANA. Each enhanced code is three numbers, separated by periods.

The first number is the *class*, which defines a general type of message. Like reply codes, a 2 indicates success, a 4 is a persistent transient failure, and a 5 is a permanent failure. There is no 1 or 3.

The second number is the *subject*, defining what part of the system this message pertains to. Unlike reply codes, we currently have eight values.

A subject of 0 indicates that there's no additional information.

A 1 is about addressing. This is a message about the sender or the recipient's address.

A 2 is about a mailbox. Mailbox errors are overwhelmingly tied to the recipient, but there's a couple cases where such messages indicate a problem with the sender.

A 3 declares this code is about the destination mail system.

A 4 is about networking and routing. It's much like 3, except it's for services that support the mail system such as LDAP, DNS, and so on.

A 5 says this code is about the mail delivery protocol.

A 6 indicates this message relates to the content of the message. This could be encoding errors, content types, and the like.

A 7 indicates this is a security or policy code.

Combining the class and the subject immediately identifies the general sort of issue. If you send mail and the server replies with an enhanced status beginning with 4.3, that means "something's going on with the destination mail system, but you can retry." A code starting with 2.1 says, "everything is okay, but here's some details about the recipient mailbox." A 5.7.anything declares "You cannot try again, per our policy." Anyone refused by policy probably did something to earn that refusal, and the sort of sender you block from mailing you will probably try again, but they own that problem.

The last digit is the *enumerated status code*, indicating a specific error. While almost any subject can be applied to each of the classes, enumerated status codes have different definitions by subject. An enumerated status code of 1 means something totally different in 4.1.1, 4.2.1, 4.3.1, and so on. The only way to identify a complete status code is to check IANA's *Simple Mail Transfer Protocol (SMTP) Enhanced Status Codes Registry,* available at `https://www.iana.org/assignments/smtp-enhanced-status-codes/smtp-enhanced-status-codes.xhtml` and almost certainly indexed by your least loathed search engine. Here are some of the more common codes you'll see, however.

2.0.0 Technically this means "other undefined status," but it usually means "command accepted and carried out."

2.1.0 The formal definition of this code is "Something about the address specified in the message caused this DSN." We'll look at DSNs in the next section. Generally, this means that the sender's address is acceptable.

2.1.5 The recipient address is valid.

4.1.8 The sender's domain does not resolve. This might be a transient DNS issue or a rebooting backend server, so the sender can reasonably try again in a few.

4.2.0 The "undefined retryable status" message means that an otherwise undescribed issue on the recipient's system is preventing delivery. You'll often see this with greylisting.

4.4.1 The "no answer from host" status is logged when the sender can't reach the destination server.

5.7.1 Message Refused. The destination server is explicitly blocking the sender. This is used for spammers, harassers, or other bad actors.

Enhanced codes most often appear combined with the reply code. Look at the previous section, where we sent mail by hand, for examples. You'll also see them in the log. One major driver in their development was for use in Delivery Status Notifications.

Delivery Status Notifications

Users want to know if emails they send are received, read, or go astray. *Delivery Status Notifications*, or *DSNs*, fulfill that role. Most often these notices are not returned to the human sender, instead appearing in error logs or SMTP transactions. One purpose behind the design of extended status codes was to support a detailed system of DSNs.

Message senders might want to know when recipients read their messages, and some clients let users request DSNs. It turns out that when those same senders receive messages in turn, they aren't so keen on letting others know they've read their email. Many people prefer privacy about when they read emails. Additionally, email clients can only see when a message has been opened, not when the recipient actually reads the text. While a few enterprise systems like Microsoft Exchange still offer unreliable "read receipt" notices, they're not built on DSNs.

The place you'll most often see DSNs is in mail system logs or bounce messages. DSNs are always enhanced status codes.

Greylisting

Email wasned in an era when hardware was pricey and redundancy was not in the budget. As hardware was not fault-tolerant, the protocol had to be. SMTP reserves 400 reply codes specifically for "I won't accept this message right now, but please do try again later." Legitimate MTAs accept that message and try again a few minutes or an hour later, or immediately detour to the backup MTA. Spambots use sloppy SMTP stacks so they can race through millions of email addresses. They'll probably try to contact you again, once they work through their list of victims. That might take days. Anti-spam activists will add them to a DNS block list (DNSBL) well before then. That leaves an obvious solution: the first time any SMTP client contacts your MTA, tell it to come back later. Keep a list of the servers that return, and accept their mail immediately from now on.

The legitimate hosts will try again. The illegitimate ones who do return won't make it past your anti-spam defenses. Unlike block lists, this approach is called *greylisting*.

Greylisting is a divisive technique. The first time a site mails your server, greylisting delays messages anywhere from a couple minutes to a couple hours. If people in your organization insist that email is instantaneous despite all evidence to the contrary, that's a problem. If some web site uses email to send authentication codes that are only valid for ten minutes, that's a problem. (The problem is that the web site is delivering ephemeral data via an unsuitable protocol, but it's still a problem.) Some domains use large server farms of MTAs, and resend attempts almost never come from the same IP address. That's definitely a problem.

Some folks get great results from greylisting and very little pain. Some find the problems outweigh the benefits. As with everything in systems administration, you have the privilege of choosing your preferred suffering. Even if you don't use greylisting, your email system must tolerate MTAs that do. Greylisting is indistinguishable from temporary failures.

One fun thing about greylisting is that you might accidentally deploy it. Postscreen (Chapter 9) includes deep inspection functions that are not deliberate greylisting, but the effects are indistinguishable from greylisting. Rspamd (Chapter 14) implements deliberate greylisting. If you want a more flexible greylisting policy server, consider Postgrey (http://postgrey.schweikert.ch/).

Backscatter

If an MTA is going to reject a message, it should do so during the SMTP conversation. Your MTA should never accept a message, close the connection, and then generate a new message back to the sender saying "Sorry, I can't deliver this." Such messages are called *backscatter*, and are always bad. It can even be used as an attack vector!

Backscatter is generally the result of spam. If a spammer forges your email address as a source for their junk, you might get dozens or hundreds of "your message was undeliverable/objectionable/ forbidden" notices. Misconfigurations can also generate backscatter.

If your server generates a new message addressed to the apparent source of an email, there's a good chance that it's replying to spam. The replies will, at best, annoy a completely unrelated person and at worse get yur server flagged as a spam generator. Automated replies to undeliverable messages usually contain the message, so your backscatter will include the junk that caused the problem in the first place!

Accept only deliverable mail. Refuse the rest during the initial SMTP connection.

DNS Block Lists

Most spam comes from malware-infected computers, or *spambots*. The computer owner is probably unaware of the infection. Large ISPs usually block port 25 to keep infected consumer machines from spewing garbage, which is annoying for knowledgeable folks who want to run MTAs at home but does keep the ISP's support load manageable. Badly maintained servers also get infected, however, and those have unfiltered Internet connections.

Spam fighters formed organizations to track infected hosts. When a new spam source is identified, its IP address is added to a list. Systems are constantly compromised and transformed into spam sources. They are secured and repaired, but at a less steady rate. You must check the block list every time a host requests an SMTP connection. These block lists are distributed via DNS, and are called *DNS Block Lists* (DNSBL). (You'll also see *Reputation Block Lists*, or RBLs, but that term is trademarked.) By refusing all mail from hosts on a reliable block list, you immediately stop the overwhelming majority of spam.

That's the catch: a *reliable* block list.

This is the Internet. Just as anyone can run a web site, anyone can publish a block list—and you can't tell by the name. These projects were overwhelmingly founded by infuriated geeks, and often grew beyond their original intent and scale. "Spam Eating Monkey" is a highly trustworthy list provider, while some official-looking lists should more properly be named "HTML Email Is Immoral And I Carry A Grudge."

How do you find reliable block lists? Spamhaus (`https://spamhaus.org`) is the largest and best-known, but others exist and you shouldn't rely on only one. Talk to your fellow sysadmins and see who they use. You'll also find blocklist test tools all over the Internet, often provided by commercial services as part of their efforts to persuade you to outsource your email. These tools include a list of block lists that they check. I've used MX Toolbox (`https://mxtoolbox.com`) for decades, but the best way for me to destroy a company is by mentioning it in a book, so look around.

DNSBLs are not perfect. Newly infected systems might spew thousands of spams before they're identified and added to a list. Hosts can be added in error or because of temporary problems. If you misconfigure your MTA and become an open relay, you'll go on a list—even if you catch your error immediately and fix the problem in three minutes, anti-spam software will catch junk relayed through your host and add you to these lists.

People also maintain DNSBL lists like "domains registered in the last week" or "domains identified in a spam trap." Which should you use? That depends entirely on your personal spam tolerance and the software you're using. If you check the EHLO statement against a DNSBL for checking domains in the message body, it won't work well.

Each DNSBL has its own editorial policy. You might want an aggressive DNSBL that blocks anything vaguely suspicious, or a more tolerant list. For demonstration I use Spamhaus ZEN (`https://www.spamhaus.org`) and SpamRATS (`https://www.spamrats.com`). Both are free for small non-commercial MTAs. Check each DNSBL provider to get the correct zone to query to access the list—and remember, you can't usefully query these from public resolvers.

Developing DNSBLs

"Whenever a host sends spam it gets added to a block list" sounds straightforward enough, but it covers a multitude of problems. What is spam? How is it identified? You could call it "unsolicited commercial email," but I have gotten spam encouraging me to convert to a particular faith. Your belief that everyone should convert to a strict vegan diet might be non-commercial, sincere, and even good for the continued existence of the human race, but if you send it to half a million random mailboxes in an hour it's spam.

The real test is: does the recipient want the message? Did they ask for it? Is this part of an ongoing discussion or relationship?

Spammers collect email addresses by buying lists and crawling web sites. Those lists are often full of obsolete email addresses, but the sellers don't care. If a conference publishes a list of attendees and their email addresses, those addresses are bait for spam. DNSBL maintainers leverage this to create *spam traps*, email addresses that have never sent mail and should never receive it. They publicize spam trap addresses on dedicated web pages, and spammers pick that up. Anything sent to a spam trap is, by definition, unwanted. The sending host might immediately get added to a block list.

Email addresses that are no longer in use by people can be redeployed as spam traps. If someone leaves an organization and their email address is shut down, messages to that address should bounce. Responsible correspondents will stop contacting that address. After a couple years, anything sent to that address is probably but not necessarily spam. An old friend might reach out now and then and get a bounce. A host attempting to email several defunct email addresses a few years after they were disabled is almost certainly sending spam.

Spam is also identified by message contents. If we know that a particular domain name is used by malware or scammers, any emails containing that domain name in the header or the body is probably spam.

A block list maintainer might also add a host to the block list for suspicious behavior. A server that attempts to reply to every spam message it receives is making life more difficult for thousands of sysadmins. That kind of behavior can get you blocked.

Finally, there's the time-honored method of someone reading a message and dropping it in the spam folder. Those messages can be analyzed for common elements.

DNSBL Delivery

Most block lists are queried via DNS. This is why your mail systems must have their own recursive nameservers. Block lists limit the number of queries they accept from a single IP, and Google's public resolvers quickly overflow those limits. When the limits overflow, queries are either ignored or always answered with either "block" or "accept." Your server will either cheerfully accept all the spam, or refuse all mail.

Some block lists are also delivered via protocols like *Border Gateway Protocol* (BGP). If you're an experienced network operator, you might consider adding a blocklist BGP feed to your network border. Blocking known spammers from connecting to your network would protect every host in your network. Anyone who knows enough BGP to implement this understands the risks. For everyone else: when your network manager says they won't do it, they have good reasons.[14]

Anti-spam block lists are highly dynamic, and not usually downloadable. Downloading an entire block list would be inefficient, as the number of hosts that poke your server will be a tiny fraction of the spam-generating hosts on the Internet. You must configure your systems to query the list over one of the supported methods. We will focus on DNS queries.

Some block list providers also offer other types of block lists that change more slowly, and those might be downloadable. Examples include Spamhaus' Don't Route Or Peer (DROP) list of addresses that regional registries assigned to known criminal operations, and the Extended DROP list that contains sub-allocations to criminals. The content of such block lists are also included in the broader DNS checks, though, so there's no need to download them.

Postfix supports DNSBL checks via postscreen(8) (Chapter 9).

DNSBL Queries and Responses

RFC 5782 describes the full block list protocol, but here's the basics.

A DNSBL zone resembles the reverse zones used in `in-addr.arpa`. IP addresses are listed in reverse order, so that the more specific identifiers appear first. This appears within the block list zone. The block zone has brief caching times, so changes are distributed within an hour or two. Suppose I run an DNSBL with the zone `spam.mwl.io`. You want to check the DNSBL for the host `192.0.2.84`. Reverse the IP address (84.2.0.192) and stick it in front of the block list zone.

---

14   That reason might be "incompetence," but *do* treasure coworkers who understand their limits.

```
$ dig 84.2.0.192.spam.mwl.io +short
$
```

No results (or NXDOMAIN) means that the address is not on the block list.

```
$ dig 85.2.0.192.spam.mwl.io +short
127.0.0.9
127.0.0.2
127.0.0.4
```

A response of 127.0.0.2 means that this host *is* on the block list. All block list responses are in 127/8 so that if the list gets misused, it won't damage the network. Responses of other 127/8 IP addresses give more detail about why this address is blocked. These codes are blocklist-specific. You might find a human-readable TXT record that offers a rationale, though.

```
$ dig 85.2.0.192.spam.mwl.io +short txt
"Believes that Luke was the hero of Star Wars when it
   was clearly Marcia Lucas"
```

Again: not all block lists are equal.

Milters

Reliable MTAs like Postfix are deliberately simple. They do not analyze the content of messages, or even validate add-on protocols like SPF and DKIM. Instead, most mail systems use a mail filter (or *milter*) interface to hand these tasks off to external daemons. Milters were created for Sendmail, but quickly became the Unix standard. The word *milter* might mean the API, a program, or the filter itself.

Milters let specialized, unprivileged programs perform specific processing of messages and provide feedback on how the MTA should treat the message. A milter might validate SPF and tell Postfix to accept or reject incoming messages based on the results of that validation. A milter can analyze a message body and provide a spam score that clients can use to evaluate messages. Postfix offers two ways to call milters.

Some milters should be applied to mail arriving over the network via SMTP. This is generally mail arriving from foreign networks on port 25, but might include submissions on port 465. Postfix calls these *SMTP-only filters*. Such mail should be checked for compliance to policies like SPF and DKIM, then further evaluated by antivirus and antispam software. To apply a milter to every listening SMTP server, use the `smtpd_milters` option in `main.cf`. If you want to apply the milter to only a particular service, such as mail arriving from the public via port 25, add `smtpd_milters` as to the service entry in `master.cf`. We'll see examples throughout this book.

Not all messages arrive via SMTP. Mail originating from the local host arrives via command line or a program like cron(8). Mail from user clients arrives via the submission service. Yes, the submission protocol uses an authenticated SMTP session, but it's a separate process than the one accepting random mail from the public (Chapter 5). Submitted mail gets handed to the public-facing port 25 SMTP server through purely internal non-SMTP processes. Just as you wouldn't want to require the public to authenticate to your port 25 mail, you wouldn't want to apply SPF checks to mail arriving via submission. Postfix calls these *non-SMTP milters*. They are mostly used for adding authentication information to outgoing mail. Configure non-SMTP milters with the `non_smtpd_milters` option. We'll use `smptd_milters` to connect Postfix to rspamd in Chapter 7.

Milters are external programs, and fail independently of Postfix. Maybe they crash, or maybe you're restarting them. By default, when Postfix can't reach a milter it answers SMTP requests with a temporary failure. If you discover you have a buggy milter that crashes too frequently, you could use `milter_default_action` to accept messages even when a configured milter doesn't answer or is unavailable.

```
milter_default_action = accept
```

You could also permanently `reject` incoming mail when one of your milters fails, but that annoys and confuses external senders.

Message Forwarding

There are two traditional methods of resending received messages to another recipient, bouncing and forwarding.

Bounce, like *server*, is an overloaded word with multiple meanings depending on context. An undeliverable email bounces from the recipient's server. As a user, however, *bouncing* a message is resending the message exactly as it was received, with a new sender in the envelope but an otherwise unchanged header and body. The recipient sees the message exactly as if they were the original recipient. Validators for SPF and DKIM often declare bounced messages to be invalid, and many MTAs today refuse to accept their users bouncing messages to other accounts.

Forwarding creates a brand new message with the original either encapsulated as an attachment or inline, and includes the forwarder's email address and other information. SPF and DKIM checkers do not evaluate attachments or message bodies, so the destination server can validate these messages.

Mailing lists might arguably be considered message forwarders, but modern mailing lists alter headers and add new authentication information to each message. Those messages do not show up as attachments, but neither are they identical to the original message the way bounced messages would be.

Now that you can figure out what your mail system is trying to tell you, let's set up Postfix and Dovecot.

Chapter 3: Postfix and Dovecot Setup

Postfix is a popular freely-available open-source mail server software that has been continuously debugged for decades, making it an excellent choice for an Internet-facing mail system. Your operating system probably provides several Postfix packages. Choose the package that integrates support for your preferred database.

Postfix Components

In keeping with the general Unix philosophy, Postfix includes several small programs that each handle a specific mail handling task. Each program offers one or more named *services* that support moving messages from one part of the email system to another. It also includes programs intended for managing the email system.

Services

All Postfix configuration files live in `/etc/postfix/` or `/usr/local/etc/postfix`. For convenience, this book refers to `/etc/postfix`. Most of these programs read their configuration from `main.cf`.

The master(8) daemon supervises the Postfix suite, starting each smaller program as needed. Control Postfix's core functions by configuring the master daemon in `master.cf`.

New mail gets placed in a `maildrop` directory. The pickup(8) daemon watches for new messages and hands them to cleanup(8).

The cleanup(8) program inspects it and performs needed corrections such as adding missing headers, removing duplicate recipients, setting up blind carbon copies, and so on. It inserts the message into the queue and adds it to the queue manager's list.

The mail queue manager qmgr(8) tracks messages in the mail queue and invokes other programs to attempt to deliver them. It handles delayed mail separately from new mail, so that attempts to deliver mail with problems does not slow down new messages.

Brand new mail generated on the local system or by IMAP clients is handed to the trivial-rewrite(8) daemon, which normalizes destination email addresses according to local policy before allowing it to proceed.

Once a message's destination email address has been normalized, the queue manager can hand it to another program. Mail bound for other servers gets handed to smtp(8). Postfix's local(8) and virtual(8) programs are designed for Unix-style mailboxes and virtual mailboxes respectively, but we'll replace both with Dovecot delivery agents so that clients can configure server-side filtering.

Postfix supports a variety of special options. Its *transport* feature can route mail to specific domains through a particular relay, UUCP, or even a shell script. It can rearrange email headers any way you wish. We won't cover those rare environments: once you understand how Postfix works, configuring Postfix is straightforward. (Configuring UUCP, not so much.)

Commands

Postfix includes several programs for managing system activity. We'll discuss many of these throughout this book, but here's an overview.

The postconf(1) program aggregates system configuration, giving a unified view of Postfix's built-in defaults and configuration file settings. It can also change those settings for you.

The postfix(1) program controls Postfix. It lets you stop and start the system, or reload the configuration files. It has several additional features for repairs and upgrades. Many systemd-based Linuxes handle Postfix services poorly, so you'll need to use `postfix` rather than `systemctl`.[15]

The Postfix queue management program, postqueue(1), lets you manage the various mail queues and verify queue integrity.

The postsuper(1) program lets you manually poke various parts of Postfix.

---

15   Those systemctl implementations do not exclusively fumble Postfix. They fumble *everything.*

Many of the Postfix sub-programs are meant to be called by Postfix, not by human beings. Most Postfix installs stash them someplace where it hopes you won't find them, usually `/usr/local/libexec/postfix` on BSD or `/usr/lib/postfix/sbin` directory on Debian.

Postfix Configuration Options

Modern mail exchangers need to speak the current SMTP protocol, but if they're designed for broad use they must also support older implementations of SMTP. It's easy to declare that you'll only communicate with modern MTAs, but your organization compels differently. That critical client that your entire business depends on? They haven't updated their mail system since the last time Yoda lost his temper, but you have to exchange messages with them. While a basic Postfix configuration will let you exchange messages with most servers, `main.cf` supports almost a thousand options that let you cope with almost any condition. Every option is documented in postconf(5).

How can anyone cope with Postfix's thousand configuration options? The trite answer is "more easily than a typical-two thousand-line Sendmail configuration" but more practically, a typical environment needs only a handful of options. Each configuration option consists of an option name, an equals sign, and a value.

```
home_mailbox = Maildir/
myhostname = mail.mwl.io
```

Certain options can take multiple arguments or accept environment variables.

```
debugger_command =
   PATH=/bin:/usr/bin:/usr/local/bin:/usr/X11R6/bin
   ddd $daemon_directory/$process_name $process_id
   & sleep 5
```

How can you possibly manage all of these?

You can't, so try not to.

Your operating system almost certainly ships with a default configuration. Start there. Debian offers a `main.cf` that contains what the package maintainers consider the minimum for a working mail system. FreeBSD's `main.cf.sample` is the same, plus a couple dozen commented-out examples that a reasonable site might need.

Each configuration option is also usable as a variable. Once you define an option, you can use it in another configuration setting by putting a $ in front of it. Here I set the configuration option `mydestination` to be equivalent to the option `myhostname`.

```
mydestination = $myhostname
```

Changing `myhostname` automatically changes `mydestination`.

Unlike many other programs, breaking up long lines rarely requires a backslash. A line that begins with whitespace is assumed to be a continuation of the previous line. Here I set `mynetworks` to a list of four values.

```
mynetworks = 127.0.0.0/8
  [::1]/128
  198.51.100.128/26
  [2001:db8:bad:c0de::]/64
```

Postfix is smart enough to aggregate these into a single line entry.

Statements in `main.cf` are processed in order. Rule order is irrelevant most of the time, but if you start using some of the anti-spam features described later, that order is vital. The first matching configuration statement wins, so if you put "refuse mail from these hosts" in front of "accept mail from these hosts," a host on both lists will get blocked.

Many configuration options have names that begin with `smtpd`, while other options have names beginning with `smtp`. It's easy to confuse `smtp_tls_security_level` with `smtpd_tls_security_level`. Settings that begin with `smtpd_` affect the running daemon that receives mail. Ones that start with `smtp_` affect the outbound SMTP sessions that send mail. This division lets you establish settings like "we accept mail however it comes, but only send mail over TLS."

postconf(1)

The postconf(1) program can be used to examine and change the current configuration. While Postfix's configuration files are human-readable, each configuration option has a default value compiled into Postfix. Each can be overriden in the configuration file. It's easy to get confused.

To get a complete list of options, run `postconf -d`. Save this to a file for easy reference.

 # postconf -d > main.cf.default

A glance at this file offers a bewildering number of options, but most of them apply only to edge cases.[16] This book discusses only those that are most useful for running a small mail system.

Out of all of those options, which have been explicitly set in `main.cf`? You could run `grep -v` and strip out the comments and blank lines, or you could ask `postconf` with the -n flag.

 # postconf -n > postconf-n

The most interesting configuration options are those that have been set to a non-default value. An explicitly configured setting isn't the same as non-default, however. I often explicitly set default values to remind me of the basics. Use comm(1) to compare the current configuration with the default settings. The `comm` program expects sorted output, but `postconf` sorts its output by default. Be sure to

---

16   The Internet is composed entirely of edge cases. Some of them are as sharp as laser swords.

put the output of `postconf -n` as the first argument and the default settings second, so that we print the non-default options.[17]

```
# comm -23 postconf-n main.cf.default
compatibility_level = 3.7
mynetworks_style = host
smtp_tls_CApath = /etc/ssl/certs
```

The maintainers of this package believe that these settings are the bare minimum that might—*might*—give you email. More probably, these are the settings that every Postfix install needs on this operating system. What do these mean?

The `compatibility_level` option tells Postfix to log backwards-compatibility warnings after an upgrade. This is a brand-new install of Postfix 3.7, so why have a compatibility warning? We don't need tshis now, but one day we might upgrade to 3.8. The upgraded daemons will look at *main.cf*, see this warning, and say "Ah! I need to parse 3.7 options, but log warnings that they're being used and point people at the new options." Postfix doesn't arbitrarily rename options, and it's pretty feature-complete at this point, but an existing option might be split into parts for more precise mail handling. Once you've cleaned up any of these warnings, change `compatibility_level` to the current Postfix version.

MTAs have a list of hosts that they trust to not send spam. This might be the range of IP addresses supporting the organization's desktops and servers. The `mynetworks_style` option tells Postfix which hosts to trust by default. Setting this to `host` means that Postfix trusts only the host it's installed on, and won't relay mail from anywhere on the network. It will accept mail to be delivered to the local host. To forward email from unauthenticated clients, you must explicitly configure acceptable address ranges. This is also a sensible default on today's Internet.

Email can use TLS. The `smtp_tls_CApath` option tells Postfix where to find this host's trusted X.509 Certificate Authority certificates.

Some packages set more options by default, but options all follow this general pattern.

---

17   The postconf(1) manual page includes a different example of how to compare these, but it's not portable between shells and thus unworthy of our attention.

Viewing Postfix Components

Postfix includes many smaller programs and services that might or might not be in use in any environment. The master(8) daemon starts these programs as per the default configuration, as overridden by `master.cf`. The postconf(1) program's –M flag parses all of this and presents what master(8) intends to start.

```
# postconf -M
smtp      inet  n    -    n    -      -    smtpd
pickup    unix  n    -    n    60     1    pickup
cleanup   unix  n    -    n    -      0    cleanup
qmgr      unix  n    -    n    300    1    qmgr
...
```

These might not all be running constantly. They might not even be separate daemons. But if master(8) needs support from a service, this is how it invokes and configures that service.

The first column is the service name. This snippet shows the essential Postfix services: smtp, pickup, cleanup, and qmgr. The smtp service listens to the network, where the others process received mail as discussed earlier this chapter.

The second column declares how this service connects to the system. Anything listed as inet listens to the network, while unix entries indicate a Unix socket. Postfix communicates internally mostly via sockets.

The third field indicates if this is a private service. "Private" services are internal to Postfix and the sysadmin cannot interact with them. As the sysadmin you can tell Postfix to send and receive mail, flush or erase the queue, and so on. You can configure other services like internal error handling or the log, but you can't interact with them.

The fourth field tells if this service is unprivileged. Most of Postfix runs as an unprivileged user such as **postfix**. Certain features, like delivering mail to users, must run as **root**. A – indicates this service is unprivileged. An n declares that this service needs **root**.

97

The fifth field declares if this service runs chrooted in
/var/spool/postfix. In a default install, this is always n for no. Many
of these services can be run in a chroot, but you must first add device
nodes and log sockets to the queue directory. That's a highly operating-
system-dependent process. Once Postfix is running correctly, you can
investigate chroots on your own.

The sixth field is the wake-up timer. If there's a number here,
the master process pokes these services at intervals of that many
seconds. The pickup daemon gets prodded to check for mail every
sixty seconds. The queue manager is told to process the queue every
five minutes.

The seventh field is the number of processes that this service can
run. A dash indicates Postfix can run up to the default limit of 100.
Here' Postfix will start up to 100 smtp(8) daemons as it needs to
handle its MTA duties. When a service bottlenecks or overwhelms
the system, you might think of setting or raising this limit, but some
services can only run one daemon at a time and others will not work if
you set any limits on them. Every service has a manual page. Consult
it before changing any process limits.

Last we have the command name and any arguments or options.

Running postconf -M gives a view of the entire system, but if you
want to see the configuration of a specific component, give its name
as an argument. To see how often the queue manager retries delayed
mail, check qmgr.

```
# postconf -M qmgr
qmgr     unix  n     -       n       300     1       qmgr
```

Maybe I don't know if this particular host is running the
submission service that accepts client emails.

```
# postconf -M submission
postconf: warning: unmatched request: "submission"
```

This Postfix install doesn't know anything about that service. We'll
edit *master.cf* to enable it in Chapter 5.

Commands versus Editors

You can edit *main.cf* and other Postfix configuration files with a text editor, or you can use postconf(1) to make the changes. Which is correct?

Both, and neither.

The more important question is, how are you managing your servers? If you use an automation system like Ansible to command your fleet of hosts, you're already using command-driven configuration. If you're running a single artisanal server, you're comfortable with firing up a proper text editor and making changes directly in the file. Perhaps you store your configuration files in a version control system and push them to production. Use whichever method works for you. This book uses both methods.

Set a configuration option at the command line by giving the option and its value in quotes as an argument.

```
# postconf "home_mailbox=Maildir/"
```

Unlike programs like vipw(1) or visudo(1), `postconf` performs no validity tests. If you use postconf to set the option `UseTheForceLuke` to `yes`, it will do so. You will see "unused parameter" warnings when restarting Postfix, but postconf won't warn you in advance. That's harmless. If you move your X.509 CA certificates and set the option `smtp_ssl_CApath` instead of `smtp_tls_CApath`, that's not so harmless.

Any time you change *main.cf* or another configuration file, you must reload or restart Postfix.

Reloading or Restarting Postfix

Postfix's various services work best when they are started and stopped in a particular order or on their own schedule. Postfix uses the postfix(1) program for managing these core functions and more.

Fire up Postfix with the `start` option.

```
# postfix start
postfix/postfix-script: starting the Postfix mail system
```

To shut Postfix down cleanly, use the `stop` option.

```
# postfix stop
postfix/postfix-script: stopping the Postfix mail system
```

Configuration changes are a little more complex. Postfix programs notice configuration changes only at startup, or when told to look. Some Postfix daemons run persistently. Others self-terminate after handling a certain number of requests or after a specific duration. The queue manager, for example, gets started every ten minutes. If you change a setting relevant to the queue manager, that change takes effect the next time the queue manager runs. If you change something relevant to master(8), the only way Postfix will notice is when you reload or restart Postfix. Rather than sorting out if a particular change will be picked up automatically, it's best to make Postfix services reread their configuration files with `reload`.

```
# postfix reload
postfix/postfix-script: refreshing the Postfix
    mail system
```

These look a lot like features provided by programs like service(8) and systemctl(8). Should you use `postfix`, or rely on your operating system's management features? It shouldn't matter, but it might. In most Unixes, programs like service(8) call `postfix` in a manner appropriate for that operating system. Use whichever you prefer. If you find that one tool doesn't work in a particular situation or is missing a feature provided by the other, ask for support and (if needed) file a bug report.

Before doing anything else, configure how Postfix handles incoming mail.

Postfix Essentials

An MTA must know what domain it sends mail as, which domains it accepts mail for, and which clients it will relay mail for. These three things are not necessarily the same! Organizations that need (or have been sold) complicated mail systems often have separate sending and receiving systems, and perhaps an additional layer of client-facing servers if the salesman got *really* lucky. For our test systems, however, we'll start by making each the sole MTA for their domain.

Why can't Postfix just pull this from the operating system? An MTA sending messages via SMTP must identify itself by a fully qualified domain name (FQDN). SMTP can't use a short hostname like `mail`: it requires full names like `mail.solveamurder.org`. No two Unixes agree on how the system should store or retrieve the FQDN. Some Unixes use the fully qualified domain name as the hostname, so that hostname(1) retrieves it. Others remove domain information from the hostname. Worse, highly experienced systems administrators disagree vehemently on this topic and override their system's defaults. Some Postfix package maintainers assume that the system has no clue about its own FQDN and hard-code one for you, while others assume that the system provides complete and accurate information and rely on it. In complicated mail systems, the host's FQDN is not the FQDN Postfix should use to send mail. Every default approach fails for someone. The wisest package maintainers realize that they have no control over any of this and shove the entire problem where it belongs: on you.

We could read the configuration files, consider all the possibilities, and create a hypothetical understanding of Postfix's configuration. Or we could configure sensible defaults on the most vital options and not worry about any of this. We'll do that.

Set Mailbox Format

Chapter 1 discussed the two common mailbox formats, mbox and Maildir. While mbox is fine for a host that doesn't handle much mail, a message store should always use Maildir. We'll be sending and receiving messages as we build and test, so set the mailbox format before doing anything else.

The option `home_mailbox` controls how Postfix stores incoming mail. By default it is empty, letting the system stash incoming mail wherever it likes—usually in */var/mail*. By giving `home_mailbox` a value, you're telling Postfix to add new messages to a file with that name in the user's home directory. A filename that ends in a slash instructs Postfix to use Maildir format, while filenames mean mbox. Here we set `home_mbox` to use the standard Maildir directory, *$HOME/Maildir*.[18]

```
home_mailbox = Maildir/
```

Restart Postfix and send a test mail.

```
# echo "very first message" | \
  mailx -s "message 1" mwlucas@localhost
```

If you go to your home directory on this machine, you'll see a new *Maildir* directory. It contains the default *cur*, *new*, and *tmp* folders. Look inside new and you'll find a file with a long name. This is your new email message. Examine the headers.

```
Return-Path: <root@mail.localdomain>
X-Original-To: mwlucas@localhost
Delivered-To: mwlucas@localhost
Received: by mail.localdomain (Postfix, from userid 0)
   id 55B3710CC1; Thu,  8 Jun 2023 14:05:30 -0400 (EDT)
To: mwlucas@localhost
Subject: message 1
Message-Id: <20230608180530.55B3710CC1@mail.localdomain>
Date: Thu,  8 Jun 2023 14:05:30 -0400 (EDT)
From: Charlie Root <root@mail.localdomain>
```

---

18   If you get clever and set home_mailbox to *mbox/* your fellow admins will ruin your life by any and all means available. Don't ask me how I know.

As we saw in the last chapter, the Return-Path header tells a mail exchanger where to send bounced messages. This message is supposed to be bounced to `root@mail.localdomain`. That's not valid on the public Internet. This is from an unconfigured mail system that doesn't know its domain name. Headers like `Received` and `Message-Id` reinforce this. You must configure this Postfix install.

Set the Hostname and Domain

The option `myhostname` tells Postfix what it should use for the local host's name. Postfix uses myhostname as a default for many other options, and uses it as part of other options. Even if hostname(1) returns the host's FQDN, always set `myhostname` in *main.cf*.

Similarly, the option `mydomain` sets the local domain name. Postfix defaults to using `myhostname` minus the first term. Postfix uses the local domain as the default for many other options.

Technically, you don't need to set both. Postfix takes a decent guess if hostname(1) returns a FQDN or not. Give your mail system all the information it needs to work even if an operating system update, organizational policy change, or sysadmin with different biases alters the output of `hostname`. Set both.

```
myhostname = mail.ratoperatedvehicle.com
mydomain = ratoperatedvehicle.com
```

We'll use these to further configure Postfix.

Outbound Mail Domain

You must define which domain or domains Postfix will send from. Postfix will use this information to polish any emails it receives from clients, so that it can transform email from **mwl** into something with a valid address.

We'll cover virtual domains in Chapter 4. For now, we're configuring mail from the hostname as discussed in Chapter 1. Use the **myorigin** option to tell Postfix the entity it's sending mail from. This machine should default to sending mail as its own hostname. We've already set that as an option, so we can reuse it.

```
myorigin = $myhostname
```

Remember, mail to your hostname-free domain is better served as a virtual domain.

Inbound Mail Domain

Shouldn't an MTA receive mail for the same domains it sends mail from? Most commonly yes—but not always. Define which hosts or domains Postfix accepts mail for with the mydestination option. The default is to accept mail for $myhostname and **localhost**, but make that explicit.

```
mydestination = $myhostname localhost.$mydomain localhost
```

Why specify both localhost.$mydomain and localhost? Different programs on the host might try to send mail with different address formats. It's easier to accept the common legitimate formats than identify and change the software.

Trusted IP Addresses

If Postfix trusts an IP address, it will forward any messages originating from that address anywhere on the Internet. Blindly trusting IP addresses means that any compromised system desktop or server can become a Death Star of Spam and land your MTA on dozens of blacklists in minutes. Servers that send unauthenticated status and alarm messages should transmit everything to your main mail system.[19] Desktop clients should authenticate before being permitted to send mail outside your network.

Postfix defaults to trusting only the local machine, but a package maintainer might change that default. Use the mynetworks_style option to explicitly declare one of two types of trusted IP addresses. Set it to host to trust only the local host, or subnet to blindly trust every host on the local network no matter how much garbage they're spewing or where said garbage claims to originate from.

```
mynetworks_style = host
```

---

19   Only a real human can properly ignore alarms.

If an intruder breaks into this system your host could still spew the aforementioned torrent of garbage, but that's a much smaller attack surface than your entire network.

If you do need to trust particular IP addresses that are not just "everything local to this host," look at the `mynetworks` option in the next chapter.

X.509 Certificates

There's no reason not to use a valid X.509 certificate when deploying a mail system today. Valid certificates are now free, and you should understand how to manage them. If you need guidance, my book *TLS Mastery* (Tilted Windmill Press, 2021) discusses X.509 certificates and TLS in explicit detail.

Postfix expects all certificates in PEM format. The main question is when working with X.509, how do you store your key files? Traditionally, one file contains the private key and another contains the certificate as well as any intermediate certificates. (Not including the intermediate certificate is perhaps the most common error in configuring TLS.) The file containing the certificate and intermediate certificates is called the *chain* file. Some server software other than Postfix even expects you to combine the key file with the chain file to avoid rare race conditions. Either way, specify the server's certificate files with `smtpd_tls_chain_files`.

With separate key and chain files, specify the key first and then the chain.

```
smtpd_tls_chain_files =
  /etc/certs/solveamurder.org/privkey.pem,
  /etc/certs/solveamurder.org/fullchain.pem
```

If you have a single combined key/chain file, use it as the only argument.

```
smtpd_tls_chain_files =
  /etc/certs/solveamurder.org/keyWithChain.pem
```

If you have multiple certificates with different algorithms, list them one after the other.

```
smtpd_tls_chain_files =
  /etc/certs/solveamurder.org/rsa-privkey.pem,
  /etc/certs/solveamurder.org/rsa-fullchain.pem,
  /etc/certs/solveamurder.org/ecdsa-privkey.pem,
  /etc/certs/solveamurder.org/ecdsa-fullchain.pem
```

The manual will show that there are corresponding smtp_ options for sending mail, but there's no need to configure a certificate for sending messages unless the receiver requires client authentication.

Standard TLS

Once your server can prove who it is, permit TLS-encrypted sessions with the options `smtpd_tls_security_level` and `smtp_tls_security_level`. A value of `none` disables TLS, while `encrypt` requires TLS. The preferred value, `may`, offers TLS and uses it when available.

```
smtpd_tls_security_level = may
smtp_tls_security_level = may
```

The settings for receiving and sending mail don't need to be identical. Depending on your organization's security policy, you might declare that any mail you send must use TLS but will still accept non-TLS messages. It's up to you.

Postfix errs on the side of compatibility, and leaves older TLS versions and weaker algorithms enabled. Like many people, they consider that poor encryption is better than falling back to plaintext.

Strong TLS

Some people want to insist on not only using TLS on all connections, but using modern TLS. They prefer the possibility of losing messages to the risk of insecure transport—not only disabling all versions of TLS older than 1.2, but refusing all weak ciphers. They consider that servers so old that they can't speak TLS 1.2 probably have cooties. You can indulge your biases, at least until they interfere with getting work done.

Use the two `_tls_security_level` options to require encryption, and then set `smtpd_tls_protocols` and `smtp_tls_protocols` to define acceptable TLS versions for sending and receiving messages.

```
smtpd_tls_security_level = encrypt
smtp_tls_security_level = encrypt
smtpd_tls_protocols = >=TLSv1.2
smtp_tls_protocols = >=TLSv1.2
```

The options `smtpd_tls_mandatory_protocols` and `smtp_tls_mandatory_protocols` apply to connections where TLS is mandatory. I generally set these to their non-mandatory equivalents.

```
smtpd_tls_mandatory_protocols = $smtpd_tls_protocols
smtp_tls_mandatory_protocols = $smtp_tls_protocols
```

If you want to restrict TLS 1.2 to strong ciphers, use `smtpd_tls_ciphers` and `smtpd_tls_mandatory_ciphers` for accepting mail, and `smtp_tls_ciphers` and `smtp_tls_mandatory_ciphers` for sending mail. Setting these to *high* uses OpenSSL's HIGH cipher list. The `_mandatory_` versions dictate what protocols and ciphers can be used when a connection host requires TLS. You can future-proof those options by setting them to use the non-mandatory options.

```
smtp_tls_ciphers = high
smtp_tls_mandatory_ciphers = $smtp_tls_ciphers
```

You could lock down TLS further, but it's rarely effective. MTAs don't necessarily verify X.509 certificates, so disabling anonymous ciphers gains nothing.

Use `testssl.sh` (**https://testssl.sh/**) to validate that your server's TLS on incoming messages is set the way you like. It should report that all versions of SSL are disabled and that only your selected TLS versions and ciphers active. Warnings about "anonymous NULL Ciphers" and "server cipher order" are irrelevant for SMTP.

```
# testssl.sh -t smtp mail.ratoperatedvehicle.com:25
```

For maximum TLS, enable DANE validation on outbound mail.

TLS with DANE

You can't validate certificate authenticity on the public Internet unless the remote site explicitly instructs you to do so. We'll look at MTA-STS in Chapter 15, but configuring DANE validation for outbound messages is much simpler.

DANE requires DNSSEC. Your host's resolver should be configured to validate DNSSEC queries. Tell Postfix to make queries with DNSSEC with the `smtp_dns_support_level` option.

```
smtp_dns_support_level=dnssec
```

With that support enabled, you can tell Postfix to check for and validate TLSA records for DANE.

```
smtp_tls_security_level = dane
```

If the remote server has no TLSA records available, TLS falls back to `may`. If TLSA records exist but aren't usable, the connection falls back to `encrypt`.

Enabling DANE for inbound messages has nothing to do with Postfix. That requires publishing TLSA records for the server's certificate and synchronizing TLSA record updates with certificate renewals. Senders do all the work of DANE validation.

TLS Logging

Postfix does not log any TLS activity by default, but troubleshooting demands it. The `smtp_tls_loglevel` option controls logging of outbound TLS activity, while `smtpd_tls_loglevel` manages logging of inbound TLS.

The default, 0, does no logging.

Setting either to 1 logs a summary of TLS activity, such as if TLS was used, if a certificate was validated, or if a certificate was invalid.

At 2, you get OpenSSL handshake logging and basic Postfix TLS operations. Only use this for brief periods, when troubleshooting..

3 gives you hexadecimal and ASCII dumps of TLS negotiations.

At 4, Postfix logs the complete contents of the TLS session. This level is strongly discouraged for performance reasons, and could disclose private information.

```
smtpd_tls_loglevel=1
smtp_tls_loglevel=1
```

I routinely log at level 1.

Testing Postfix

In theory, your Postfix install can now send and receive mail to and from the local hostname. This is a proper theory, because it's falsifiable. Test the configuration on both of your test hosts. Start by opening the mail log in a separate terminal window.

```
# tail -f /var/log/maillog
```

Now send yourself a mail on both local systems, without using the full address.

```
# echo "mail to myself" | mailx -s "self-test" mwlucas
```

This mail should go to your account on this host, such as `mwlucas@mail.ratoperatedvehicle.com`, and appear nearly instantaneously. If the log declares that Postfix is trying to send it to the bare domain address, such as `mwlucas@ratoperatedvehicle.com` without the `mail` in the middle, you messed up `$myorigin`. If the message is delivered, view the file in *~Maildir/new*. The `Return-Path`, `Delivered-To`, and `To` headers should all contain complete email addresses.

That works? Great. You can remove that test message from your Maildir. Repeat the test, using the complete email address as the recipient.

```
# echo "mail to myself with full address" | \
  mailx -s "self-test" \
  mwlucas@mail.ratoperatedvehicle.com
```

That should also get delivered locally.

Now the acid test. You have two machines. Have each send a mail to the remote host. Here, on `mail.ratoperatedvehicle.com`, I send mail to my account on my other test host.

```
# echo "mail to remote host" | \
  mailx -s "self-test" mwlucas@mail.solveamurder.org
```

You should see activity in the logs on both hosts. Within a few seconds, the mail from one host should arrive at the other and be accepted. Look at that message. The `Return-Path` and `From` headers should give the source email address. The `X-Original-To`, `Delivered-To`, and `To` headers should have the destination address.

Accounts and Addresses

Your test system is set up the same way most twentieth-century mail systems were. Each email address is associated with a Unix account. Adding a Unix account automatically creates a matching email address. Email addresses without Unix accounts are processed by the aliases file as discussed in Chapter 1. If an address has neither an account nor an alias, the address is invalid.

This is undesirable for most modern systems, even if you're truly running email for only yourself. If you want additional accounts for friends, family, or a small organization, it's a disaster. Perhaps my half-Wookie-but-balding uncle needs an email account at the family domain, but I know for a fact that he answers every hair restoration spam and he doesn't understand the difference between Netflix and his cell phone. His email should not be tied to a Unix account or, indeed, any system access whatsoever.

We will disassociate Unix accounts from email addresses in Chapter 4.

Queue Management

The great thing about tests is that they fail, giving you the chance to fix problems before your coworkers see them. When you're testing mail, however, you will create undeliverable messages. Undeliverable messages will fester in the queue for several days, cluttering the log and spawning regular warning messages, until Postfix gives up trying to deliver the message and gives the sender a failure notice.

For the kind of testing we're doing, those retries are pointless—or worse, you'll change something to make those messages deliverable and suddenly the recipients will receive heaps of old test messages. Save yourself trouble and remove messages that you know are undeliverable from the queue.

The postqueue(1) command lets you view the queue. It can also tell postfix(1) to attempt to deliver delayed messages, but right now use the -p flag to see what's lingering.

```
# postqueue -p
-Queue ID-  --Size-- ----Arrival Time---- -Sender/Recipient-------
4EB6A10094       360 Fri Jun  9 15:46:42  root@ratoperatedvehicle.com
(connect to ratoperatedvehicle.com 192.0.2.11:25: Operation timed out)
                                         mwlucas@ratoperatedvehicle.com
```

This queue contains one message. The message-ID is 4EB6A10094. The sender is `root@ratoperatedvehicle.com`. The current delivery error message is in parentheses. We see the destination host, `ratoperatedvehicle.com`, and its IP address. The actual error is "Operation timed out." The recipient, `mwlucas@ratoperatedvehicle.com`, appears last.

This message is an error. I was on `mail.ratoperatedvehicle.com` and attempted to send a mail to the local account `mwlucas`. Postfix's myorigin was set to ratoperatedvehicle.com, however. The missing parts of the address were set to `ratoperatedvehicle.com`, and my test server attempted to send a mail to that host. While the host `ratoperatedvehicle.com` does have a web site with videos of rat driving tiny cars, it lacks an MTA. This connection will never complete. In a few days, Postfix will report that this message is undeliverable.

I don't need Postfix's efforts to retry this doomed message cluttering up my mail log. Use postsuper(1) to remove it from the queue, with -d to give the message-ID.

```
# postsuper -d 4EB6A10094
postsuper: 4EB6A10094: removed
postsuper: Deleted: 1 message
```

The failed message is gone.

You can eradicate the queue with ALL argument.

```
# postsuper -d ALL
```

Should you routinely go into the queue and remove undeliverable messages? Probably not. Users need to see bounce messages. They're educational.

Perhaps you've fixed an error elsewhere that caused mail to back up, and want Postfix to try to deliver all outstanding messages. Use the -f flag to force an immediate redelivery attempt.

```
# postqueue -f
```

You now have two vaguely functional mail systems. Don't try to use them in public yet! You need to configure the surrounding services and install protections before trying to talk to the world.

Dovecot Essentials

Postfix faces the world, but Dovecot faces the users. Much like Postfix, Dovecot is a suite of programs that work together to provide multiple client-facing mail services like IMAP, authentication, and filtering. Supporting filtering requires that you weave Dovecot a little more deeply into the SMTP server than you might expect, but it's in the sysadmin's control.

Dovecot provides a very modular sample configuration through heavily-commented include files. It is designed to quickly set up the most common services, and only coincidentally reduces beginner support questions. This configuration includes services we don't need and less secure options, so we won't use them as-is. The sample files ending in .conf are intended to be loaded into a default configuration, while the files ending in .ext are less frequently needed. The examples are extremely useful when you decide to connect Dovecot to a database, LDAP server, or OAuth2 system. Any time you have a question about how Dovecot works, check the sample configuration. Restart dovecot whenever you change the configuration.

Whenever you run a Dovecot program, it tries to read the configuration file *dovecot.conf*. If it cannot read the file or process the contents, it refuses to run. For basic commands, an empty configuration works.

 # touch /etc/dovecot/dovecot.conf

You don't need to set any options right now, but let's look at the configuration style. Each setting contains an option name, an equals sign, and one or more settings. Here I list the protocols we're going to use Dovecot for, using the protocols option.

```
protocols = imap lmtp submission
```

Certain options require commas as delimiters. The listen option sets the addresses Dovecot creates sockets on. IP addresses are complicated, so they must be separated by commas.

```
listen = 203.0.113.68, 2001:db8::68, 127.0.0.1, ::1
```

Services have their own stanzas, allowing per-service configuration by setting off sections with brackets. Here's some example snippets we'll set up later in the book.

```
service imap-login {
  inet_listener imap {
  port=0
  }

inet_listener imaps {
  port=993
  ssl = yes
  }
}
```

Dovecot supports many protocols and the configurations can get very complicated. Dovecot lets you split a configuration into multiple files and pull them in with an `!include` statement.

```
!include *.conf
```

We'll start configuring Dovecot by setting up TLS.

Dovecot TLS

Like Postfix, Dovecot processes TLS with the ubiquitous OpenSSL toolkit. Like many programs, including OpenSSL, it still calls TLS "SSL." Go with it. Set the `ssl` option to required to insist all connections use either pure TLS or STARTTLS, as the service allows.

If a service uses STARTTLS, the client can decide if they're going to engage TLS or not. The server can't control their decision. What Dovecot can do, however, is declare that it will not accept credentials transmitted in plain text.

```
disable_plaintext_auth = yes
```

Dovecot considers connections from the local host secure. If you test the STARTTLS requirement from the host running Dovecot you'll find it accepts plain text credentials. It refuses unencrypted credentials from other hosts, however.

The catch with Dovecot's TLS is that only privileged users may read X.509 private key files. Sometimes, unprivileged or even restricted users need to run Dovecot programs for reasons that have nothing to do with TLS. They'll read *dovecot.conf*, encounter TLS certificate information, fail to read those files, and quit before doing anything useful.

Dovecot provides the `!include_try` option for these situations. The `include_try` statement means "try to include this configuration, but ignore any errors and go on." We'll split the X.509 certificate information into a separate file and `include_try` it. Your *dovecot.conf* needs these statements.

```
ssl = yes
!include_try tls-dovecot.conf
```

Create a separate file, `tls-dovecot.conf` for your certificate details. Use `ssl_cert` and `ssl_key` to give the path to the full certificate chain and the private key.

```
ssl_cert = </var/acme/certs/mail.ratoperatedvehicle.com/fullchain.pem
ssl_key = </var/acme/certs/mail.ratoperatedvehicle.com/privkey.pem
```

The =< syntax instructs Dovecot to use the file's contents as the value. You don't want Dovecot to try to use the path to the key file as the key!

With this, privileged users can run Dovecot commands and read the key files. When an unprivileged user runs a Dovecot command, the command will fail to read the key files but shrug and carry on.

Restart Dovecot after making this change, and we'll check to see if the changes have taken effect.

doveconf(1)

Dovecot has its own configuration management program, doveconf(1). Unlike postconf(1), it doesn't change configuration files—you must use doveadm(1) for that. It can even show per-service and per-network configurations.

Running `doveconf -a` shows the current value of all options. It's over a thousand lines. The −n flag shows the options that have been changed from the default, which is probably more useful.

```
# dovecot -n
# 2.3.20 (80a5ac675d): /usr/local/etc/dovecot/dovecot.conf
# OS: FreeBSD 13.2-RELEASE-p1 amd64
# Hostname: mail.ratoperatedvehicle.com
ssl_cert =
   </var/acme/certs/mail.ratoperatedvehicle.com/fullchain.pem
ssl_key = # hidden, use -P to show it
```

Our changes are in place!

You can also query for the value of a specific option.

```
# doveconf ssl
ssl = yes
```

Use the `service` keyword to dump the configuration of all dovecot services. You'll have to search for the particular service you're interested in, but it's easier than scanning the list of all possible settings.

```
# doveconf service
service aggregator {
  chroot = .
  client_limit = 0
  ...
```

We'll use these features to set up client-facing services later in this book.

Dovecot Variables

Dovecot includes a variety of *variables*, macros that can be used in configuration files. Variables let you centralize management of SQL query strings, filter by IP address, and more. We'll illustrate with user management macros.

The variable `%u` represents the complete username. In Dovecot terms, a username is an email address, like `mwl@solveamurder.org`.

A `%n` gives the name part of the username, the bit before the @ sign.

Similarly, `%d` gives the domain part of the username, the section after the @ sign.

Finally, `%s` identifies the protocol being used. You can have separate configurations for, say, IMAP and SMTP.

Dovecot has many other macros, but this gives the idea. We'll use these to configure accounts in Chapter 4.

Doveconf Logging and Debugging

Much of the work Dovecot performs is invisible to the user. You must be able to view its logs. You could trace your syslog configuration, or you could let dovecot find the logs for you. The log subcommand to doveadm finds the logs for you.

```
# doveadm log find
Looking for log files from /var/log
Debug: /var/log/debug.log
Info: /var/log/maillog
Warning: /var/log/maillog
Error: /var/log/maillog
Fatal: /var/log/messages
Fatal: /var/log/maillog
```

Reading the log is only part of the problem. You need to get Dovecot to write detail to those logs. Use the *dovecot.conf* option `mail_debug` to make Dovecot log details.

```
mail_debug=yes
```

Debug logs grow huge. Monitor their size.

Like Postfix, Dovecot could fill a book. Also like Postfix, you don't need to know all those features. The doveadm(1) man page describes many of the features and provides excellent examples. Let's go on and see how these programs support email.

Chapter 4: Virtual Domains

Now that you have basic SMTP between two machines and can understand Postfix's complaints, let's expand your configuration to accept real mail for a domain. We'll consider how Postfix manages tables and lists. With that we can configure a virtual domain and set up DNS records for it. In Chapter 6, we'll move our virtual domains into a database for easier large-scale management.

Managing virtual email domains requires careful data management through Postfix tables.

Postfix Tables

While you can configure Postfix almost entirely in *main.cf*, moving independent sections into separate files can improve manageability. A large mail system might have thousands of accounts, or allow dozens of IP addresses to relay through it, or receive mail for hundreds of domains. Including all of these details in *main.cf* would overwhelm other configuration options. It makes sense to move such settings into separate files. External files can be *tables* or *lists*. A list contains single values, while a table is some sort of key-value array. I'll use the word "table" to refer to both.

Tables can be text files or databases.

Local Databases

Unix has implemented many different file formats and sources for data in the last quarter century, and Postfix supports almost all of them. Many formats are for local files. Postfix includes postmap(1) to create files in these formats. You can also use remote databases like MariaDB, LDAP, or (if you've given up) NIS. To see which formats your install supports, run postconf -m.

```
# postconf -m
btree
cidr
environ
...
```

You'll often hear these local databases called *hash files*. Originally a hash file was a specific format, but over decades that term has been catastrophically distorted until people apply it to almost any type of local database file. There's the primordial Berkeley db file, btree files, DBM files, SDBM files, and more. Over drinks one might credibly argue that sqlite is backed by a hash file, but at that point someone pulls a blaster, the whole bar erupts, and you have to apologize for the mess. Postfix supports many of these local hash file formats, but your install might not. Berkeley db files, or *hash files*, are fine for almost all uses. Hash files normally have a .*db* extension, although filename extensions are treacherous and must not be trusted.

Most packages on most operating systems support a couple dozen different types. This book expects your software will support the MySQL (MariaDB) and proxy formats as well as hash files.

We'll use the aliases file as an example. We discussed *aliases* back in Chapter 1. An alias is a system-wide message forwarding, so that email sent to one address on the host can be redirected to a real account. Whenever you update the aliases file you must run postalias to regenerate the database. This is a classic Unix feature, but Postfix extends that concept and stores most tables as local databases.

Postfix prefers database files because they are quickly readable and pre-parsed. Reading a text file is so slow that Postfix reads and parses the file only at startup. Changes to the text file mean reloading Postfix. A database file can be queried like a database, so changes can be made without bothering the running daemons. Does everything need to be a database? Not necessarily. I have hosts that only accept mail from localhost and that will never change, so I don't bother with a database. Our examples start with text files and proceed to databases.

Postfix databases are key-value stores. Consider a sample line from the aliases file.

```
root:    mw1
```

The key is `root`, and the value is `mw1`. Mail to the user **root** is redirected to the user **mw1**.

The option `default_database_type` sets the default local database format. Check that setting with `postconf -d`.

```
$ postconf -d default_database_type
default_database_type = hash
```

This install defaults to Berkeley db files. Convert a text file to the default database type with the postmap(1) command. The file bad-domains contains a list of sites and addresses we don't want to accept mail from, which we'll discuss later.

```
filthyewokwhowontshutup@gmail.com REJECT
@mw1.io  REJECT
…
```

Convert this to a hash file with postmap.

```
# postmap bad-domains
```

This creates the file *bad-domains.db*, which Postfix can read without reloading.

Querying Databases

Query databases with postmap's -q option. Give -q two arguments, the item you want to check and the table. While postfix has special tools for managing the aliases file, `postmap` can perform basic lookups. Here I want to know the value of `root` in the aliases databases.

```
# postmap -q root aliases
mw1
```

To dump an entire database, use the -s option.

```
# postmap -s relay-clients.cidr
127.0.0.0/8     OK
[::1]/128       OK
...
```

You'll see references to postmap being able to edit the database. If you want to add or remove entries from databases, you can! The problem is, these operations affect only the database file—not the source text file. The next time you run postmap to transform the text file into a database file, those edits will be overwritten. Always update the text file and convert it to the database file. If you want to manage these tables in a database, use a real database as discussed in Chapter 6.

Postfix includes specific tools for managing the aliases file according to traditional Unix practices.

The Postfix Aliases File

We touched on the format of the aliases file in Chapter 1. Use postconf -d to see where Postfix expects to find the aliases file and how it will use it.

```
$ postconf -d | grep aliases
alias_database = hash:/etc/aliases
alias_maps = hash:/etc/aliases
newaliases_path = /usr/local/bin/newaliases
```

The alias_database option shows the path to the aliases file. Here it's the traditional /etc/aliases. The alias_maps option gives the format and location of the local database. Some operating systems behave weirdly when you change the location of these files. If you want your aliases file in /etc/postfix, links or symlinks from the expected location can help.

Finally, `newaliases_path` lets you know where Postfix installed `newaliases`. Every time you edit the text aliases file, run Postfix's `newaliases` to update the corresponding hash file. Many Unix tools can update a hash file, but it's best to use Postfix's native support. If newaliases gives you trouble, verify that your system doesn't have multiple `newaliases` commands—or that you're running the correct one.

The `postalias` command can also search the aliases database, much like postmap(1). If you want to know where Postfix will send mail for a local address, use the -q option and give the account. This system has an unprivileged account for sshd(8), sshd. If I send mail to that account, who receives it?

```
$ postalias -q sshd aliases
root
```

Okay, it goes somewhere. But I know perfectly well that nobody reads email to root on this system. Hopefully it gets sent to a real user?

```
$ postalias -q root aliases
mw1@solveamurder.org
```

Ah. I really *must* delegate that to someone competent.

Dump the entire database with the -s option.

```
$ postalias -s aliases
root:     mw1@mw1.io
postmaster:     root
_dhcp:   root
...
```

Like `postmap`, you'll see references to `postalias` being able to edit the database. Also like postmap, these changes affect only the database file and not the source text file.

IP Address Tables

In Chapter 3 we used the `mynetworks_style` option to say that remote hosts could not freely relay through this host.

```
mynetworks_style = host
```

You'll often have other hosts that need to relay messages through your system. Your ecommerce web server farm must send receipts to customers, but you probably don't want to manage a complete mail system on each server. Configure those servers to relay everything through your MTA. Configure your mail system to accept and forward messages from those addresses using the `mynetworks` option.

When you have a short list of IP addresses that isn't likely to change, you might include them directly inside `main.cf`. Here I replicate using `mynetworks_style=host` by specifying a list of **localhost** IP addresses inside the config file.

```
mynetworks = 127.0.0.0/8 [::1]/128
```

`127.0.0.0/8` is the block of IPv4 localhost addresses, while `::1/128` is the IPv6 localhost address. IPv6 addresses must appear in square brackets, with the prefix length outside the brackets. You don't know which IP stack a client might prefer, so include both. All IP addresses must be in *Classless Inter-Domain Routing* (CIDR) format. Anything not on the list is denied permission to relay messages through Postfix.

Suppose your ecommerce servers use the addresses `198.51.100.128/26` and `2001:db8:bad:c0de::/64`. You want your mail system to relay messages from these hosts. Add these to **mynetworks**.

```
mynetworks = 127.0.0.0/8 [::1]/128 198.51.100.128/26
    [2001:db8:bad:c0de::]/64
```

Reload Postfix and check your work with `postconf`.

```
# postconf mynetworks
mynetworks = 127.0.0.0/8 [::1]/128 198.51.100.128/26
    [2001:db8:bad:c0de::]/64
```

Perhaps the hosts in 198.51.100.136/29 are for testing, and should never send mail to the outside world. You can exclude those from the list while still allowing the rest of 198.51.100.128/26 by using an exclamation point. Lists are read from left to right, and Postfix stops checking on the first match, so list the exclusion before the permitted addresses.

```
mynetworks = 127.0.0.0/8 [::1]/128 !198.51.100.136/29
  198.51.100.128/26 [2001:db8:bad:c0de::]/64
```

This is getting uncomfortably long and complicated for a configuration file entry. I could list each address block on its own line, but that makes the configuration file even longer.

```
mynetworks = 127.0.0.0/8
  [::1]/128
  !198.51.100.136/29
  198.51.100.128/26
  [2001:db8:bad:c0de::]/64
```

Our growing organization will add additional servers. Let's fling this list into a separate file.

External File

Rather than cluttering up *main.cf* with a long table, we can tell *main.cf* to include an outside file. This *main.cf* entry tells Postfix to check the file */etc/postfix/relay-clients* for the value of this option.

```
mynetworks = /etc/postfix/relay-clients
```

The file *relay-clients* contains a list of permitted IP addresses. You could put them all on one line, but only if you want to make the file less readable.

```
127.0.0.0/8
[::1]/128
!198.51.100.136/29
198.51.100.128/26
[2001:db8:bad:c0de::]/64
```

Reload Postfix, and it will now read the table contents from the file.

```
# postconf mynetworks
mynetworks = /etc/postfix/relay-clients
```

Postfix programs read text files only when reloaded or started. If you want Postfix to react dynamically to changes in external files, use a hash file or database.

Postfix CIDR Tables

IP addresses are such a common configuration parameter than Postfix has specific support for them. A Postfix CIDR table is still a text file and is only reread when you reload or restart the daemon. Specify a table with the table type, a colon, and the path to the database file.
`mynetworks = cidr:/etc/postfix/relay-clients.cidr`

A CIDR table contains one network block per line, with an accompanying OK or REJECT statement. The list is processed in order, and processing stops on the first match. Addresses not on the list will be rejected. Here's our existing list of relay clients in that format.

```
127.0.0.0/8               OK
[::1]/128                 OK
198.51.100.136/29         REJECT
198.51.100.128/26         OK
[2001:db8:bad:c0de::]/64  OK
```

You must reload Postfix whenever you change a text address table. In most environments, client addresses rarely change. Don't make CIDR tables hash files; they don't work well.

Postfix Access Tables

The CIDR table we just saw is an example of an *access database*. Each item in the list is attached to an OK or a REJECT. An access database lets you dictate which messages you accept or refuse.

Postfix includes configuration items that let you check individual email addresses, accounts, domains, and more. Perhaps your server accepts mail from a certain IP address—but a later configuration setting rejects it based on the MAIL FROM a particular message uses. This is an important protection. Suppose a spammer breaks into one of your web servers. The server is behind a packet filter, so they must relay their junk through your MTA. Postfix will accept mail from that IP address, but when the spammer sets their outbound domain to theirs, Postfix will reject it.

Each access table has three possible settings, but you'll mostly see ACCEPT (or OK), and REJECT. *OK* means "this is fine, pass it on." *REJECT* is a refusal.

There is a third option, but it's almost never explicitly stated and you probably won't ever see it in a table. *DUNNO* appears implicitly at the end of every table. It means "This table has no opinion on accepting or rejecting this message." Processing continues, and the next option gets its chance. The CIDR table above ends in an implicit DUNNO. Only use DUNNO explicitly in a table if the documentation for that table specifically declares it is necessary. You might see it if you dig deep into debugging output.

Suppose you have a table that says "automatically accept messages from these IP addresses" and another that says "reject all mails from these IP addresses." What happens if a source IP is on both lists? Suppose a domain name appears twice, once with ACCEPT and once with REJECT? That depends on the context.

If a key-value list includes the same key twice, `postmap` complains. Depending on how the database is used, Postfix might use the first or last entry. Save yourself pain; when `postmap` complains, pay attention.

If you give a parameter twice in *main.cf* (or service twice in *master.cf*), Postfix logs a warning and uses the last one.

If you have a non-database key-value file, like a CIDR table, the first match wins.

If you use multiple access databases for restrictions (such as in the `smtpd_option_restrictions` settings), the first match wins.

We'll use tables and access databases throughout configuring our server.

Local Delivery Agents

As Chapter 1 discusses, the Local Delivery Agent (LDA) accepts messages from the MTA and delivers them to the user's mailbox. Postfix comes with the local(8) LDA, which does an admirable job of accepting files and sticking them in directories. That's all we've needed so far. If you're running email in production, though, you probably want features like filtering, mailbox extensions, and virtual domains. At this point we'll use the LDA provided with Dovecot, dovecot-lda(1).

There's one user `dovecot-lda` cannot deliver mail to: **root**. Users must be able to edit and delete their own messages, so `dovecot-lda` runs as the destination user. For safety reasons it won't run as **root**, so it cannot deliver mail to **root**. Be sure the aliases file forwards mail to **root** to an actual user.

Postfix exports several environment variables to the LDA. The full list is available in postconf(5), but the critical ones are $SENDER (the email's sender) and $RECIPIENT (the recipient).

The Postfix option `mailbox_command` sets the LDA. It's normally blank, which instructs the system to use local(8). Use the full path to `dovecot-lda`. Use the -f flag to specify the sender, and -a the recipient.

```
mailbox_command =
  /usr/libexec/dovecot-lda -f "$SENDER" -a "$RECIPIENT"
```

Reload Postfix. In one terminal window, run `tail -f` on your mail log. In another, send a test mail.

```
$ echo "dovecot test" | mailx -s "dovecot test" mwlucas
```

Your mail log should show Postfix calling `dovecot-lda` with the arguments you specified, and then `dovecot-lda` putting it in your mailbox. Check your mail directory and you should see a new message. If the mail log shows an error either you missed something or your Unix's default *dovecot.conf* has incomplete or inaccurate crud that sabotages simple local deliveries. We'll look at configuring dovecot-lda(8) shortly.

With Dovecot's LDA in place, we can look at virtual hosts.

Virtual Hosts

Exactly like the word *server*, technology professionals have folded, spindled, and generally overloaded the phrase *virtual server* into meaninglessness. In their defense, system capabilities have increased exponentially for decades and 1985's unthinkable dream is today's triviality.

Originally hosts could only receive requests addressed to them, whether they be for mail or Gopher or even ultra-advanced protocols like HTTP 0.9. The new and exciting "virtual server" feature allowed a host to respond to incoming requests addressed to a hostname other than its own. My web server has a hostname of `www.ratoperatedvehicle.com`, but it also accepts requests for `ratoperatedvehicle.com`. That's a virtual host. A commercial web server probably hosts hundreds or thousands of sites this way. Similarly, the mail system we've been building has a hostname like `mail.solveamurder.org`, but we want it to accept mail addressed to users at bare `solveamurder.org`. That's a virtual email server. We'll call that a "virtual host" like in the old days, to differentiate it from the term "virtual server" commonly used to describe an operating system install running in a virtual machine.

Using virtual hosts for your production domains offer advantages over the test configuration we've been using. Sending mail directly to the host requires each valid email address have a Unix account. Your common email address should not be tied to a system account. If someone wants to attack my MTA, the email address `mwl@mwl.io` offers no clue about my system account name. Intruders are welcome to attack the nonexistent shell account `mwl` as much as they like; it will generate IP addresses to feed to my packet filter.

The configuration of a virtual host is entirely separate from the main host's email, and even the host's configuration. Once you set up your first virtual email host, the configuration is easily replicable for additional domains. The kind of sysadmin who wants to run their own email almost certainly has registered multiple domain names.

Postfix allows mapping virtual domains to Unix accounts, but that's a stopgap solution for a slowly growing system. You could also use them to support a parent domain—that is, receiving mail for `ratoperatedvehicle.com` on `mail.ratoperatedvehicle.com`. In most cases purely virtual domains not tied to any system account are more sustainable, so we will focus on them. A host can have both types of account.

Email configuration quickly grows complicated, and tools exist to manage that complexity. We will do a basic setup by hand so you understand how the system hooks together, then switch to using a database-backed administration system in Chapter 6.

Configuring a Virtual Host

Supporting a virtual host means informing Postfix of the virtual hosts and the email addresses therein, configuring Dovecot for those domains and addresses, and configuring an agent to deliver mail to those virtual hosts.

Postfix and Virtual Hosts

While mail to the hostname places messages in the user's account, a virtual host needs a user to own received messages and a directory to store them in.

I recommend using a dedicated filesystem or a ZFS dataset for mail messages. Each virtual host gets its own directory beneath the mount point. Postfix and Dovecot will manage the mailbox contents. In these examples, virtual domain mailboxes go under */vhosts*.

You'll need an unprivileged account for owning virtual host mail. We created the **vmail** user in Chapter 1 for exactly this purpose.

Once you have these, configure virtual hosts in *main.cf*. Postfix has over thirty options for virtual hosts, all beginning with `virtual_`. Here are the minimum options needed to establish the virtual host `ratoperatedvehicle.com` on the host `mail.ratoperatedvehicle.com`.

```
virtual_mailbox_domains = ratoperatedvehicle.com
virtual_mailbox_base = /vhosts
virtual_mailbox_maps = hash:/etc/postfix/virtual-mailboxes
virtual_alias_maps = hash:/etc/postfix/virtual-aliases
```

The option `virtual_mailbox_domains` lists the virtual hosts this Postfix install accepts mail for. We have only one virtual domain, but can add more later.

With `virtual_mailbox_base`, we tell Postfix where to store incoming mail. Each domain will get a directory beneath this, with user accounts in further subdirectories.

The file given by `virtual_mailbox_maps` lists the valid accounts for each virtual host, and is stored as a local database. Postfix hash files expect a key and a value, so this file needs two columns. Technically we need only a list, but this file will get leveraged later to declare who has permission to send mail as this user, so add a second column with the same information. (We'll see how this works in Chapter 5.) Here I create a single account, `mwl@ratoperatedvehicle.com.`, in the file */etc/postfix/virtual-mailboxes*.

```
mwl@ratoperatedvehicle.com mwl@ratoperatedvehicle.com
```

Each domain needs aliases. The `virtual_alias_maps` option tells Postfix where to find information on per-domain aliases. My virtual host needs the standard aliases discussed in Chapter 1, and they should be sent to my account at that domain. The `virtual_alias_maps` option points at the file */etc/postfix/virtual-aliases*, so that's where I create the standard aliases.

```
postmaster@ratoperatedvehicle.com   mwl@ratoperatedvehicle.com
hostmaster@ratoperatedvehicle.com   mwl@ratoperatedvehicle.com
webmaster@ratoperatedvehicle.com    mwl@ratoperatedvehicle.com
abuse@ratoperatedvehicle.com        mwl@ratoperatedvehicle.com
```

Update the databases after editing these files.

```
# postmap virtual-mailboxes virtual-aliases
```

You'll see references to the options `virtual_uid_maps` and `virtual_gid_maps`. These support Postfix's delivery agent for virtual domains, but we'll be using Dovecot's delivery agents.

Postfix now knows about these accounts, and can accept mail for them. Now to get them delivered to user accounts.

Dovecot Password File

Removing email accounts from the host might protect the operating system, but email account information must exist somewhere. We'll store it in Dovecot. Before email virtual hosts were invented, Dovecot read usernames and passwords from `/etc/passwd`. Today, the Dovecot password database retains compatibility with `/etc/passwd`. Using an actual file on the system limits your management abilities, but Dovecot grew support for other data sources through the time-honored method of "run this query and format the results like `/etc/passwd`." We will deploy an SQL back end in Chapter 6, but must understand the password file format to do so.

The password file contains eight fields. The `/etc/passwd` gecos (real name) and shell fields are ignored and unused, but Dovecot keeps them to retain compatibility.

username:password-hash:uid:gid:ignored:home:ignored:extras

The *username* is the full email address. Usernames are normalized to lower case. You can play all sorts of Dovecot tricks to change this, but having the email address be the account name is accepted practice.

You can generate the password hash with dovecot-pw(1), as we'll see in the next chapter.

The *uid* and *gid* set the owner of the files on disk. This email account might not have an operating system account, but files require an owner. In our example, we'll use the system user **vmail** for our UID and GID.

The *home* sets the user's home directory.

You could add extras at the end, but don't.

All you need for message delivery is the email address followed by five colons. Your password file will eventually need actual passwords, but for now declare only that the email address exists. You don't even need all the colons, as Dovecot ignores the last two fields.

```
mwl@ratoperatedvehicle.com:::::
```

We will use other Dovecot features to set several other fields to default values in the next section.

Dovecot User Database

Dovecot user accounts require three pieces of information: a user database, a password database, and the location where user email gets stored. We'll start with the simplest possible system, just enough to deliver mail to your account, and expand later.

The Dovecot password database contains the user's password and any pre-login account details. Use the `passdb` option to define the password database in */etc/dovecot/dovecot.conf*.

```
passdb {
  driver = passwd-file
  args = /etc/dovecot/passwd
}
```

The `driver` option defines the type of system we're storing passwords in. It might be an LDAP or SQL database, a key-value store like Redis, or an external program. Dovecot can even combine multiple databases. For now we're using a password file compatible with */etc/passwd*, although we'll replace that with a database in Chapter 6.

The `args` option lets us declare how the driver will be used. The last argument must be the file containing the password database, or the configuration to connect to it. We don't need any of the complex options, so just give the path to our password file.

The Dovecot user database contains information needed after the user has authenticated. It can be the same as the password database, or it might be split out for performance reasons. Again, this is a small server so we'll use the same database. Define the user database with the `userdb` option in *dovecot.conf*.

```
userdb {
  driver = passwd-file
  args = /etc/dovecot/passwd
  default_fields = uid=vmail gid=vmail home=/vhosts/%d/%n
}
```

The `driver` and `args` options are exactly like those in `passdb`. The `default_fields` option is new, however. To simplify your password database, and to help separate storage administration from user management, you can define default values for user account information.

The `uid` and `gid` options let you define Unix accounts that own the on-disk mail files, saving you the trouble of duplicating entries in the host's password file. Use the UID and GID of the system's **vmail** user we set up earlier.

The `home` option sets the user's home directory. You can hard-code a home directory into the user database to override this setting for select users, but setting a default ensures consistent file storage. This example takes advantage of Dovecot variables, as discussed in Chapter 3. Remember, `%n` represents the part of the email address before the @, and `%d` what comes before. Each user's home directory will default to */vhosts/domain/name*.

Why have two separate options if we're using the same data source? For a small mail system, it doesn't matter. An enterprise that needs load balancers for their web servers and clusters all their databases might need two separate databases, however.

Once the user has a home directory, you can tell Dovecot where to put the user's mail and what format to use. Our virtual users do not need any of the usual detritus a shell account acquires; their home directory exists solely to store email. Use the `mail_location` *dovecot.conf* option to tell Dovecot to use the Maildir format, and to stick mail directly in the user's home directory.

```
mail_location = maildir:~
```

Now to weld Dovecot and Postfix together.

Local Mail Transport Protocol (LMTP)

Once you start hosting virtual domains and adding a few users you'll discover that some people receive more messages than any sane person could desire. The dovecot-lda(1) program works great for processing individual messages, but it spawns a new process for each incoming mail. Once multiple messages start arriving simultaneously it's much more efficient to use a dedicated daemon for local delivery, via the Local Mail Transport Protocol (LMTP).

Why have a separate protocol for local email? LMTP is a heavily trimmed-down version of SMTP. LMTP doesn't need queues; either it delivers the message to the user's inbox and reports success, or can't deliver and reports an error. The SMTP daemon handles any queuing. Standard LMTP is designed for trusted environments, so it has zero access controls. If you can reach the LMTP server, you can use it. If you have separate hosts for the message store and the mail exchanger, you can use LMTP between them and protect the service with packet filters, firewalls, and a Sith Lord with a six-bladed lightsaber and constipation. For a single server, though, use LMTP over a Unix socket.

Much like Postfix, Dovecot contains many small services. Each is configured and enabled separately. Here's a *dovecot.conf* configuration to make Dovecot provide an LMTP listener where Postfix can access it, and to activate it with a protocols statement.

```
protocols lmtp

service = lmtp {
  unix_listener /var/spool/postfix/private/dovecot-lmtp {
    group = postfix
    mode = 0600
    user = postfix
  }
}
```

We start with the `service` statement, informing Dovecot that this configuration is for LMTP.

The `unix_listener` statement creates a Unix socket. The directory */var/spool/postfix* is the **postfix** user's home directory, and the *private* subdirectory is readable only by that user. The socket is named *dovecot-lmtp* because Postfix has its own LMTP server and we need to explicitly avoid it.

The next three entries define the user, group, and permissions on the socket. Only Postfix may communicate with this listener. You must include the leading zero on the permissions.

Restart `dovecot`, and the socket should appear. If it doesn't, verify that the `protocols` statement includes `lmtp`. Dovecot will parse this configuration without that statement, but it won't activate LMTP unless you declare it should.[20] Once the socket exists, configure Postfix.

Postfix Virtual Delivery Agent

While the `mailbox_command` option sets the delivery agent for email addresses with associated Unix accounts, Postfix uses the *main.cf* `virtual_transport` option to set the delivery agent for virtual domains, like so.

```
virtual_transport = lmtp:unix:private/dovecot-lmtp
```

This tells Postfix to use LMTP, via a Unix socket, located at *private/dovecot-lmtp*. This path is relative to Postfix's `queue_directory` setting, */var/spool/postfix* on my host. Set this and restart Postfix.

Theoretically, enabling LMTP would let you remove all knowledge about user accounts from Postfix. In practice, that generates backscatter. Postfix uses the `virtual_mailbox_maps` and `virtual_alias_maps` options to identify which email addresses it should accept mail for.

---

20   "Is it turned on?"

Testing Your Virtual Mailbox

Configuring a virtual host requires a whole bunch of pieces, and you probably messed up somewhere. Test your work. In one terminal, run `tail -f` on your mail log. In the other, send a test message.

```
# echo "lmtp test message" | mailx -s \
  "lmtp test message" mwl@ratoperatedvehicle.com
```

If this works, the mail log should show delivery. Dovecot should create the directory */vhosts/ratoperatedvehicle.com/mwl*, and that directory should contain Maildir's *cur*, *new*, and *tmp* folders. You'll also see several files of metadata Dovecot needs for client-facing services.

If you don't see this, stop. Review the log. See where the system broke. Do not proceed until you can receive mail at your first account. Once your first account works, you could add additional accounts.

LMTP in Headers

LMTP is a stripped-down SMTP, so it adds a `Received` header at the top of the message.

```
Received: from mail.ratoperatedvehicle.com
  by mail.ratoperatedvehicle.com with LMTP
  id ozleJvaMfGVmZwEAkO8d9g
  (envelope-from <mwlucas@mwl.io>)
  for <mwl@ratoperatedvehicle.com>; Fri, 15 Dec 2023
    12:29:26 -0500
```

The header plainly declares this message was delivered via LMTP.

We're using LMTP on the local host, so it's very simple. If your LMTP configuration involves multiple hosts you might see instead LMTPA (for LMTP with SMTP AUTH), LMTPS for LMTP over TLS, or LMTPSA for LMTP with both TLS and SMTP AUTH.

If everything functions, we can proceed to client-facing services.

Chapter 5: IMAP and Submission

Your server can send and receive mail, but you probably don't want to use cat(1) and rm(1) as your client. It's time to configure your server to support proper email clients. The *Internet Message Access Protocol* (IMAP) allows clients to synchronize messages between a client and server. It's used for desktop and phone clients like Thunderdbird and Outlook, as well as web-based email systems like Roundcube.

While synchronizing mail folders between client and server is dandy, most users also want to send messages. Postfix's *submission* service allows authenticated clients to send mail through the server. If you offer an unauthenticated submission service spammers will use you to sell Wookie enhancement supplements, so we'll have Postfix authenticate SMTP submissions against the Dovecot IMAP user database before accepting messages. Authenticated SMTP is commonly called *SMTP AUTH*.

We'll look at configuring user accounts for IMAP, configuring and testing IMAP, and configuring the submission service.

Dovecot User Passwords

In Chapter 4 we told Dovecot about virtual host accounts. To access mail via IMAP, though, those accounts must have passwords. While Dovecot can access user account information from LDAP or SQL, at this point we're using a password file. Chapter 6 discusses using a database backend.

As with all ethical password systems, Dovecot stores password hashes rather than actual passwords. Never store your users' actual passwords, only the hashes!

Password Algorithms

The doveadm-pw(1) command is the password management interface. Dovecot supports many different popular and obscure password algorithms, depending on how your package was built. To get a complete list of algorithms, run `doveadm pw -1`.

```
$ doveadm pw -1
SHA1 SSHA512 SCRAM-SHA-256 BLF-CRYPT...
```

What are all these algorithms, and why do you care? Most often, you don't.

You just need to pick one to run on your server. (Clients don't care what algorithm the server uses.)

Dovecot's documentation as of the publication of this book declares that ARGON2I or ARGON2ID are the preferred algorithms. Blowfish (BLF-CRYPT) comes next. In 2010 the NIST recommended the PBKDF2 algorithm, although in 2023 NIST declared they would be revising their recommendation. If nothing else, the salted SHA512 scheme, SSHA512, is supported almost everywhere.[21] Many of the other algorithms supported come straight from OpenSSL, and are not suitable for production use. Do not use them unless your organization's security policy insists you follow dangerously outdated standards. Some of my servers do not support either ARGON2I algorithm, so we'll use Blowfish.

Use `doveadm pw` to translate passwords into hashes. Specify the algorithm with `-s`.

```
# doveadm pw -s blf-crypt
Enter new password:
```

Enter the password when prompted, verify it, and `doveadm` returns the password hash.

```
{BLF-CRYPT}$2y$05$I1DVkOhpTBKE.ZCfY4AJcujHv/U91/001WS...
```

---

21   Please do note my anti-recommendation for the LANMAN algorithm.

If you want to enter a password as part of the command itself, know that the plain-text password will appear in the system's process list, your shell history, and anything else that tracks which commands get run. It's poor practice, but you can do it by adding the –p flag and the password.

```
# doveadm pw -s blf-crypt -p ThisIsFoolish
{BLF-CRYPT}$2y$05$7H9wb7ptUOqQ7WRTRRxrZOMyzdmreK59wof...
```

Once you have the password hash, what do you do with it?

The Password File

We set up a password file in Chapter 4, but it contained only addresses. Now we'll add a password.

If you are literally the only user on your system, managing your password in a password file is not unreasonable. If you have multiple users, however, storing password hashes in a real database and providing a web-based front end will be much more maintainable. We'll use a password file to show you how the system works, then migrate to a database later.

The password hash is the second entry in the Dovecot password file. Take the hashed password and put it in the account line.

```
mwl@ratoperatedvehicle.com:{BLF-CRYPT}$2y$05$36zh...::::
```

With this, the account can now authenticate. Hopefully.

Dovecot User Lookups

Now that this account has a password, you can test authentication at the Dovecot level. Use the doveadm-auth(1) `lookup` feature to verify that the dovecot password database sees the account.

```
# doveadm auth lookup mwl@ratoperatedvehicle.com
passdb: mwl@ratoperatedvehicle.com
  user     : mwl@ratoperatedvehicle.com
```

The account is in the password file. I did that part correctly. Dovecot has separate configurations for the user and password databases, though, so we should verify that as well. Use doveadm-user(1) to check the user database.

```
# doveadm user mw1@ratoperatedvehicle.com
field   value
uid     5000
gid     5000
home    /vhosts/ratoperatedvehicle.com/mw1
mail    maildir:~
```

It exists, and the information looks correct. The UID and GID come from the system's **vmail** user, and have nothing to do with the virtual user except as a placeholder.

Now let's see if we set the password correctly, using the `auth test` subcommand. Give the username as an argument.

```
# doveadm auth test mw1@ratoperatedvehicle.com
Password:
```

Enter the password, and doveadm will verify it.

```
passdb: mw1@ratoperatedvehicle.com auth succeeded
extra fields:
 user=mw1@ratoperatedvehicle.com
```

If you're comfy ignoring risks, you could also give the password as the final argument.

```
# doveadm auth test mw1@ratoperatedvehicle.com ThisIsFoolish
```

To read the user's information from both the password and the user databases, simulate a full login with the `auth login` subcommand.

```
# doveadm auth login mw1@ratoperatedvehicle.com
Password:
passdb: mw1@ratoperatedvehicle.com auth succeeded
extra fields:
 user=mw1@ratoperatedvehicle.com
userdb extra fields:
 mw1@ratoperatedvehicle.com
 uid=5000
 gid=5000
 home=/vhosts/ratoperatedvehicle.com/mw1
 auth_mech=PLAIN
```

This is exactly what we set in the Dovecot configuration and password files. If an actual client can't authenticate, we know the password is correct but the plumbing between the client and the database is busted.

Let's set up that plumbing now.

Internet Message Access Protocol

Dovecot provides IMAP letting clients access their messages. It also supports POP3, but that's decades obsolete and if anyone demands it tell them it's time to free their PalmPilot. Once your virtual hosts have accounts with passwords, enabling IMAP is simple.

Find the `protocols` statement in *dovecot.conf*. Add `imap` to the list.

```
protocols = lmtp imap
```

Don't restart `dovecot` yet! Like telnet and FTP, IMAP was originally unencrypted and ran on port 143. Encrypted connections, tunneling IMAP over TLS, are known as IMAPS and run on port 993. You have an X.509 certificate, so you should permit connections only over TLS. We configured TLS back in Chapter 3, so Dovecot will automatically enable TLS versions of any protocol you turn on. Disable unencrypted IMAP by telling Dovecot to run that service on port 0.

```
service imap-login {
  inet_listener imap {
     port=0
  }
}
```

Dovecot's `imap-login` service handles user connections. The `inet_listener` option controls how Dovecot accepts network connections. Setting unencrypted IMAP to listen on port zero disables it.

Dovecot supports many user authentication methods. Most of them were created when X.509 certificates were too expensive to deploy everywhere, and use complicated cryptographic techniques to secure credentials. By only permitting client connections over TLS, you can permit simple authentication methods. The most common IMAP authentication method is called PLAIN, and is Dovecot's default. Microsoft clients such as Microsoft Outlook and Microsoft Mail do not support this standard; rather, they have a tweaked version called LOGIN. Dovecot supports LOGIN, but not by default. If you support Microsoft clients, enable LOGIN with the `auth_mechanisms` option.

```
auth_mechanisms = plain login
```

That's it. Restart Dovecot, and it should listen for clients on TCP port 993 but not 143.

Double-check that you still have some test mails in your account, and proceed to testing.

Testing IMAP with OpenSSL

Like most email-related protocols, IMAP is text-based. You can connect to the service using netcat or OpenSSL, authenticate, and read your messages without a client. Different netcat clients offer varying support for TLS connections via a multitude of command-line flags, or might not even support TLS at all, so we'll talk to the IMAP server with the always-consistent openssl(1). The command has this format:

```
# openssl s_client -quiet -connect server:port
```

The `s_client` keyword is an OpenSSL sub-command that tells OpenSSL it's connecting to a TLS-protected service. The `-quiet` tells OpenSSL to skip printing all of the TLS detail. All I want to know is that TLS works. The `-connect` option lets us aim OpenSSL at a TCP port. Finally, give the target hostname and port. I want to connect to mail.ratoperatedvehicle.com on the IMAPS port, 993.

```
# openssl s_client -quiet \
 -connect mail.ratoperatedvehicle.com:993
depth=2 C = US, O = Internet Security Research Group, CN
= ISRG Root X1
verify return:1
depth=1 C = US, O = Let's Encrypt, CN = R3
verify return:1
depth=0 CN = mail.ratoperatedvehicle.com
verify return:1
```

I told OpenSSL to be quiet about the details of TLS, but it insists on printing a few of those details so I do my best to ignore them. Then we get actual IMAP information.

```
* OK [CAPABILITY IMAP4rev1 SASL-IR LOGIN-REFERRALS ID
ENABLE IDLE LITERAL+ AUTH=PLAIN] Dovecot ready.
```

The OK indicates that Dovecot is ready and willing to serve my requests. Following that we have a list of features this server supports. The protocol version (IMAP4rev1) might be important for debugging other servers. For now, the AUTH=PLAIN statement declares that the server accepts logins via text usernames and passwords.

IMAP does not provide a command prompt. If there's a blank line, the server is either waiting for you to do something or is so overloaded it can't answer you. Go ahead and issue a command. Commands are case-insensitive.

Every IMAP command starts with a *tag*. A tag is a text string identifying this command. IMAP allows multiplexing commands to be served asynchronously. You could put all of your test commands in a single long command and let the server execute them in order. Simplify your debugging. Don't get fancy. Issue one command at a time. I habitually use the word *tag* as my tag, but it could be anything. Some IMAP servers even get annoyed if you reuse tags within a session.

First, log in. The `login` command takes two arguments, the account and the password. My account is `mwl@ratoperatedvehicle.com`, and I provide my password.

```
tag login mwl@ratoperatedvehicle.com MyRealPasswordIPromise
tag OK [CAPABILITY IMAP4rev1 SASL-IR LOGIN-REFERRALS ID
ENABLE IDLE SORT SORT=DISPLAY THREAD=REFERENCES THREAD=REFS
THREAD=ORDEREDSUBJECT MULTIAPPEND URL-PARTIAL CATENATE UN-
SELECT CHILDREN NAMESPACE UIDPLUS LIST-EXTENDED I18NLEVEL=1
CONDSTORE QRESYNC ESEARCH ESORT SEARCHRES WITHIN CONTEXT=-
SEARCH LIST-STATUS BINARY MOVE SNIPPET=FUZZY PREVIEW=FUZZY
PREVIEW STATUS=SIZE SAVEDATE LITERAL+ NOTIFY] Logged in
```

We now know that basic login functions work. Clients can authenticate. But since we're here, let's see what's in this mailbox. The LIST command takes two arguments, the folder to list and the messages within that one. I want to see everything.

tagg list "" "*"

I misspelled *tag*? Oops. Tag names don't matter, remember? The IMAP server returns a list of mailboxes.

```
* LIST (\HasNoChildren) "." futurepain
* LIST (\HasNoChildren) "." errors
* LIST (\HasNoChildren \UnMarked) "." ignore
* LIST (\HasNoChildren) "." Trash
* LIST (\HasNoChildren) "." INBOX
tagg OK List completed (0.001 + 0.000 secs).
```

With IMAP every user has an INBOX folder, even if it's empty. Even if the directory doesn't exist on the server. Other folders are directories where messages are or have been stored. Let's take a look at the inbox, see what's new.

ttag select INBOX

```
* FLAGS (\Answered \Flagged \Deleted \Seen \Draft Old)
* OK [PERMANENTFLAGS (\Answered \Flagged \Deleted \Seen
\Draft Old \*)] Flags permitted.
```

Dovecot remembers flags that the client can set. Flags are how clients mark certain messages as seen, or replied to, or drafts, or so on.

```
* 3 EXISTS
* 0 RECENT
```

I have three messages. "Recent" messages have appeared since the last time a client accessed this mailbox.

```
* OK [UNSEEN 3] First unseen.
* OK [UIDVALIDITY 1691091894] UIDs valid
* OK [UIDNEXT 8] Predicted next UID
ttag OK [READ-WRITE] Select completed (0.001 + 0.000 secs).
```

Message 3 has not been seen yet, however. The details about UIDs are not relevant to us. I want to see message 3, so I use the FETCH command. FETCH would let you query headers, grab just message bodies, or whatever, but the RFC822 option lets you view an entire message.

tag fetch 3 rfc822
```
* 3 FETCH (FLAGS (\Seen) RFC822 {843}
```

The response tells us that Dovecot understands the command and will comply.

```
Return-Path: <mwlucas@mail.ratoperatedvehicle.com>
Delivered-To: mwl@ratoperatedvehicle.com
...
Subject: yet another test
Message-ID: <ZPoCFqXn5zyx6OEx@mail.ratoperatedvehicle.com>
MIME-Version: 1.0
Content-Type: text/plain; charset=us-ascii
Content-Disposition: inline

Did you really create this message just so you'd have some-
thing to show in the book?
)
tag OK Fetch completed (0.001 + 0.000 secs).
```

Yes. Yes, I did.

This suffices to verify that the IMAP server accepts logins and retrieves messages. You can be confident that a correctly configured client will work.

Testing IMAP with Mutt

Email clients like Outlook and Thunderbird expect to communicate with a fully functional mail system. You don't have one yet. Testing your IMAP configuration requires a client that handles IMAP separately from sending mail. If you are already cozy with your preferred mail client and can make it test receiving separately from sending, use it. Configure an IMAP account in your client, try to connect, and see what happens.

If you don't have such a client, I recommend mutt (http://www.mutt.org). One advantage mutt has over other mail clients is that you can run it on the server, letting you test features like IMAP and mail submission without worrying about the network between your desktop and your server. You should have already configured your packet filter as discussed in Chapter 1, but you couldn't test it until something was listening on those ports.

Mutt is a command-line email client, by default displaying only text. That's fine—the question is not "can we view the pretty spam?" but "can we log into IMAP and view our messages?" Mutt reads its configuration from the `.muttrc` file in your home directory. If you're already using mutt for an existing account, create a new `.muttrc` for testing. Set the options `imap_user`, `spoolfile`, and `folder` to use IMAP.

```
set imap_user = mwl@ratoperatedvehicle.com
set spoolfile = imaps://mail.ratoperatedvehicle.com/
set folder = imaps://mail.ratoperatedvehicle.com/
```

The `imap_user` option gives your username.

The `spoolfile` is the location where the system stores your new mail. Older sysadmins would know this as `/var/mail/username`. The `imaps` scheme tells mutt that the spoolfile is on your IMAP server.

The `folder` option tells mutt where to look for your mailboxes. Again, instruct it to look at the IMAP server.

These options should suffice, but we're talking about computers so something will go wrong. Run `tail -f` on the Dovecot log (probably the mail log, but see Chapter 3 if you have trouble). In another terminal, run mutt. You should see mutt declare which encryption algorithms it negotiated with the server, and then get a password prompt. Enter your password, and your mailbox should appear.

```
q:Quit  d:Del  u:Undel  s:Save  m:Mail  r:Reply  g:Group  ?:He
   1      Aug 07 Lucas     (0.5K) default maildir test 2


---Mutt: =INBOX [Msgs:1 0.5K]---(date/date)-----------(all)---
```

The line at the top lists helpful commands. Below that, each mail message appears on its own line. This mailbox has one message, a previous test. Mutt lists the date the message was sent, the sender's name, the message size, the mailbox, and the message subject. Use the up and down arrows to move between messages, ENTER to view a message, and i to return to this index. Delete messages with d.

Mutt prefixes folder names with an equal sign. To save this test message to a folder, use the s command and then give a folder name like =test. You can move between folders by giving the c command and the target folder name. If you want to see all your folders, use c and then a question mark. You can then arrow up and down between folders.

If you can see your mailbox, you configured your client correctly. If you can't, read the error message both from mutt and Dovecot's error log and troubleshoot.[22] Once IMAP works, you can proceed to Postfix's submission service.

Submission Service

One critical function of an MTA is *refusing* mail.

A standard MTA accepts messages destined for accounts on the local host. If I send a mail to mwl@solveamurder.org and it reaches the MTA for solveamurder.org, the MTA should either accept the mail or declare that the account doesn't exist. An MTA also has a list of IP addresses that it will forward messages for. If I have a herd of ecommerce servers on the network 2001:db8:bad:c0de:cafe::/64 and I set up an MTA to handle those messages, that MTA needs to accept messages from those addresses and send them on to their recipients. (Installing a real mail program on the clients and having them use SMTP AUTH would be better.)

It's everyone else that's the problem. Your organization's members should send their official mail via your MTA. Between telecommuting and travel, their IP addresses are unstable. You need a method to tell your server to accept and forward mail from those clients, but still reject spammers.

That's where the *submission* service comes from.

---

22   Once mutt works, configure it to talk to Gmail and use regexes to give your mailbox its first proper cleaning in decades.

Submission is "regular SMTP plus user authentication." It runs on port 465 with TLS, and 587 with STARTTLS. Each client provides a specially encoded username and password. If the MTA can verify them, the client can send its messages. If the MTA cannot verify the credentials, the client is rejected. Submission services usually apply different filtering and processing rules than MTAs that accept mail from the general public.

The trick with submission is that Postfix knows nothing about users or passwords. Only Dovecot has that information. When Postfix receives an email for a domain it controls, it asks Dovecot if the account exists. Anyone who has dealt with authentication for longer than a week understands that maintaining user authentication data in one and only one place is the only way to not join the Dark Side. Postfix must accept the client's authentication information and ask Dovecot if it's valid.

That's exactly what the *Simple Authentication and Security Layer* (SASL) is for. We'll configure Dovecot to answer SASL requests, then get Postfix to make them.

Dovecot SASL

Dovecot includes a sample SASL configuration, but we'll build one from scratch. As with LMTP, have Dovecot communicate with Postfix over a Unix socket and protect that socket with permissions.

```
service auth {
  unix_listener /var/spool/postfix/private/dovecot-sasl {
  mode = 0600
  user = postfix
  group = postfix
  }
}
```

This looks almost exactly like the LMTP entry. The `service` entry declares this to be an `auth` (authentication) service. The `unix_listener` entry tells Dovecot where to create a socket. The `mode`, `user`, and `group` options set the permissions on that socket. Only the user **postfix** should have access to the socket, though it

150

should be setuid. Restart `dovecot` and you should see the socket appear.

```
# ls -la dovecot-sasl
srw-------  1 postfix postfix 0 Mar 31 09:54 dovecot-sasl
```

If the permissions don't look like this, verify you included the leading zero in the mode.

Once the socket exists, use doveadm(1) to verify that SASL is working and this socket can provide authentication.

```
$ doveadm auth test \
 -a /var/spool/postfix/private/dovecot-sasl user
```

Here I test SASL authentication with my account.

```
$ doveadm auth test -a dovecot-sasl \
 mwl@ratoperatedvehicle.com
Password:
passdb: mwl@ratoperatedvehicle.com auth succeeded
```

SASL works! I could put the password at the end of the command line, if I didn't mind having my password show up in the process list and my shell history. With the Dovecot part working, I can proceed to Postfix.

Configuring Postfix SASL

Making Postfix check Dovecot via SASL involves telling Postfix what SASL implementation it should use and where to find the authentication socket. This doesn't enable SASL for email submission, but simply tells Postfix that this facility exists and where to find it.

Many online examples show setting these values only for the submission service, via *master.cf*. I prefer configuring SASL providers (and any other services) in *main.cf*, so they remain consistent across any services that might need them. If I need to add SASL to some other part of Postfix later, I'll start off with a consistent configuration.

```
smtpd_sasl_type = dovecot
smtpd_sasl_path = private/dovecot-sasl
smtpd_sasl_security_options=noanonymous
smtpd_sasl_local_domain=$myhostname
smtpd_sender_login_maps=$virtual_alias_maps
```

The `smptd_sasl_type` option tells Postfix which SASL implementation it's talking to. While SASL is a standard, every implementation has its own quirks.

Postfix needs to know how to reach the SASL provider. The option `smtpd_sasl_path` gives the location of the provider's Unix socket. This path is relative to the `queue_directory` setting, which defaults to `/var/spool/postfix`. We configured Dovecot to create its authentication socket at `/var/spool/postfix/private/dovecot-sasl`, so set this to *private/dovecot-sasl*. (Some Linuxes get twitchy and require a full path, or refuse a full path, so if you have trouble check your Linux variant's documentation or just muck with the path and see what happens.)

The variable `smtpd_sasl_security_options` lets you tweak switches in the SASL protocol. You could do things like require mutual authentication, disallow plaintext, and a couple other rarely-useful features. SASL supports anonymous authentication. Like Windows' "guest" account and LDAP's anonymous bindings, this has been demonstrated as a predictably bad idea.[23] Set `smtpd_sasl_security_options` to *noanonymous* to disable this historical weakness.

Every SASL provider knows the scope of its authority. Dovecot defaults to using the local hostname. This isn't for access control so much as verifying clients are talking to the correct security provider. To have Postfix match that, set `smtpd_sasl_local_domain` to the local hostname.

Allowing authenticated connections is necessary but not sufficient. You also need to verify that the person sending a message owns the account they're sending mail from. I don't want **flunky@ratoperatedvehicle.com** sending email as **ceo@ratoperatedvehicle.com**! The `smtpd_sender_login_maps` option connects Dovecot accounts to email accounts. In Chapter 4 we

---

23   When very smart technologists are divided between "This will work well" and "This will end in wretched sobbing," the smart money bets on misery.

used `virtual_alias_maps` to provide the list of valid email accounts. At the moment that's the file `/etc/postfix/virtual-mailboxes`. We'll double-purpose that file to map Dovecot accounts to Postfix addresses. Look at an entry from that file.

`mw1@ratoperatedvehicle.com mw1@ratoperatedvehicle.com`

Each address is listed twice. Part of that is because a hash file expects to see a key and a value. The other reason is so that we can use it to map Dovecot and Postfix accounts. The first column defines a Postfix virtual mailbox. The second column gives the Dovecot login that owns that account. The file format is truly:

postfix-account-name dovecot-user

This entry says that the Postfix address `mw1@ratoperatedvehicle.com` is owned by the Dovecot user `mw1@ratoperatedvehicle.com`.

You could point `smtpd_sender_login_maps` straight at the alias file, but if you migrate from a password file to a database you'll have to update multiple *main.cf* entries. It's best to point `virtual_alias_maps` to the authoritative list, and anything else that needs that list to `$virtual_alias_maps` so that changes flow transparently through the configuration.

Now you can configure the submission service itself.

Connecting SASL to Submission: master.cf

Dovecot now provides SASL, and Postfix knows about it. We haven't attached that SASL to any of Postfix's component services. We don't want to call SASL every time the MTA receives email from the public Internet. Rather, we want SASL called any time an email hits the submission service. Up until now, we've configured Postfix in *main.cf*. It's time to adjust the master(8) daemon via *master.cf*.

Postfix includes many smaller daemons and services. On a default install submission is not among them, but verify on your system using postconf(1).

```
# postconf -M submission
postconf: warning: unmatched request: "submission"
```

If submission is already running, you'll need to find and edit the configuration.

Entries in *master.cf* have the same eight columns shown in `postconf -M`. Here's the default entry for smtp, the service that listens on port 25 and accepts palatable email from the outside world.

```
smtp    inet  n        -      n       -        -            smtpd
```

We went through the entries in Chapter 3, but as a reminder they are:

- the service name
- how the service communicates to the world
- is the service private
- is the service unprivileged
- is the service chrooted
- how often is the service woken up
- the maximum number of processes
- the command line

This entry shows that the `smtp` service communicates via the Internet, is not private, and uses the command `smtpd`. It's perhaps the most visible Postfix service, and mostly works by default. The smtpd(8) process reads its options from *main.cf*.

Postfix's submission service is provided by the same smtpd(8) program that handles external mail. They both speak SMTP, after all. The problem is, we need Postfix to handle submission very differently than MTA-to-MTA mail exchange. This `smtpd` process must listen on a different port and permit connections from any IP address, but any connecting client must authenticate. We must extensively override both Postfix's defaults and the *main.cf* settings. Use the `-o` option to impose those overrides. Right now, do not put spaces around any equals signs.

As with many Unix configuration files, in *master.cf* a hash mark (#) indicates the start of a comment and lines with text are configuration entries. Postfix is slightly different in that lines starting with white space are a continuation of the previous line. A service entry can be extremely lengthy, and allowing entries to wrap to the next line is the only way to retain your sanity. Unfortunately, that whitespace rule only applies to complete statements. Splitting a long statement into multiple lines requires braces, as we'll see shortly.

The default *master.cf* includes a commented-out example of a submission service that includes all sorts of useful possibilities. Feel free to look through that to get an idea of the available options, but we'll build a simple submission service that will suffice for most users. For reasons that will become obvious shortly, I suggest adding this to the end of *master.cf*.

```
smtpds inet n - n - - smtpd
  -o syslog_name=postfix-submission
  -o smtpd_tls_wrappermode=yes
  -o { smtpd_client_restrictions=permit_mynetworks,
      permit_sasl_authenticated,reject }
  -o smtpd_sender_restrictions=
  reject_sender_login_mismatch
  -o { smtpd_recipient_restrictions=
  reject_non_fqdn_recipient,
  reject_unknown_recipient_domain,
  permit_sasl_authenticated,reject }
```

The first line is a standard *master.cf* entry. The service is called *submission*. It listens to the network. It is not private, it runs unprivileged, is not chrooted. This service runs constantly so it is not woken up, and there is no limit on how many processes it can use. The last entry is the command to be run, smtpd.

So far this is the same command as the smtp service, the first entry in *master.cf*. All of those indented -o lines that follow are arguments to this instance of smtpd(8). The leading whitespace means each can be on its own line.

By setting syslog_name, you tell postfix to use a different name in the mail log. This eases troubleshooting.

The option `smtpd_tls_wrappermode` tells Postfix to wrap all connections in TLS, period.

By default, the submission service accepts mail from anyone. The `smtpd_client_restrictions` option lets you tighten that down. Rules are applied in order, and the first match wins. Postfix supports many client restrictions, letting you fine-tune who can use this. You can permit access based on authentication, IP addresses, client TLS certificates, and more. If you must restrict access to your submission service, definitely investigate this option in the manual. This small mail system applies three rules. First, `permit_mynetworks` declares that hosts in mynetworks can send mail through the submission service. These hosts can already send mail through the standard SMTP service, but certain software expects to use submission. The `permit_sasl_authenticated` option passes messages from clients that authenticated via SASL. Finally, `reject` says to refuse all other clients.

The `smtpd_client_restrictions` option appears in braces. The braces allow using whitespace, including newlines, within an option statement. If an option statement is long, split it with braces.

Even once you know a user can send mail, you'll need additional integrity and sanity checks. The `smtpd_sender_restrictions` option lets you impose rules on senders. You should always use *reject_sender_login_mismatch* here to verify that the sender's email address in the submitted message matches the Dovecot SASL username, as *main.cf* defines in `smtpd_sender_login_maps`. This prevents the janitor from sending mail as the CEO. Postfix supports many options of interest to large organizations, but this one is a must for most organizations. If you are truly the only user of this system, and you want to send mail as any of your accounts or aliases, you might drop this.

You should also check incoming mail for obvious daftness, using the option `smtpd_recipient_restrictions`. This lets you reject obviously undeliverable mail as quickly as possible, reducing system load. Like other Postfix options, the first matching option wins. First, email addresses should be complete, like `LordVader@galacticempire.gov`. If a user enters a truncated address like `LordVader` the server should immediately reject it. The *reject_non_fqdn_recipient* setting does that. Similarly, if the sender tries to send mail to a nonexistent domain the server should refuse to accept it. Use *reject_unknown_recipient_domain* to enable that check. We then allow authenticated clients to send messages with *permit_sasl_authenticated*, and just to be certain *reject* everything else.

Reload Postfix. You can now test mail submission from a client.

Submission Testing and Troubleshooting

If you configured everything perfectly and your Unix's Postfix package maintainer didn't change the default settings too much, your email client should be able to submit mail to your MTA. You can't yet send mail to the general public, but you have a second test server with known-working addresses. If my account `mwl@ratoperatedvehicle.com` can email my account `mwl@mail.solveamurder.org`, submission worked.

If it doesn't work, things get interesting.

First, check the error log. Submission uses the same mail log as MTA-to-MTA logs. Watch the log, capture the error message, and try to figure it out. If that fails, abandon the client and directly interrogate the submission service.

Interrogating the Submission Service

Don't leap straight to OpenSSL or a TLS-aware netcat. Submission doesn't take a straight username and password. Instead, you need a login string. If you're supporting Microsoft clients, you need two. A *login string* or *authentication string* is a precisely formatted username and/or password, encoded in base64. Base64 is not an encryption method, but rather a way to transparently transfer binaries as plain text. Passwords are not binary data, but they should include special characters that protocols might consider escapes. Figure out your authentication string before starting debugging.

Postfix's default authentication method is called PLAIN. A PLAIN login string is a single line encoded into base64. You'll see lots of examples using `echo`, but `echo` is not portable between shells let alone between operating systems. Use printf(1)—not the shell's built-in `printf` with its extensions and incompatibilities, but the standalone POSIX-compliant program. You'll probably have to specify it by full path.

You need a program to convert the output to base64. Every Unix has one, in a package if nothing else. I'm using base64(1), but you'll find that feature in uuencode(1) and OpenSSL and elsewhere.

```
$ /usr/bin/printf '\0username\0password' | base64
```

With my account name and sample password, I would run:

```
$ /usr/bin/printf \
  '\0mwl@ratoperatedvehicle.com\0ThisIsFoolish?!' \
  | base64
AG13bEByYXRvcGVyYXR1ZHZlaGljbGUuY29tAFRoaXNJc0Zvb2xpc...
```

Record the authentication string for later.

Microsoft clients use the LOGIN authentication method. It also uses base64, but encodes the username and password separately. It also doesn't require those pesky null bytes.

```
$ /usr/bin/printf 'mwl@ratoperatedvehicle.com' | base64
bXdsQHJhdG9wZXJhdGVkdmVoaWNsZS5jb20=
$ /usr/bin/printf 'ThisIsFoolish?!' | base64
VGhpc0lzRm9vbGlzaD8h
```

Record these.

Remember, base64 is not encryption. It is *encoding*. It's another way of describing the exact same characters and is trivially reversible.

```
$ echo 'AG13bEByYXRvcGVyYXR1ZHZlaGljbGUu...' | base64 -d
mwl@ratoperatedvehicle.comThisIsFoolish?!
```

Now that you have the auth string you can connect to the submission service.

```
$ openssl s_client -quiet -connect host:port
```

Here we use OpenSSL's `s_client`, much like testing IMAPS. We then connect to a host and a port. To test submission on `mail.ratoperatedvehicle.com`, we would run:

```
$ openssl s_client -quiet \
  -connect mail.ratoperatedvehicle.com:465
```

We'll get a few lines of OpenSSL output, followed by a message from the submission server.

```
220 mail.ratoperatedvehicle.com ESMTP Postfix
```

So far, this looks like normal SMTP. Introduce the host you are connecting from.

```
ehlo desktop.mwl.io
250-mail.ratoperatedvehicle.com
250-PIPELINING
...
250 CHUNKING
```

Authenticate before trying anything else. To log in with the PLAIN method, use the command `auth plain` and your precomputed login string.

```
auth plain AG13bEByYXRvcGVyYXRlZHZlaGljbGUuY29tADk5
235 2.7.0 Authentication successful
```

To test the Microsoft-friendly LOGIN method, enter `auth login`.

```
auth login
334 VXN1cm5hbWU6
```

Postfix has switched to base64, as per the Microsoft standard. This decodes as `Username:` and expects your username. Enter it.

```
bXdsQHJhdG9wZXJhdGVkdmVoaWNsZS5jb20=
334 UGFzc3dvcmQ6
```

Postfix prompts you with a base64 `Password:` prompt. Enter your base64 password.

```
VGhpc01zRm9vbGlzaD8h
235 2.7.0 Authentication successful
```

Whatever method you use, getting the "Authentication successful" message means that Postfix's submission process can speak to Dovecot's authentication socket, and Dovecot recognizes your password. This much of the system works. Proceed to send an email from this account.

```
mail from:<mwl@ratoperatedvehicle.com>
250 2.1.0 Ok
rcpt to:<mwl@mwl.io>
250 2.1.5 Ok
data
354 End data with <CR><LF>.<CR><LF>
submit by hand.
.
250 2.0.0 Ok: queued as 77D1C81A6
quit
221 2.0.0 Bye
```

If manual submission works and the message gets sent, but your fancy desktop client can't send mail, try mutt.

Submitting Mail With Mutt

Just as mutt can speak IMAP without traversing the network, it can send mail via the submission service. Mutt defaults to transmitting mail via sendmail(8), but with the smtp_url option you can instruct it to use the submission service.

```
set smtp_url = "smtp://username@host:port"
```

The *username* is your IMAP username. The *host* is the host where your submission service runs. The port will be 465. This option should appear directly after your IMAP configuration, like so.

```
set imap_user = mwl@ratoperatedvehicle.com
set spoolfile = imaps://mail.ratoperatedvehicle.com/
set folder = imaps://mail.ratoperatedvehicle.com/
set smtp_url =
  "smtps://$imap_user@mail.ratoperatedvehicle.com"
set ssl_starttls = no
```

I defined $imap_user earlier in my *.muttrc*, so I reuse it in smtp_url. My mail exchanger is **mail.ratoperatedvehicle.com**. With this entry, I can send mail via mutt.

Open mutt and log into your IMAP mailbox. Hit m to compose a message. You'll be asked for the recipient. Enter your test account on the other server—in my case, `mwl@mail.solveamurder.org`. Mutt then asks for a subject. When you enter one, mutt dumps you into your text editor. Write a short message and exit the editor. Mutt drops you into a screen where you can double-check the recipient and the subject. If everything looks right, hit y to send the mail. Depending on how your mutt is packaged it might prompt you for your password again, or not. Hit q to exit mutt.

If you can send mail via mutt from the server, but not from your fancy desktop client, either your client is misconfigured, there is some sort of network filter in place preventing you from communicating with the server, or you have stumbled upon one of the wonderful edge cases that abound in systems administration. Dig deeper into the logs.

Submission and Headers

Messages record each SMTP server they pass through with the `Received` header. Take a look at your test message headers and you should see something like this.

```
Received: from [203.0.113.65] (ceodesktop.mwl.io
  [198.51.100.9]) by mail.ratoperatedvehicle.com
  (Postfix) with ESMTPSA id 36ACB49F29 for
  <mwl@ratoperatedvehicle.com>; Fri, 15 Dec 2023
  12:36:06 -0500 (EST)
```

In addition to the usual date and time and message ID, you'll see both the original IP without any NAT (`203.0.113.65`) and the address the server saw as the connection source (`198.51.100.9`). There's also a new protocol keyword, ESMTPSA. No, there's not a whole new protocol for submission. This keyword says *how* the message was submitted. ESMTPA indicates that the message arrived via SMTP AUTH. ESMTPS indicates the message arrived on a TLS-encrypted SMTP connection. ESMTPSA declares the submission used both TLS and SMTP AUTH.

Now let's set up to manage several users.

Chapter 6: Database Back Ends

Text file configuration works great for settings that rarely change. If your mail system is truly only for you, then text files will probably be fine. When you have a larger number of users or a more dynamic environment, however, you need more flexible management. That means a database. And a front end to manage that database, because routinely running raw SQL commands would require memorizing the database structure and that would consume brain space better utilized for something else. Anything else.

Before starting, verify that your Postfix install supports your chosen database. Run `postconf -m` to list all the supported lookup table types and check for your chosen database engine. Also verify that `proxy` is a supported lookup table.

Many folks have written database-driven Postfix management systems. Some of them are even adequate. This book will use PostfixAdmin (`https://postfixadmin.github.io/postfixadmin/`), but primarily to illustrate database-backed Postfix and Dovecot. We won't go through the web interface, because web interfaces change frequently. Once you've migrated from managing Postfix via text files, your most common question is "where did they hide the menu for this setting?"

One pleasant PostfixAdmin feature is that it lets you delegate control of domains to users. If you have a semi-technical buddy who wants email for their domain, you can give them an account and let them take charge of it. One unpleasant PostfixAdmin feature is that it lets you delegate control of domains to users. They'll get confused, change settings randomly, hopelessly scramble their domains, and beg for help. We won't cover delegating control of domains to other users, but the web interface makes it straightforward. We will mention when features are related to delegating domains, though.

Installing PostfixAdmin

PostfixAdmin runs on PHP and a database. We'll use MariaDB, as discussed in Chapter 0. Before installing it, however, check the current version on the PostfixAdmin web site and compare it to that in your operating system's package repository. Like all system management software PostfixAdmin is security-sensitive, and installing an obsolete version is a great way to offer your resources to intruders and spammers. If the package is current, use it; if not, grab the latest stable version from the web site.

You'll find official, current instructions for installing PostfixAdmin on their web site, and many packages include those official instructions. Publishing a walkthrough in this book invites them to change their entire procedure, but we'll try it.

PostfixAdmin Users

PostfixAdmin has four tiers of users. Each level of user can see only the features relevant to them.

The *setup password* is used only for initial configuration and upgrades. This is the equivalent to `root` in single user mode. You must configure a setup password before trying to configure PostfixAdmin.

The *Superadmin* resembles `root` in normal use. It can set up new domains and email addresses. It can delegate domains to other users.

A *domain administrator* controls one or more domains on your server, within limits established by the Superadmin. If a domain administrator screws up their domain, the Superadmin can come in and straighten it out. Domain administrators are relevant for larger systems. We won't discuss them, but they're pretty straightforward to figure out in the web interface.

Finally, *regular users* have email accounts. They can log into PostfixAdmin to change their passwords.

Database Setup

PostfixAdmin requires a database, a database user, and a password for that user. Write these down before starting. We'll use the database name *slurry*, the user *garbage*, and the password *MailIsTheWorst!1*.

Create the database and the user, then tie the two together. Log into your database as an administrator and run the following commands.

```
> create database slurry;
> create user 'garbage'@'localhost' identified by 'MailIsTheWorst!1';
> grant all privileges on slurry.* to 'garbage'@'localhost';
> flush privileges;
```

We'll set up the database tables through the PostfixAdmin interface, but don't lose the note where you recorded the database information.

Dovecot Stats Writer

Dovecot keeps statistics and logs, and PostfixAdmin needs access to add to them. Dovecot's default configuration creates the Unix socket */var/run/dovecot/stats-writer* to receive reports from Dovecot programs. That socket is usually accessible only to the user **root** and the group **dovecot**, and only they can write to the socket. Your web server probably runs as something like **www** or **www-data**,[24] so it cannot connect to the socket. The Internet is full of horrible advice to make the socket world-writeable. Don't do that. Don't *ever* do that.

Grant access with group permissions. No, don't add **www** to the **dovecot** group! That grants the web server far too much access to Dovecot's innards. Create a new group that includes both **dovecot** and **www**, then grant that group permission to the socket. I created the group **mailglue**. Here's a *dovecot.conf* snippet that changes the group ownership on the socket.

```
service stats {
  unix_listener stats-writer {
    group=mailglue
  }
}
```

This grants the access PostfixAdmin requires, and nothing more.

---

24   If your web server runs as **root**, accessing a local Unix socket will not be amongst your problems.

Web Server and PHP Setup

The PostfixAdmin package should pull in all necessary PHP modules, although you'll probably need to verify that it included the modules for your selected database engine. Configure your web server to parse PHP and install whatever PHP accelerators you like. Verify that *php.ini* sets the same time zone as the host. Otherwise, PostfixAdmin logins will fail.

```
date.timezone = Tatooine/Mos_Eisley
```

A web interface means a web server. If you're using ACME to get your X.509 certificate, you probably already have one. If not, get one. Have the unencrypted site redirect to the TLS-protected one.

The package will install PostfixAdmin somewhere on your disk. Figure out where that is. For my host, that's */usr/local/www/postfixadmin*. This directory contains the configuration files, functions, and so on. The subdirectory *public* contains the web portion of PostfixAdmin and must be available somewhere on your web site, or as its own virtual host. I avoid using obvious locations like **https://example.com/postfixadmin**, preferring locations meaningful to me but opaque to outsiders. Here's an Apache *httpd.conf* snippet that makes PostfixAdmin accessible on my site.

```
<Directory "/usr/local/www/postfixadmin33/public">
  Require all granted
</Directory>
Alias /jabba /usr/local/www/postfixadmin33/public
```

Restart your web server and verify that you get a PostfixAdmin page at your chosen URL. That page will be stuffed with errors. Don't try to configure PostfixAdmin before fixing them.

PostfixAdmin Setup Password

To protect new installs, PostfixAdmin requires you to define a setup password before installing. While every other password goes in the database, this password goes in the configuration file. You can't store a password in a database if you don't yet have a database.

The setup password must be stored as a hash. You can use the PostfixAdmin setup page to generate the hash, or just use a php(1) command.

```
$ php -r "echo password_hash('YourPasswordHere', PASSWORD_DEFAULT);"
$2y$10$ajIeqP7LolK3tPCg/37ze.CuOTLv.ML93Z7LivLq8UMWF/W73bpA2
```

There is no newline at the end of the output, so your command prompt gets appended to the end. Copy the hash without that prompt and have it on hand before configuring PostfixAdmin.

PostfixAdmin Back End Configuration

The main PostfixAdmin directory has a configuration file, `config.inc.php`, that contains all the options and their default settings. Upgrades replace it, so any changes you make will disappear. Instead, create `config.local.php` and put your configuration in there. Your local configuration must include:

- the database type and location
- database authentication credentials
- password hashing algorithm
- the hash of the setup password
- a statement that you have provided this configuration

The config file uses standard PHP syntax. Here is a minimal configuration using the database created earlier this chapter, the hash of the setup password we just generated, and the salted SHA512 algorithm selected in Chapter 5.

```php
<?php
$CONF['database_type'] = 'mysqli';
$CONF['database_host'] = '127.0.0.1';
$CONF['database_user'] = 'garbage';
$CONF['database_password'] = 'MailIsTheWorst!1';
$CONF['database_name'] = 'slurry';
$CONF['encrypt'] = 'dovecot:BLF-CRYPT';
$CONF['setup_password'] = '$2y$10$3ybxsh278eAlZKlLf...';
$CONF['configured'] = true;
?>
```

The `database_type`, `database_host`, and `database_name` options tell PostfixAdmin how to query the database, where to find it, while `database_user` and `database_password` provide authentication credentials.

The `encrypt` option selects an algorithm for hashing the database's passwords records. We're using Dovecot tools and the Blowfish algorithm. You can change algorithms later, but as with the system password files, it will only affect new accounts and changed passwords. Existing hashes do not change.

The `setup_password` option needs the previously generated password hash.

The `configured` option tells the PostfixAdmin setup routine that a sysadmin has looked at the configuration options and set non-default choices, so it is safe to initialize the database.

With this infrastructure set, we can set up PostfixAdmin.

PostfixAdmin Setup

Browse to the *setup.php* page in the PostfixAdmin directory. Enter the setup password. PostfixAdmin will inspect your environment, create database tables, and verify that it can access everything it needs.

You must address any errors before proceeding. What kind of errors might you get? That depends entirely on your operating system and the package maintainer. Read the errors carefully. PostfixAdmin tries to be helpful and provide context for errors, but sometimes that context isn't relevant to your specific error. Some errors can be addressed with *config.local.php* options. Look at *config.inc.php* for a full list of the available options and their default settings.

Many PostfixAdmin installs expect to run the dovepw(1) command, but Dovecot replaced that with `doveadm pw`. A check of *config.inc.php* unveils the `dovecotpw` option, which you can use to correct this.

```
$CONF['dovecotpw'] = "/usr/local/bin/doveadm pw";
```

The doveadm(1) command expects to parse *dovecot.conf*, including all the files it references. That's why the TLS configuration in Chapter 5 is fault-tolerant.

Once all the errors are cleared, leaving only warnings about support for databases you aren't using, you can create a Superadmin account. This is essentially `root` for PostfixAdmin. It's the account you'll use for creating virtual hosts and your first users. Create the user, then log in as them.

As the Superadmin, you can create a domain and then a user in that domain. At this point, the database is not connected to Postfix so you won't see your test domains or the users you created in Chapter 4. Recreate them here. The limits suggested are for delegating control of domains to other users. You can set them to anything you like. I'll add the domain `ratoperatedvehicle.com`, and the user `mwl@ratoperatedvehicle.com`. PostfixAdmin lets you define a password validity duration, but studies have shown that scheduled password rotation reduces security.[25] Set the validity duration to 0 to not require password rotation.

Also create a second account. You'll use this to verify that Postfix is reading from the database, not the text files. I'll add `drivers@ratoperatedvehicle.com`.

At this point, PostfixAdmin is ready for Postfix. If you're so inclined, it's also a good time to study the database. See which tables exist and how they store data. When you're comfortable, proceed to Postfix.

---

25   NIST document 800-63b Appendix A from 2017 discusses exactly why password expiration is bad, but I don't expect enterprises to change their practices until roughly never. Besides, PCI DSS 4.0 from 2023 declares that passwords must change every 90 days. We are all doomed.

Configure Postfix for a Database

Postfix's text configuration files are simply but strictly formatted. Information must appear in a certain order, marked by non-negotiable tags. Replacing them with a database means crafting queries that reproduce those configuration files. Postfix accepts minor changes, such as not requiring delimiters, but overall the database queries must resemble the text files they replace.

Mind you, "replacing" a text file with a database is something of a misnomer. If you store Postfix's virtual hosts in a database, Postfix will still have an external virtual hosts file. The file contains the instructions for connecting to the database and the query needed to generate the virtual hosts table. Adding and removing entries doesn't change those files, however.

Postfix Proxymap

A busy Postfix server might constantly query the database. Even tiny servers occasionally get pummeled. Starting up individual database connections isn't exactly computationally expensive on modern hardware, but if your host starts up a new database query every time it moves an email from one part of the stack to another, they add up. Postfix aggregates database queries with proxymap(8). The `proxymap` program opens a single database connection and handles all queries for the various Postfix programs.

The word `proxy` in a configuration entry tells Postfix to route these requests through the proxy.

Postfix can also use proxymap(8) to bypass chroot restrictions for specified tables, and to aggregate writes to avoid file locking issues.

Proxymap is enabled by default in *master.cf*.

Postfix Database Configuration

PostfixAdmin includes information about configuring Postfix to talk to its database in the file *POSTFIX_CONF.txt*. Rather than making you hand-craft Postfix configuration files, the file is also a bash script that asks for your database information and writes proposed files in

170

a temporary directory. (The files are MySQL-compatible, and will require minor query string changes if you're using Postgres or SQLite.) Most packages install *POSTFIX_CONF.txt* in a documentation directory.

```
$ bash POSTFIX_CONF.txt
/tmp/postfixadmin-wYfSPx
```

This is the temporary directory where your files will be written. You're then prompted for the database details.

```
Database host? (often localhost)
localhost
Database name?
slurry
Database user?
garbage
Database password?
MailIsTheWorst!1
Config files have been written to
 /tmp/postfixadmin-wYfSPx.
Please check their content and move them to
 /etc/postfix/sql/.
Do not forget to edit /etc/postfix/main.cf as described
 in POSTFIX_CONF.txt.
```

Review a couple of these files. You'll see database connection information, then a query that produces the information Postfix expects.

These files contain plain-text database passwords, so they should not be readable by the world. I don't want Postfix to be able to write to these files either, but it must be able to read them. Create the directory */etc/postfix/sql* and give it appropriate protective permissions.

```
# mkdir -m 750 /etc/postfix/sql
# tar -C /tmp/postfixadmin-wYfSPx/ -cf- . | \
    tar -C /etc/postfix/sql/ -xf-
# chown -R root:postfix /etc/postfix/sql
# find /etc/postfix/sql -mindepth 1 -exec chmod 0640 {} +
```

These files are as secure as Unix permits. Now configure Postfix to read them.

main.cf and Databases

We defined virtual domains with the `main.cf` options
`virtual_mailbox_domains`, `virtual_alias_maps`, and
`virtual_mailbox_maps`. Change all of these to use the database-
backed configurations. The database configuration files that
PostfixAdmin created for us have names that resemble the options
they belong to. Do not blindly follow my instructions; always check
the top of `POSTFIX_CONF.txt` for the instructions on your version.
(They'll be close, but minor changes happen.)

The `virtual_mailbox_domains` option lists the virtual
domains this host accepts mail for. Point it at the file
`mysql_virtual_domain_maps.cf`.

```
virtual_mailbox_domains =
proxy:mysql:/etc/postfix/sql/mysql_virtual_domains_maps.cf
```

Let's take this apart. The `proxy` statement tells Postfix to aggregate
database queries through proxymap(8). The `mysql` statement informs
Postfix that this data source is MySQL-compatible. We then have the
path to the file containing the query details.

The `virtual_alias_maps` option gives aliases for virtual hosts.
Aliases come in several varieties, and can be expressed best by using
multiple database tables.

```
virtual_alias_maps =
  proxy:mysql:/etc/postfix/sql/mysql_virtual_alias_maps.cf,
  proxy:mysql:/etc/postfix/sql/mysql_virtual_alias_domain_maps.cf,
  proxy:mysql:/etc/postfix/sql/mysql_virtual_alias_domain_catchall.cf
```

The mailbox definitions in `virtual_mailbox_maps` fit into two
database table, one for the accounts and one for the aliases tied to
those account.

```
virtual_mailbox_maps =
  proxy:mysql:/etc/postfix/sql/mysql_virtual_mailbox_maps.cf,
  proxy:mysql:/etc/postfix/sql/mysql_virtual_alias_domain_mailbox.cf
```

Watch the error log and restart Postfix. If you don't see unusual
error messages, it should work. Fire up your test mail client and see if
you can send mail to your main test address.

If that works, send mail to the account that you created brand-new within PostfixAdmin. It should bounce, but the bounce message should include a Dovecot error. Remember, virtual accounts must be configured in both Postfix and Dovecot. We've told Postfix to check the database for user accounts. A bounce with a Dovecot error means that Postfix accepted the message, but Dovecot did not. Postfix is reading the database.

That frees us to configure Dovecot.

Configuring Dovecot for a Database

Dovecot uses a password database with pre-authentication information and a user database with post-authentication information. While Dovecot uses Unix-compatible password files, when it queries a database it expects only the information relevant for each function.

Create a separate configuration file for your database configuration, */etc/dovecot/dovecot-sql.conf*. As this file contains security-sensitive passwords, it should be owned by the user root and the group dovecot, and not world-readable.

```
# touch dovecot-sql.conf
# chown root:dovecot dovecot-sql.conf
# chmod 640 dovecot-sql.conf
```

Your SQL configuration file needs four parts: the connection information, the password query, the user query, and an iteration query.

Connection Information

Dovecot needs to know the database information, the database type, and the default password hashing algorithm. Start by defining the database with a connect statement.

```
connect = host=hostname dbname=database user=username
  password=password
```

Fill in the information for our database. You don't need to escape special characters in the password, but test spaces carefully.

```
connect = host=localhost dbname=slurry user=garbage
  password=MailIsTheWorst!1
```

Use the `driver` option to set the database type. Dovecot can use Postgres, SQLite, or MySQL.

```
driver=mysql
```

The conveniently named `default_pass_scheme` option sets the default password hashing algorithm. Everything else in this stack uses Dovecot's Blowfish support, but we're in Dovecot so we don't have to specify the application.

```
default_pass_scheme = BLF-CRYPT
```

After these, you get to play with SQL. Dovecot's documentation provides sample SQL queries for both MySQL and Postgres. They work fine, so long as you followed exactly their recommended setup. No application's recommendations precisely match any other application's recommendations. That's okay. Modifying the queries is not terrible.

The Iterate Query

The iterate query returns a list of all active users. That's pretty standard across PostfixAdmin installs.

```
iterate_query = SELECT username as user FROM mailbox
  WHERE active = '1'
```

Log into your MySQL client and run this query yourself, to verify it works.

The Password Query

The password query is expected to return a specific username and password hash. It can use all of the Dovecot variables discussed in Chapter 3 like %u, %d, and so on. A Dovecot username is the complete email address, or %u. (The query results are not checked for these variables, so if your username happens to include %d it won't get expanded.)

The minor catch is that the username field must be called "user" and the hash "password." The PostfixAdmin database stores the user in the "username" field. Your SQL query must use an alias to remap the query. The PostfixAdmin designers couldn't have the database column names match both Postfix and Dovecot expectations.[26]

```
password_query = select username as user,password \
    from mailbox where username = '%u' and active='1'
```

Log into your database and run this query using your test user for `%u`. If you haven't changed the PostfixAdmin database, it should work as written. The user query is more trouble.

The User Query

The user query needs to return a properly formatted user database entry, including the home directory, user and group IDs, and any quotas. Parts of this depend on where you chose to store your virtual mailboxes and what system user owns them. The example provides all the SQL logic you need, but you must update the constants for your system.

Here's a query skeleton.

```
user_query = select concat \
    ('mailbox-location/',maildir) as home, \
    owner-uid as uid, owner-gid as gid, \
    CONCAT('*:bytes=', quota) AS quota_rule \
    FROM mailbox \
    WHERE username ='%u' and active='1'
```

The *mailbox-location* is the directory where your mailboxes are stored. This is the same as `virtual_mailbox_base` from Postfix's `main.cf`. My installation uses `/vhosts`. Dovecot provides the user's mail directory as the variable `maildir`. The query glues these into the path to the user's files on disk.

---

26   I'm not complaining. If *I* had to choose between "annoy Postfix" and "annoy Dovecot," I would become an intergalactic smuggler and borrow money from a sketchy mob boss.

The *owner-uid* and *owner-gid* are the system users that own the mailbox files and directories.

Here's the final query for the configuration used in this book.

```
user_query = select concat ('/vhosts/',maildir) \
    as home, 5000 as uid, 5000 as gid, \
    CONCAT('*:bytes=', quota) AS quota_rule \
    FROM mailbox WHERE username ='%u' and active='1'
```

Definitely run your query by hand, with your test user. Check the path, UID, and GID against your system.

Put all three of these queries in *dovecot-sql.conf*.

Telling Dovecot About the Database

The *passdb* and *userdb* options in *dovecot.conf* tell Dovecot how to find the user and password databases. Remove the entries that point to password files. When you switch to using an actual database, both can use the same configuration.

```
passdb {
  driver = sql
  args = /etc/dovecot/dovecot-sql.conf
}

userdb {
  driver = sql
  args = /etc/dovecot/dovecot-sql.conf
}
```

The `driver` option tells Dovecot to use SQL, and the `args` option gives the path to the configuration. Restart Dovecot and you're ready to go!

Except for whatever you messed up.

Testing the Dovecot Database

Watch the Dovecot log with `tail -f`. Open `mutt` on the local system and try to log in with IMAP. It should require the password you entered in PostfixAdmin's web interface. If your queries are incorrect or you have some other configuration error, you won't be able to log in and you'll get a log message.

If that works, use `mutt` to send a mail to the new test account that you created via PostfixAdmin. The log should show it delivered.

Once you can send messages from one account to the other on the local system, add that new test account to your desktop client. The desktop client should be able to log in and download that test message. This verifies that IMAP works.

Your desktop client should be able to mail from one of your server's accounts to the others, demonstrating that basic SMTP still works. If that functions, test submission and relaying by having that account mail an account on your other test host. Does Postfix complain that your account doesn't own your account? You probably set the `smtpd_sender_login_maps` option to the password file rather than `$virtual_alias_maps` like I told you.

When any test fails, stop immediately. Read the log. Debug the problem before proceeding.

Once all parts of the database-backed mail system work, you can start preparing your mail system to face the world.

Chapter 7: Rspamd Essentials

Good systems use the least resource-intensive methods to deal with the most common cases. Tools like `postscreen` and DNSBLs cost-effectively eliminate a large amount of spam. Classifying messages based on content is computationally expensive and requires a specialized tool. Many are available, but we'll focus on rspamd.

Rspamd (`https://rspamd.com`) started life as a Bayesian spam filtering system, but its extensible design led people to write additional functions. Like many open-source software suites, it's freely available but support is available through Rspamd Ltd. It includes the core software, many modules, the rspamadm(1) management tool, and a web interface. It uses Redis for data storage. Rather than Unix sockets, rspamd uses network ports to communicate between processes. Of all the programs your mail system needs, the combination of rspamd and Redis are probably the most resource-intensive.

Configuring a spam tester might seem premature—after all, we haven't even told the world how to send mail to our domain! Rspamd also supports several less resource-intensive functions, however, such as validating SPF records and handling DKIM, and you absolutely need these before letting random people mail you. You could use outside tools for these, but SPF and DKIM support are among rspamd's lightest features. Before we get into teaching rspamd how to perform fancy statistical analysis, we'll set it up for these simpler functions and return to it as needed.

Evaluating spam is a matter of inspecting an individual mail's characteristics and assigning points to each. Some characteristics hint that the mail is valid ham; others imply spam. Each characteristic gets a point value. If a message accumulates enough points, it's flagged as spam. Does a message include a malformed, encrypted, or executable

179

attachment? That's bad, add points. Does it have valid DKIM, SPF, and DMARC? Promising, knock off points. Does it include Unicode characters commonly used to spoof your language, does the reverse DNS not match the hostname, or does the hostname in the EHLO not exist in DNS? Points! If the message body contains a URL known to be used for phishing, the message wins *all* the points. Win enough points and rspamd declares the message to be spam. Low enough, and rspamd passes the ham.

A deep understanding of rspamd requires reading source code and studying antispam forums. You can effectively deploy rspamd without that, so long as you're prepared to occasionally dig in to figure out strangeness.

Some rspamd features duplicate features in Postfix. Postscreen's intrusive checks work like greylisting. Rspamd includes a greylisting module. Which should you use? Both, or neither, sort of. Once you add exceptions for large mail systems, postscreen is much less resource-intensive than rspamd. That's not a matter of programming skill: rspamd is optimized for digging deep into messages, and is efficient at doing so. If a message makes it through postscreen's intrusive checks, but rspamd decides that the message content is sufficiently suspicious, it can also greylist. You can disable or strengthen all of these as you desire.

Any spam checking system raises privacy concerns. The rspamd dashboard shows the subject lines of every mail your recipients get and what rspamd did with that message. Rspamd can check links and email addresses within message bodies against external block lists, but that requires sending all the email addresses and links inside your messages to that external block list. Do I really want some outsider knowing I receive lots of links to `https://forums.OverthrowTheEmpire.org`? Forget comfort—is that even *safe?* You have an opinion, but someone receiving messages on content that's illegal where they live, where the server is, where the block list is hosted, or where the block list operator lives might have a different opinion. You're in the middle of it. Rspamd's defaults split the difference by enabling tests that block known spambots, but not enabling blocklist-based content analysis. Rspamd also uses *fuzzy hashes*, which break up message content according to predefined rules, computes hashes for those chunks, and compares the hashes against a list of hashes of known spam maintained by `rspamd.com`. One match is suspicious. Multiple matches in one message is extremely suspicious.

You have no way of knowing in advance how a fresh rspamd install will react to the specific blend of email you and your users receive. While we all get spam offering to elevate us to the Galactic Council in thirty days, my routine email looks nothing like yours. Start any deployment by telling rspamd to never impede messages, only to add headers showing the test results. As you gain confidence in rspamd and train it to detect your personal spam and ham, increase the sensitivity.

Managing rspamd requires Universal Configuration Language. You also need Redis. We'll briefly discuss both.

Universal Configuration Language

Have you ever looked at a JSON configuration and thought, *That could be a regular Unix text file*? Or wondered why a developer used text when JSON or YAML would have been better? YAML and JSON and Unix text all represent similar data in different formats. Each format has strengths, weaknesses, and syntactical idiosyncrasies that please their devotees. JSON might be a configuration store that can be extended until it is complete, but it's not designed to be written by hand and very few people advocate doing so. YAML looks writable, until it fails to validate. Even plain text goes wrong when you miss a semicolon or a quote. Every format is full of failure.

Universal Configuration Language (UCL) brings all these failures together. UCL-aware tools can read Unix-style text configurations as well as various JSONs, YAML, and messagepack. They can output configurations in any of these formats. If it makes sense for you to configure an application in YAML, do that. If someone else needs the same application to use Unix-style text configuration, that's fine. UCL also simplifies programmatic configuration changes. Rspamd uses UCL for all its configuration files.

UCL calls the text format *configuration*. It borrows heavily from nginx's strict format. Here's a snippet of rspamd configuration in configuration. (That sentence shows why this book refers to the format called *configuration* as *unix-style*.)

```
options {
  cache_file = "/var/db/rspamd/symbols.cache";
  one_shot = false;
  map_watch_interval = 300;
  map_file_watch_multiplier = 0.100000;
  dynamic_conf = "/var/db/rspamd/rspamd_dynamic";
...}
```

This format is almost instinctive for any sysadmin or programmer. Here's the exact same thing in JSON.

```
"options": {
  "cache_file": "/var/db/rspamd/symbols.cache",
  "one_shot": false,
  "map_watch_interval": 300,
  "map_file_watch_multiplier": 0.100000,
  "dynamic_conf": "/var/db/rspamd/rspamd_dynamic",
  ...
```

Which should you use? Whichever you like. Rspamd's default configuration files use a mix of JSON and unix-style.

UCL Features

UCL's JSON format does not adhere to the strictest JSON. Top objects don't need braces, quotes can be skipped, and you can use = instead of :. Additionally, an object or array can have a trailing comma.

Many Unix configurations expect boolean settings, like true or false, on and off, and so on. You can use *true, yes,* or *on* interchangeably. Similarly, *false, no,* and *off* are all interchangeable. Use whatever makes sense in context. If you need any of these as strings, put them in quotation marks.

Arguments about base two versus base ten have plagued computing for decades, and will continue to do so until long after I am blissfully liberated from computing. UCL supports the usual k, m, and g labels for multipliers as well as kb, mb, and gb. The versions that end in *b* are calculated in base two, while the bare abbreviations use base ten.[27] 500mb is not the same as 500m. Tune your systems however you wish.

Preface single-line comments with a hash mark (#), while multi-line comments can use the traditional C-style /* and */. UCL supports nested comments.

Includes and Variables

UCL allows the developer to use a variety of macros and variables. Macros have names beginning with a period (for example, .lightsaber). Variables begin with a dollar sign, such as $DROIDTYPE. UCL defines the macro .include and establishes a rich syntax for pulling in other files and how the contents of those files should be treated. Rspamd's configuration heavily leverages .include statements.

A common risk for including files is defining the same setting multiple times. Maybe your main configuration file sets DEBUG to *0*, while one included file sets it to *YES* and another sets it to *wookie*. Each program deals with such conflicts in a manner that the programmer thought appropriate. Sometimes the last one wins. Sometimes the program refuses to accept the configuration, perhaps providing an error message of varying usefulness. Maybe it picks one. Who knows? UCL explicitly addresses this matter through a *priority* system. You can define priorities for different include files, explicitly declaring which files have precedence. Priority runs from 0 to 15. The default priority is 0, meaning that default settings can be overwritten by anything. By setting a priority for an include file, you can tell UCL which file wins.

---

27   I can almost hear some poor developer shriek, "I refuse to listen to this squabble any longer. Take this solution and leave the chat. While you can."

Rspamd typically uses includes in three ways. Here's a snippet of the *options* section.

```
...
options {
  pidfile = "$RUNDIR/rspamd.pid";
  .include "$CONFDIR/options.inc"
  .include(try=true; priority=1,duplicate=merge)
     "$LOCAL_CONFDIR/local.d/options.inc"
  .include(try=true; priority=10)
     "$LOCAL_CONFDIR/override.d/options.inc"
}
```

The first line of the options section sets the PID file. It defines a file in the directory $RUNDIR. That's a variable defined within the rspamd code. Your operating system's rspamd package maintainer set this to conform with your operating system's expectations. We'll see how to change this later.

The next line is a simple include statement. $CONFDIR is a variable that represents the configuration directory. In our case that's */etc/rspamd*. This line reads the file *options.inc* and absorbs all the settings it finds. If *options.inc* does not exist, this configuration is invalid.

The third entry pulls in another file, $LOCAL_CONFDIR/local.d/options.inc, but the parentheses provide instructions for special handling. The try option says to try to find the target file, but keep going if it doesn't exist. This file gets a priority of 1, meaning in the case of a conflict its entries override the default settings. The duplicate statement tells how to handle duplicate entries. By merging, we allow included files to create new settings. Taken as a whole, this .include declares that the file configuration file in */etc/rspamd/local.d/options.inc* overrides what's in */etc/rspamd/options.inc* and can add new variables.

The last entry tries to include
`/etc/rspamd/override.d/options.inc`, but under very different
conditions. The priority is 10, so entries in this file are more important
than any other. There is no `duplicate` statement, so the contents
of `override.d/options.inc` entirely overwrites other settings.
Overwriting is heavy-handed, and replaces entire configuration
sections.

What does "overwriting" mean? Consider our earlier example of
settings options.

```
"options": {
  "one_shot": false,
  "cache_file": "/var/db/rspamd/symbols.cache",
  "map_watch_interval": 300,
  "map_file_watch_multiplier": 0.100000,
  "dynamic_conf": "/var/db/rspamd/rspamd_dynamic",
  …
}
```

Suppose some rspamd plugin moves the cache file, but you
want to weld it in place via an override. You might try this in
`override.d/options.inc`.

```
"options": {
  "cache_file": "/var/db/rspamd/symbols.cache"
}
```

That looks fine, right?

Here's the catch: this does not override the definition of `cache_file`.
It overrides the definition of `options`. The settings in the default
`options` section, like `one_shot`, `map_watch_interval`, and so on, are
now undefined. If you don't tell UCL to merge entries, it doesn't merge
entries.

Avoid overrides unless you're rewriting entire configuration files.

Redis

Redis is a database, but not in the way Postgres or MySQL or sqlite or hash files or notes scribbled on a napkin or Oracle are. While traditional databases prioritize getting data safely ensconced on the disk, Redis treats RAM as its primary data store. Redis has options for safely stashing data on the disk, including options that approach the reliability of traditional databases, but its primary aim is speed. Redis is a key-value store, not an SQL engine; you might think of it as a super-fast network-aware hash file. Almost every operating system has a Redis package.

Redis is changing its licensing. Forks are emerging. If you read this book after 2024, you should investigate which of those forks are prospering and consider using it instead.

Rspamd uses Redis for ephemera such as IP addresses, scores, and symbols, plus long-term storage of Bayesian statistics. If the server suffers a catastrophic outage, the ephemera does not matter. By the time you could restore it from backup, all that data would have expired. The Bayesian statistics data is important, though. The easiest way to manage the split is to have a separate Redis instance for each.

Socket Directory

While Redis can listen to the network, that's unnecessary exposure for a local-only database. Configure Redis to use faster, more efficient, and more secure Unix sockets. Rspamd needs read-write access to those sockets. Both Redis and rspamd run as unprivileged users, so we need a directory accessible to both their users. This directory will be useful for anything that rspamd and redis must share.

```
# install -d -m 0775 -o redis -g rspamd \
  /var/run/rspamd-redis
```

Even if you move rspamd and Postfix to separate machines, Redis should live on the rspamd host.[28]

---

28   If you are running a mail system with so much load that you need dedicated Redis hardware cross-connected to a beefy rspamd host, I don't know why you're reading this book. I appreciate you buying it and all, but I can't help you.

Primary Redis Configuration

Configure Redis in `/etc/redis.conf`. The sample configuration includes options for replication and TCP backlogs and keepalives, all of which are overkill for our application. The package for your operating system has already tuned the options for memory allocation. Don't change them unless you have problems, or are already a Redis expert and are skimming this section.

Redis expects you to run multiple Redis instances for separate processes. I encourage this, especially as I am easily confused, especially when dealing with outages at stupid o'clock. If I must remember that the default Redis instance is used by rspamd, the outage will last longer. Instead, I want a Redis instance clearly labeled "rspamd." Don't use the default Redis instance. Set up a specific rspamd instance. Set the common options you want in the default config, but don't start an instance from that config. Instead, create specific named Redis instances for every role and have those instances suck in your defaults.

Set the location where redis will store its on-disk data with the `dir` option. Your operating system's default is probably fine, but you need to know where that is. Set the on-disk filename with `dbfilename`.

```
dir /var/lib/redis
dbfilename dump.rdb
```

How fast Redis dumps its data to disk is dictated by how fast the in-memory data store changes. If there's been at least one change, it dumps data every hour. If there's been at least one hundred changes, it dumps every fifteen minutes. If there have been at least ten thousand changes in the last minute, it dumps. In most cases, this is fine. In the event of a crash you could lose a few messages' worth of spam training data, but the Internet has an infinite supply of spam. You'll be fine.

While Redis uses memory efficiently, a spam attack might cause its memory to balloon. Rspamd recommends restricting Redis' memory usage to half a gigabyte with the `maxmemory` option. You might be able to turn this down later, but on modern systems it's a good starting point. Redis accepts abbreviations like mb, kb, and gb. Like UCL, abbreviations that end in *b* calculate size in base 2, while abbreviations without the *b* use base 10.

```
maxmemory 500mb
```

Redis logs to its own file by default but over the long term syslog is preferable. Disable the logfile option and set the syslog-enabled and syslog-ident options.

```
#logfile /var/log/redis/redis.log
syslog-enabled yes
syslog-ident redis
```

Redis needs a PID file, given by pidfile. The default is fine, but you'll need to know where it is.

```
pidfile /var/run/redis/redis.pid
```

Disable the network by telling Redis listen to port 0 and assign a Unix socket. Use the unixsocketperm option to allow the owner and the owning group to access the socket. Earlier in this chapter we created a sockets directory owned by **rspamd** and **redis**.

```
port 0
unixsocket /var/run/rspamd-redis/redis-defaultinstance.sock
unixsocketperm 770
```

Finally, set a password for accessing the database. Yes, a password stored in a text file is not "secure," whatever that word means. Using passwords still increases the difficulty of hostile reconnaissance. Use an inconvenient password as the default setting. If this configuration is ever mistakenly used to start an instance, people will quickly realize something is wrong.

```
requirepass WhyDoesASpaceStationNeedATrashCompactor?
```

These defaults will help support the instances you actually want to run.

Redis for Rspamd

We need one Redis instance for Bayesian data and one for the rest of rspamd. Each requires its own configuration file. We'll call them *bayes* and *rspamd*. Here's `/etc/redis-bayes.conf`.

```
include /etc/redis.conf
syslog-ident redis-bayes
unixsocket /var/run/rspamd-redis/bayes.sock
pidfile /var/run/redis/bayes.pid
logfile /var/log/redis/bayes.log
dbfilename bayes.rdb
dir /var/db/redis/bayes/
requirepass LetsBlowThisThingAndGoHome
```

We start by using `include` to suck in the default values from `redis.conf`.

Each Redis process needs its own Unix socket, PID file, and log file. The `dbfile` option tells Redis where to write persistent data, and we stick this data in a directory under the default. This instance needs persistent data, so add the dump file to your backups. I also add a new syslogd identifier, so that when I get a weird log message I know what instance is complaining.

Here's a configuration for the rspamd's ephemeral Redis service, `/etc/redis-rspamd.conf`. A socket named plain old *rspamd* better go straight to `rspamd`, so I give this a more specific name.

```
include /etc/redis.conf
syslog-ident redis-rspamd
unixsocket /var/run/rspamd-redis/redis4rspamd.sock
pidfile /var/run/redis/rspamd.pid
logfile /var/log/redis/rspamd.log
dbfilename rspamd.rdb
dir /var/db/redis/rspamd/
requirepass HanShotFirst
```

Having separate passwords for each instance also serves as a double-check that you told each rspamd module to use the correct Redis instance. You don't want to discover too late that your Bayesian values were not written to disk before rebooting!

After running rspamd for a while, you might need to override other values like `maxmemory` for certain instances. That depends entirely on your environment and mail load.

Each instance has its own subdirectory in Redis' data directory. Be sure to create those directories and make **redis** their owner.

Now make your operating system start these additional Redis processes. Most Linuxes require a systemctl(8) incantation. BSDs use an */etc/rc.conf* setting. Traditional Unixes use */etc/rc.local*. Give your Unix what it wants. Verify that the processes can start, that the log files appear and show no errors, and that the TCP ports opened.

Talking to Redis

Verify that you can manually connect to the Redis instances. While you'll find fancy Redis interfaces, the redis-cli(1) tool that ships with the software is more than adequate for simple tests. Give the path to the socket of the instance you want to connect to with -s. Here, I run this command from */var/run/bayes-redis* to keep the sample output short.

```
$ redis-cli -s bayes.sock
redis bayes.sock>
```

It's connected, but only in a basic "I see the socket" sense. Give the AUTH command and the password for that instance.

```
redis bayes.sock> auth LetsBlowThisThingAndGoHome
OK
```

We can now issue commands. Use ping to see if the Redis process is listening to you.

```
redis bayes.sock> ping
PONG
```

It answers! These are brand-new freshly-started databases, so they shouldn't have any data in them. But Redis got your request and answered it. The database is ready and accessible.

If you want to see what happens in the database, use the `monitor` command.

```
redis bayes.sock> monitor
OK
```

Monitoring Redis while starting rspamd will show activity. Once rspamd has been running for a while, use the `info` command to see what it's doing. It'll offer several pages output on the software configuration, the amount of memory used, and errors. At the very end, you'll see the number of keys.

```
redis bayes.sock> info
# Server
redis_version:7.2.4
...
# Keyspace
db0:keys=128060,expires=0,avg_ttl=0
```

This database has 128,060 keys in it. We're ahead of ourselves now, though. Let's set up rspamd so we can get those keys.

Exit with the `quit` command.

Rspamd Components

Rspamd performs tests on each message. Tests define *symbols* (sometimes called *tags*) indicating the test type, the result, and the weight or point value. Symbols are in capital letters. The weight indicates how strongly this characteristic indicates spam or ham. Testing the message against the domain's SPF record could generate tags like R_SPF_ALLOW (weight -2), R_SPF_FAIL (weight +1), and R_SPF_NEUTRAL (weight 0). Symbols might be combined; if a message fails SPF, DKIM, *and* DMARC validation it gets tagged with the AUTH_NA_OR_FAIL symbol. Rspamd attaches each module's symbols to the message. You can fine-tune rules so that their weight gets multiplied under specific conditions. After the message passes through all the modules, rspamd totals the weights and provides a final score. Rspamd supports hundreds of symbols and adds more at each update.

Some symbols are defined in a configuration file in */etc/rspamd/*. Other symbols will be defined in a core rspamd rule. Those rules are mostly written in Lua, and will be in a location like */usr/share/rspamd/rules* or wherever your Unix stashes such things.

Symbols are also *grouped*. Rule groups can be enabled, disabled, or weighted. If you want to stop using a whole category of tests, check to see if they're already in a group.

Modules can utilize outside services. Chapter 8 discusses attaching DNSBLs to postscreen, to stop spammers before they reach the SMTP server. DNSBLs can provide information on domain names as well as IP addresses, though. Organizations like Spamhaus maintain block lists of domain names that show up in phishing attacks and scam mails. Rspamd has a module to check message bodies for links to these domains. Similarly, Rspamd Ltd offers lists of disposable email addresses and free email services.

Adding and removing tests is a matter of installing, enabling, or disabling modules. Each module can be configured via includes and overrides. Always check rspamd's online configuration reference before making changes: assume *nothing*.

All modules have a configuration file in `/etc/rspamd/modules.d`. As with the rest of rspamd, do not configure modules in their configuration file. Use a local file or, if you must, an override.

You can disable modules by setting `enabled` to *false* in a local file named after the module's file. Suppose you don't want rspamd to greylist. The greylisting module's configuration is `/etc/rspamd/modules.d/greylist.conf`. Create `/etc/rspamd/local.d/greylist.conf` containing only this line. `enabled=false;`

When you restart rspamd, the module will be turned off.

rspamadm(1)

Your main interface to what rspamd is doing and how it's set up is rspamadm(1). This program is for both novice and advanced users, so some of its functions won't be useful to the operator of a small mail system. See all the functions of your `rspamadm` version with the `-l` option.

```
$ rspamadm -l
```

You'll get the version number and a usage summary, and then a list of sub-commands:

```
Available commands:
  clickhouse          Retrieve information from Clickhouse
  configdump          Perform configuration file dump
  configgraph         Produces graph of Rspamd includes
  confighelp          Shows help for configuration options
...
```

If an option piques your interest, use the help command to request a detailed description.

```
$ rspamadm help configdump
```

You can also use the option itself with the `--help` argument.

```
$ rspamadm configdump --help
...
Application Options:
  -j, --json          Json output (pretty formatted)
  -C, --compact       Compacted json output
  -c, --config        Config file to test
  -h, --show-help     Show help as comments for each option
...
```

The output of `rspamadm help` *commandname* and `rspamadm` *commandname* `--help` might differ, so check both.

Some rspamadm options help you configure rspamd services or modules. They work by adding or editing local configuration files. If you have trouble, use these tools to create the initial configurations, then tune the generated configurations as needed.

rspamc(1)

The rspamd command-line client rspamc(1) is most useful for large operations or for testing a single message, but certain features are useful for smaller mail systems. One of the most useful subcommands is stat, which shows how many messages rspamd has processed and what it's done with those messages. Troubleshooting normally involves single messages, but keeping a watchful eye on the spam levels can warn you if the system is going wrong. Rspamd only updates the statistics once every sixty seconds, so don't worry if changes don't appear immediately.

```
$ rspamc stat
Results for command: stat (0.164 seconds)
Messages scanned: 1495
Messages with action reject: 1495, 100.00%
...
```

The stat_reset subcommand shows that information and resets all the counters to zero. You might decide that per-day counters are more important than ongoing scores.

We'll use the learn_ham and learn_spam subcommands to train the statistical filter.

The counters subcommand shows each symbol, its weight, how many times per minute it gets assigned, and how many times the symbol has been assigned to a message. If you don't receive enough email the per-minute counters are empty, but the number of times any symbol has been hit is useful. You could parse that output, see what your typical email looks like, and perhaps adjust symbol weights.

Other rspamc commands let you communicate with remote rspamd servers, manipulate symbols and hashes, and adjust cached data. When you're just starting with rspamd, stay with the configuration files for these.

Rspamd Documentation

You'll find a whole bunch of rspamd documentation, but pulling it all together or finding the instructions for the feature you want can be challenging.

The rspamd web site (`https://rspamd.com`) includes tutorials for the most common environments and references on less common uses. The per-module references are notably helpful when fine-tuning tests, which is the most frequent rspamd task.

Skimming a module's configuration file can offer hints about which sorts of tests the module performs.

I most often start with the module configurations in */etc/rspamd/modules.d*. Each module has a configuration file. Each file starts with a warning to not edit the file directly, then a pointer to the online documentation.

The rspamadm command offers syntax for certain modules. Running `rspamadm confighelp` *modulename* might show the module's configuration options. Not all modules have this support.

Maps

An rspamd *map* includes external information in a configuration file. Maps are usually key-value stores. Unlike a UCL `include` statement, maps might be on the local system or available over HTTP. Maps are reread upon a SIGHUP, so you can update them without entirely restarting rspamd. You can also set a fallback to be used if any part of the preferred data source is unavailable.

Consider this tidbit of */etc/rspamd/modules.d/mime_types.conf*.

```
mime_types {
  file = [
      "https://maps.rspamd.com/rspamd/mime_types.inc.zst",
      "$LOCAL_CONFDIR/local.d/maps.d/mime_types.inc.local",
      "${DBDIR}/mime_types.inc.local",
      "fallback+file://${CONFDIR}/maps.d/mime_types.inc"
  ]
  …
```

Rspamd uses MIME types to identify which tests should be applied to each part of a message. IANA assigns new MIME types independently of rspamd releases, so this list needs to be trivially updatable. Rspamd aggregates a list from several sources, separated by commas.

The primary data source listed is a file on the `rspamd.com` website.

The second data source is the file `/etc/rspamd/local.d/maps.d/mime_types.inc.local`. List any custom MIME types in that file. Also send anyone who created a custom MIME type to interrogation.

The third data source is the file `/var/db/rspamd/mime_types.inc`. The web interface stores its changes here.

Rspamd combines these three data sources into a single primary list. If any one of these data sources is unavailable, it tries the file labeled *fallback*. There's no rule in this snippet of configuration pulling in the local and web site additions, but the fallback file includes them on its own.

The contents of a map do not appear in the configuration compiled by `rspamadm`, but the data sources do.

The directory `/etc/rspamd/maps.d/` includes editable maps for many tests.

Blocklists in Rspamd

Chapter 9 discusses IP-address-based DNSBLs. Block lists can be used for more than IP addresses, though. If it can be encoded as a DNS query, it can be used in a DNSBL. Rspamd can query DNSBLs of known spammer email addresses, URLs of scams that appear in message bodies, links, and more. If you edit tests, you must verify that each test is connected to an appropriate block list.

Rspamd modules are configured by default to query appropriate block lists. Be extremely careful about overriding the block list. Perhaps you don't like the way one DNSBL manages its operation, but switching to a different DNSBL with more suitable management but the wrong sort of information will not help. A test that checks for known scam URLs in message bodies will not work if you query a DNSBL that catalogs bad FROM addresses.

Configuring Rspamd

Rspamd's configuration files live in `/etc/rspamd`. The configuration files use Universal Configuration Language (UCL). Default files are either Unix-style or JSON. The initial files are designed to easily create a functional anti-spam system that's usable across a majority of platforms and environments. We will go through the bare minimum configuration needed to assign management passwords, connect Redis, enable the web interface, and make rspamd non-intrusive so we can test it.

Rspamd simplifies its configuration files with two variables. The `LOCAL_CONFDIR` variable refers to the directory containing your rspamd configuration. In our examples, it's `/etc/rspamd`. The variable `DBDIR` gives where rspamd stores its on-disk data. For this install, it's `/var/db/rspamd`. The directory used depends on how your operating system packages rspamd.

The overrides and includes in `/etc/rspamd` look somewhat tangled, but upgrades will overwrite the default configuration files without warning. Never edit the default files. Use local configuration files and override files instead, as discussed in "Universal Configuration Files" earlier this chapter. Local files let you set individual options, while override files replace entire stanzas of configuration and forcibly overwrite options set elsewhere.

Basic tests like "how many people did this message go to?" "how many MIME attachments are in this message?" and "is the date reasonable?" are in the core rules rather than modules. Rspamd's one major feature that is not a module is *Bayesian analysis*. The *Bayes rule* is a statistical theorem for assessing probabilities. Bayesian analysis takes a group of known spam and a group of known good messages (or *ham*), and scrutinizes them for patterns. When new spam arrives in my inbox, my action of saving it to the spam folder should trigger analysis of that message. If rspamd filters a good message into my spam folder, moving it out of my inbox should trigger a fresh analysis. This continued analysis teaches rspamd what your users' mail looks like, and how to recognize the spam you get. Bayesian analysis works well when consistently trained.

Compiling the Configuration

The main rspamd configuration file is `rspamd.conf`. It's composed primarily of `include` statements for all the modules. It reads all those files, all the local files, all the override files, and all the files those include files include. It then assembles them into a single configuration. View the complete, parsed configuration with `rspamadm configdump`. Add the `-s` flag to see the comments from the original configuration files. An rspamd configuration is thousands of lines, so redirect it to a file.

```
$ rspamadm configdump -s > rspamd.config
```

The best way to fully understand rspamd is to go through this configuration line by line, looking up every option in the online configuration reference. At first, though, page through it to get an idea of how an rspamd configuration hangs together.

The dump includes symbols only if they appear in the configuration files. Symbols defined in the core rules do not appear unless you changed them.

Untangling which files rspamd is parsing feels overwhelming for new users. If you like visual representations, rspamadm's `configgraph` command can generate a formally defined graph of configuration file dependencies and what files have been parsed. If you're not certain rspamd is reading your configuration files, or you want to see how all these files fit together, generate the graph and check. You'll need Graphviz's dot(1) to convert the graph to a usable format like PNG.

```
$ rspamadm configgraph > rspamd-config.dot
$ dot -Tpng rspamd-config.dot -o rspamd.conf.png
```

You'll want to view this on a wide screen. A large, wide screen. *Wider.*

Rspamd comes with most of a working configuration. You must set up a controller password and inform the various modules of their Redis instances before using the program. Once it works, you can tweak settings.

Controller Password

Rspamd provides a worker-control process accessible as a local socket or on TCP port 11334. This controller is integral to the web interface, and supports a read-only password and a read-write password. Rspamadm's pw subcommand generates password hashes.

```
$ rspamadm pw
Enter passphrase:
$2$1yfwuq4c...
```

Set the passwords in */etc/rspamd/local.d/worker-controller.inc*. The password option is the read-only password, while enable_password is the read-write password.

```
password = "$2$1yfwuq4c..."
enable_password = "$2$1kf1q19..."
```

Even if you have no intent of accessing the controller socket or using the web interface, don't leave the controller unprotected. Assign passwords.

Redis

We configured two Redis instances earlier this chapter: one for Bayesian statistics and one for ephemera. Each of these modules or features uses a different configuration file.

The Bayesian statistics engine's default configuration settings are in */etc/rspamd/statistic.conf*. Rspamd supports setting Bayesian-analysis-specific values in a local *classifier-bayes.conf*. All you need right now is to set the Redis server.

```
backend = "redis";
servers = "/var/run/rspamd-redis/bayes.sock";
password = "LetsBlowThisThingAndGoHome";
```

Put your catchall Redis instance in
/etc/rspamd/local.d/redis.conf, with the `password` and `servers`
options.

```
password = "HanShotFirst";
servers = "/var/run/rspamd-redis/redis4rspamd.sock";
```

Any time you work with include and override files, I recommend
double-checking your changes against the compiled configuration.
Run `rspamadm configdump` and search for your Redis sockets and
passwords to verify your work, then restart to make your changes take
effect.

Local Addresses

Most of us do not need spam protection against our local networks.
If you tell rspamd that a network is local, it does not perform DKIM,
DMARC, or SPF checks against mail from those addresses. It skips
greylisting, RBL tests, and more. The default `local_addrs` in
/etc/rspamd/options.inc includes the private addresses allocated
in RFC 6890, such as `10.0.0.0/8` and `192.168.0.0/16`. Use the
`local_addrs` option in */etc/rspamd/local.d/options.inc* to add to
this list.

```
local_addrs = [203.0.113.0/24, 2001:db8::/32]
```

Emails from these addresses will still undergo statistical analysis.

Rspamd Actions

Rspamd scores message spamminess by points. The *actions* settings are
point thresholds where rspamd either recommends the MTA take an
action or adds headers describing why the mail is suspicious. Find the
default settings in */etc/rspamd/actions.conf*.

```
reject = 15; # Reject when reaching this score
add_header = 6; # Add header when reaching this score
greylist = 4; # Apply greylisting when reaching this score
```

When a message's score reaches the `reject` value, rspamd rejects the message. Technically, rspamd does not reject the message. It recommends rejection to the MTA. The MTA could be configured to override the milter. Postfix takes rspamd's suggestions, however.

At the `add_header` level, rspamd adds a header to the message indicating that the recipient should treat it as spam. Use Sieve rules to filter these messages into a spam folder.

When the score equals `greylist` or higher, rspamd gives the sender a 451 temporary failure. The sending host's network is greylisted for five minutes.

Rspamd offers actions other than these, but most are for edge cases.

On initial deployment, we don't want rspamd to reject or slow down email. We want to see how rspamd treats messages we receive. Crank up the thresholds on the intrusive actions. Create */etc/rspamd/local.d/actions.conf* and set new values.

```
reject = 500;
greylist = 499;
add_header = 15;
```

This isn't guaranteed to pass all messages, but if 15 is normally considered unquestionable spam and an incoming message achieves a 500, we should probably reject it. We will add a "this is spam" header only with a score of 15 or greater.

Rspamd Tests

Testing all email but changing nothing is great, but we need to see the results. The *milter_headers* module can add, change, and remove message headers. Use the `extended_spam_headers` option to tell rspamd to add test results to each message's headers. Create */etc/rspamd/local.d/milter_headers.conf* with one line.

```
extended_spam_headers = true;
```

Restart rspamd.

Rspamd Web Interface

Rspamd provides a web interface for management and showing graphs. The web interface is biased towards large sites that handle a steady stream of hundreds or thousands of simultaneous messages. Many of the statistics functions don't work for tiny servers. "Number of spam messages rejected per minute" means nothing when a server receives fifty messages an hour.

The web interface lets you configure some but not all rspamd functions. Those changes are stored in a database. Changes in the web interface override changes in the configuration files. Once you start using the web interface to configure rspamd, identifying all the changes you've made is challenging. Web-based rspamd management is a one-way trip: start using it and you can't go back to configuration files. Use whichever you prefer, but be consistent.

The web interface accesses rspamd via the controller socket. You set read-only and read-write passwords in the socket earlier. The web interface uses those same passwords. If you do not want to configure rspamd through the web interface, protect yourself by using the read-only password.

You can only access the web interface from the local host, on port 11334. We can configure your web server to proxy those requests, but you should verify the site works first. Test the web interface in your terminal by using a text-only browser such as lynx.

```
$ lynx localhost:11334
```

You'll get a minimal web page that complains about lynx's lack of JavaScript support, but it confirms that a web site exists.

Now set up your web server to forward requests to it. Configure non-password access control in the web server. Here's a snippet for Apache 2.4, forwarding all requests to /rebelscum to the rspamd proxy[29] and restricting access to my office network.

---

29   Yes, I could put this at /rspamd, but why make it easy for people to guess?

```
RewriteEngine On
RewriteRule ^/rebelscum$ /rebelscum/ [R,L]
RewriteRule ^/rebelscum/(.*) http://localhost:11334/$1
[P,L]

<Location /rebelscum>
 Require ip 203.0.113.0/24
</Location>
```

Even in read-only mode, the interface offers convenient information. The menu across the top offers information on many rspamd functions. The *Status* tab offers generic statistics and graphs. The *Throughput* graph provides more detail on how rspamd classified messages. *Configuration* lets you set the action thresholds and edit certain other settings. The *Symbols* tab shows all the symbols in your rspamd install. Under *Scan*, you can paste in a message and see how rspamd would evaluate it. Finally, History shows a complete history of received messages, the symbols applied to the message, and the results of the scan.

You can now connect Postfix to rspamd. You'll get new headers on your messages but no filtering, rejection, or other changes unless the message is egregiously spammy.

Connecting Postfix to Milters

Rspamd's *proxy worker* process handles features like load balancing, mirroring traffic, and feeding requests to the scanning layer. It also offers a milter on `localhost` port 11332. Rspamd does not offer a Unix socket milter. We'll use it to demonstrate attaching Postfix to a milter.

Only mail that arrives from the Internet needs SPF validation. Your MTA validates messages that arrive via the submission service with SMTP AUTH. Only mail that arrives on port 25 should be tested for SPF compliance. You need to configure that process, which means editing `master.cf` rather than `main.cf`.

The first uncommented line in a default `master.cf` is the standard smtpd(8) process that listens on to the world on TCP port 25.

```
smtp    inet    n    -    n    -    -    smtpd
```

To apply an option to this process, add -o and the option name. The option `smtpd_milters` attaches a milter to an smptd(8) process. Multiple milters will be processed in order. Use the keyword `inet` for milters listening on a TCP port and `unix` for Unix sockets. The rspamd milter runs on port 11332 on `localhost`.

```
smtp    inet    n    -    n    -    -    smtpd
  -o smtpd_milters=inet:localhost:11332
```

Separate multiple milters with a comma. If you have long -o options, you can use braces to allow whitespace and make them easier to manage. Restart postfix, and `smtpd` will route all incoming mail through rspamd.

Does it work? Run `tail -f` on the rspamd and mail logs. Send another mail from one test host to the other. You should see activity.

Rspamd Test Headers and Symbols

Rspamd's extended spam headers adds five new headers to an email.

The `X-Spam` header declares that this message has enough points to be considered definitely, positively spam. It only appears when the message has more points than the `add_header` action's threshold.

The `X-Rspamd-Server` header records which rspamd server processed the email. Large service providers need multiple rspamd servers.

Rspamd assigns each message a queue identifier as it passes through each module. The `X-Rspamd-Queue-Id` header shows that ID, and is recorded in the system log. You can use it to identify rspamd log entries for a specific message.

With `X-Rspamd-Action`, rspamd tells you what action it recommends based on the test results.

The `X-Spamd-Result` provides the total spam score of this message, symbols for all the results, and their numerical score. Identifying and understanding these tests is the heart of tuning rspamd. We'll spend most of our time with this header.

Create a Symbols List

When you encounter a symbol in headers or the log, you'll probably want to know either the symbol's description or how to change its point value. The web interface lets you search for symbols by name. At the command line, though, digging through the rules and the configuration file is inconvenient. Before you start work, extract the symbols from the web site into a greppable list.

Use curl or wget or whatever tool your fingers know to grab the symbols list from the web site.

```
$ fetch http://localhost:11334/symbols
```

That file is compressed JSON, a hundred thousand characters on a single line. Convert it to a list with jq(1). The JSON file contains statistical and timing data, but for looking up symbols all you need are the symbol name, weight, and description.

```
$ jq -c '.[].rules[] | \
  [.symbol,.weight,.description]' symbols.json \
  > symbols.txt
```

The file *symbols.txt* contains one symbol per line. Symbols with a positive value show that the message leans towards spam, while negative values hint at ham. Each symbol has a brief description. Consider this entry.

```
["MSBL_EBL",7.500000,"MSBL emailbl (https://www.msbl.org/)"]
```

The symbol MSBL_EBL has a value of 7.5, strongly suggesting this message is spam. The description is a block list web site. Visit the site to read about the block list and how it works. Other entries are more difficult.

```
["RCVD_HELO_USER",3.0,"HELO User spam pattern"]
```

Whatever a "HELO User spam pattern" is, it's worth three points.

Unfortunately, while the description tells you what characteristics the symbol *represents*, rspamd does not provide details on why the behavior is positive or suspicious or even what this test is testing for.

An experienced spam filter operator probably already knows all about the "HELO User spam pattern," but if we want to learn more we need to find the rule definition. We can read the Lua rule definitions in `/usr/share/rspamd` or check the source code for the rules in C and try to extract meaning. Reading the test source tells me that spambots will sometimes open an SMTP conversation with the recipient's email address, as in `EHLO mwl@ratoperatedvehicle.com`. We learned that was wrong back in Chapter 2.

If the importance of a test baffles you, check the rspamd mailing list archives or search the larger Internet.

Rspamd Results on Legitimate Mail

Here's a typical `X-Spamd-Result` header for a legitimate email message from Amazon's affiliate program.

```
X-Spamd-Result: default: False [1.30 / 500.00];
 URI_COUNT_ODD(1.00)[7];
 R_PARTS_DIFFER(1.00)[100.0%];
 DMARC_POLICY_ALLOW(-0.50)[amazon.com.au,quarantine];
 FORGED_SENDER(0.30)[associates@amazon.com.au,
    202401291702330ba37c0cd7f7475badc0483049e0p
    0fe-C5GOEGCBN7OXP@bounces.amazon.com];
 R_SPF_ALLOW(-0.20)[+ip4:54.240.0.0/18:c];
 R_DKIM_ALLOW(-0.20)[amazon.com.au:
    s=p3dozbfvgms6qio3537seunjegojqglw,
    amazonses.com:s=hsbnp7p3ensaochzwyq5wwmceodymuwv];
 MIME_GOOD(-0.10)[multipart/alternative,text/plain];
 …
```

The first line declares that this test was performed with the default rspamd rules. It has a total score of 1.30 out of the 500 required.

Consider the first symbol, URI_COUNT_ODD. The description reads "Odd number of URIs in multipart/alternative message.". Why is that important, though? Rspamd does not say. You must derive the deeper meaning from your understanding of the protocols and tools. In this case, this is an HTML message. It has a plain text version. The number of links in the plain text version should be the same as the number of links in the HTML version. If they're not, that's suspicious.

The second symbol, R_PARTS_DIFFER, is described as "Text and HTML parts differ." Spammers often target only people who view HTML mail. It's not that people who read their email as text are less susceptible to scams—all humans have a hardware vulnerability to scammers.[30] The HTML mail can easily show a bright red button shrieking "Click here to claim your free landspeeder," but in plain text that link obviously leads to `blatantscamsite.com`. Spammers will often fill their plain text versions with innocent text pulled from Project Gutenberg or other innocuous sources, in the hope that the text will confuse Bayesian analysis. The plain text version also does not include emojis, though, so this test is only worth one point.

The web interface describes DMARC_POLICY_ALLOW as "DMARC permit policy." You'll find several symbols for DMARC. Each symbol describes different ways a message could pass DMARC. Successful DMARC is worth half a point.

The FORGED_SENDER symbol looks suspicious, doesn't it? It's described as "Sender is forged (different From: header and smtp MAIL FROM: addresses)." The message claims to be from a normal-looking Amazon address, but the actual MAIL FROM is a long string of letters and numbers at `bounces.amazon.com`. Why is forged email only worth 0.3 points? Automation. Your organization's web server probably sends mail as the user `www`, but you need it to show up as `billing@` or `bounties@` or whatever.

Going further down, we have successful SPF and DKIM, and correct MIME. Add all this up, and you get a score of 1.3.

This particular message ran more tests, however.

```
RCPT_COUNT_ONE(0.00)[1];
ASN(0.00)[asn:16509, ipnet:54.240.24.0/22, country:US];
MIME_TRACE(0.00)[0:+,1:+,2:~];
MISSING_XM_UA(0.00)[];
ARC_NA(0.00)[];
DWL_DNSWL_NONE(0.00)[amazonses.com:dkim];
RCVD_IN_DNSWL_NONE(0.00)[54.240.25.3:from];
```

---

30   People who believe they are too smart to be scammed are among the people most likely to be scammed.

```
RCVD_COUNT_ZERO(0.00)[0];
FROM_NEQ_ENVFROM(0.00)[associates@amazon.com.au,
    202401291702330ba37c0cd7f7475badc0483049e0p0fe-
    C5GOEGCBN7OXP@bounces.amazon.com];
TO_MATCH_ENVRCPT_ALL(0.00)[];
DKIM_TRACE(0.00)[amazon.com.au:+,amazonses.com:+]
```

All these tests have a weight of zero. Each describes a condition detected in the email, but the default rspamd rules declared them irrelevant. It's worth investigating these symbols to see if they might indicate spammy behavior in your environment. They might also lead you to symbols that this message didn't match, but would indicate suspicious messages. The symbols list shows that RCPT_COUNT_ONE means this message was addressed to one recipient. That's normal on my tiny server. A handful of recipients would be normal. A search for the broader RCPT_COUNT shows symbols for two recipients, 3-5 recipients, 7-11 recipients, and so on up to "over 50." That might be interesting.

Rspamd Results on Scam Mail

The default score for "definitely spam" is 6 and "reject this mail" is 15, but this spectacular missive achieved an impressive score of 38.9.

```
X-Spamd-Result: default: False [38.90 / 500.00];
  FUZZY_DENIED(12.00)[1:9052c3c872:1.00:txt];
  MSBL_EBL(7.50)[agentmichealfbi@gmail.com:email,
    agentmichealfbi@gmail.com:replyto];
  RCVD_HELO_USER(3.00)[];
  FORGED_MUA_OUTLOOK(3.00)[];
  MISSING_MID(2.50)[];
  HFILTER_HOSTNAME_UNKNOWN(2.50)[];
  RBL_SENDERSCORE(2.00)[148.135.13.66:from];
  RBL_VIRUSFREE_BOTNET(2.00)[148.135.13.66:from];
  MISSING_TO(2.00)[];
  RECEIVED_SPAMHAUS_XBL(1.00)[103.169.216.1:received];
  AUTH_NA(1.00)[];
  OLD_X_MAILER(0.40)[];
  RCVD_NO_TLS_LAST(0.10)[];
  MIME_GOOD(-0.10)[text/plain];
  ...
X-Spam: Yes
```

The FUZZY_DENIED symbol means that the body of the text resembles text identified as spam in Rspamd Inc's fuzzy hash service. A weight of 12 indicates that much of this message matches identified spam.

MSBL_EBL's description says that the message is from a host on the MSBL block list, and gives a web page that describes the block list and how it works. Rspamd trusts this list, and assigns it 7.5 points.

The next symbol is RCVD_HELO_USER. It's described as "HELO User spam pattern." For more details, you'll have to read the Lua code defining the test for the symbol.

FORGED_MUA_OUTLOOK is pretty easy to understand. The description is "Forged Outlook MUA." The sender faked some message headers to try to pretend that the message was sent from Microsoft's desktop client, but did it badly. You might dislike using Outlook as a client, but a fake Outlook is even worse—and worth a solid three points.

MISSING_MID? What is a MID, and why do we care? It's described as "Message-ID header is missing." All legitimate MTAs apply a Message-ID header, but whatever's sending this couldn't bother.

According to the description, HFILTER_HOSTNAME_ UNKNOWN appears when the sending MTA has no reverse DNS. Actual MTAs need correct forward and reverse DNS. With a weight of 2.5, this rule is serious.

The next two symbols, beginning with RBL, reference two different block lists the sending host appears on.

MISSING_TO tells us the original message has no To: header. Another MTA failure.

The RECEIVED_SPAMHAUS_XBL symbol tells us that the sender is on the Spamhaus XBL, the Exploit and Botnet Filter. The sender is not a virus or an intruder. It is merely residing on a host that is controlled by a virus or intruder. That's worth a point.

AUTH_NA might look inexplicable, but the description says it's a simple lack of SPF, DKIM, DMARC, or even ARC. Like the lack of reverse DNS, this is a hint that this host was not intended to send mail.

The OLD_X_MAILER header indicates that the header indicates this was sent by an old mail client. Not only is the spambot poorly forging Outlook , it's forging an old version.

RCVD_NO_TLS_LAST indicates that this message was delivered without TLS. TLS is generally preferred, but it is not yet so widely deployed that it can be required. This is only 0.1 points.

This spambot is failing at pretending to be a legitimate mail client, and the host is not a legitimate mail server. The spammer didn't even bother to configure an SPF record for their garbage. MIME_GOOD shows that they *did*, however, correctly configure their message to show HTML and text versions. That part is user-visible, so they had to do it correctly.

After these, we see the usual list of zero-point symbols.

Finally, there's an X-Spam header. If the message scores more points than the add_header action, rspamd adds this header to say the message is spam. You can filter on it.

With rspamd installed, you can risk informing the world that your mail system exists.

Chapter 8: MX and SPF Records

The Domain Name System (DNS) is the world's most successful distributed database. Email systems consult it for information about which hosts perform which roles, as well as supporting other security and integrity checks. As Chapter 0 said, you must know basic DNS to run email. Making your messages deliverable requires placing a lot of data in DNS. We'll start with the two basic records: MX and SPF.

An MX record declares which hosts receive mail for a domain. It's how other MTAs find your MTA. Chances are, your domain name's DNS entry points at your web site. If someone opens up their browser and tries to visit `https://solveamurder.org`, I want that request to go to my web site. My email for that domain is hosted on a different host, `mail.solveamurder.org`. I could say that my email address is `mwl@mail.solveamurder.org`, but most users prefer the simpler `mwl@solveamurder.org`. And what if the mail server for solveamurder.org has a completely unrelated hostname, like `mail.rebelalliance.galaxy`? MX records steer the world to the correct MTA.

SPF records declare which hosts can send mail for a domain, and help systems assess if a message is spam or not. Rspamd will validate SPF for you.

MX Records

A *mail exchanger (MX)* record tells the world which hosts receive mail for a domain. It dates from 1986 and has a very simple format.

```
Domain   TTL   IN   MX   Priority   Host
```

The *domain* is the domain this record is for.

The optional *TTL* is how long recursive servers may cache this record, exactly like every other DNS record. The optional *IN* declares this to be an Internet record, and the *MX* declares this is a mail exchanger record.

211

The *priority* lets you establish backup MTAs. Today we have geographic load balancing and virtual servers and high-availability clusters that let you share one IP address between multiple pieces of hardware and network locations, but in 1986 we did not have geographical load distribution or CDNs or even VRRP or CARP. All of those tools are poorly compatible with SMTP, and cause more deliverability problems than the backup system built into SMTP. Backup servers required a different hostname and IP address. The host with the lowest priority is the primary MTA, while higher numbers are less preferable backups.

Finally, the host name for the domain's MTA. This must be the name of an A or AAAA record; it cannot be a CNAME (alias).

Here's the record for one of my domains, without any of the usual zone file shorthand.

```
ratoperatedvehicle.com.  3600  MX  10  mail.ratoperatedvehicle.com.
```

The *domain* is the destination domain. This record is for `ratoperatedvehicle.com`. The TTL is 3600 seconds, or one hour. It's an Internet MX record. The priority is 10, a common choice for "primary MTA." Finally, we have the hostname, `mail.ratoperatedvehicle.com`.

When an external MTA has an email addressed to an account at `ratoperatedvehicle.com`, it checks for an MX record. This record instructs it to send any mail for that domain to the host `mail.ratoperatedvehicle.com`.

MX records do not have to point to hosts in their domain. Here's one of my other domains.

```
tiltedwindmillpress.com. 3600   MX   10 mail.mwl.io.
```

Mail intended for the domain `tiltedwindmillpress.com` is directed to the host `mail.mwl.io`.

If a domain does not have an MX record, MTAs will fall back to checking for an A or AAAA record that matches the domain name. This is an ancient fallback and not recommended.

Backup MTAs

The `priority` setting prompts everyone to ask: how do I set up a backup MTA? These days, now that we have clusters and virtual floating IPs and everything's cloudy, configuring a completely different IP to handle email feels baroque. You're welcome to use all those modern high-availability techniques, but the backup MTA dates from when hardware could not be resilient so the protocol had to be.

A backup MTA doesn't work the way most folks think. Consider a domain with these MX records.

```
ratoperatedvehicle.com  MX  10 mail.ratoperatedvehicle.com.
ratoperatedvehicle.com  MX  20 mail.solveamurder.org.
```

The first record, with priority 10, declares that `mail.ratoperatedvehicle.com` is the primary MTA for the domain `ratoperatedvehicle.com`. The second record, priority 20, declares that `mail.solveamurder.org` is the backup MTA. Simple enough.

The standard declares that MTAs always send messages to the host with the lowest priority value, unless that host cannot be reached or responds improperly. If the recipient MTA cannot accept the message, the sending MTA sends the message to the backup server. The backup MTA queues those messages until the primary reappears, at which point it dumps its queued messages onto the primary.

The standard does not reflect what people do. Exactly what happens depends on the MTA software and the error returned by the primary MTA. If the primary MTA cannot be reached or does not respond on port 25, the sending MTA tries the backup MTA. That's all clear-cut.

But if the primary MTA responds with any part of SMTP, different software behaves differently. Consider 400 errors, for temporary problems. If your primary MTA returns 400 errors, Sendmail and Postfix clients immediately try the backup MX. Gmail and Microsoft queue the message and try again whenever they get around to it.

Mail can stay queued for days. Older systems allow up to five days. That was reasonable when server repairs meant "contact the manufacturer, have a disk drive the size of a coffin sent here via emergency freight, and tell the technicians down in the docking bay to have the forklift ready." Today, one day seems common. Even if your MTA hardware gets dropped into molten lava and you take the opportunity to entirely rebuild it in a fancy black case with an ominous-sounding ventilation system, most organizations can install a new server in a day.

What does a backup MTA give you? It queues incoming mail. When the primary MTA reappears, the backup forwards the queue to it. That's all.

A backup MTA can reduce the error messages seen by senders. Some MTAs are configured to notify users that a message could not be delivered yet. These messages usually start off with "This message could not be delivered in the last four hours because the recipient isn't answering, but we're still trying." Many users who get this message immediately contact their helpdesk and demand that the local mail administrator immediately fix the recipient's server.[31] When a backup MTA accepts the message, the user does not get that notification. I prefer that the mail system inform folks that I haven't received their mail, let alone read it—especially if they sent urgent messages over a protocol that permits five days for delivery.

Should you have a backup MTA? That's a personal decision. Personally, I don't bother. Emails can queue on the sender's system as easily as they can lounge in mine. Other sysadmins say that they want to always accept mail and never even hint to outsiders that there's a problem.

Backup mail exchangers are often less well protected than the primaries, so the most sophisticated spammers entirely skip the primary and send everything at the backup. You must synchronize spam protections and user account information between the primary

---

31   I have been educating users for thirty years. Perhaps I should abandon those efforts in favor of a hobby where success is theoretically possible.

and backup MTAs, or your backup will become a sewer running straight to your user inboxes and generate thousands of bounced emails from nonexistent accounts. Other spammers spurn the backup MX entirely, and if the primary is unavailable they move on. Spambots must spew as much sewage as possible before they are caught. I suspect that in the wretched hives of scum and villainy where spammers hang out, the debate over which method is more effective gets just as fierce as our debates on how to stop them.

Why do this instead of using a load balancer? SMTP is not HTTP. A delay of a second or two is meaningless, especially considering the five-day window. Load balancers do not improve deliverability, and actually make certain deliverability problems worse. The SMTP protocol says to connect to a different IP, and hiding multiple MTAs behind a load balancer only confuses troubleshooting.

Testing the MX Record

Once you have an MX record for each of your test domains, other MTAs can send messages to them. Previously, I tested that my host `mail.solveamurder.org` could mail accounts at `mwl@mail.ratoperatedvehicle.com`. With the `ratoperatedvehicle.com` MX in place, I can now mail `mwl@ratoperatedvehicle.com` from *any* mail service. Start by sending mail from your other test host. If that works, you might try from a free mail provider. This is also a good test to see if that free mail provider leaks previously unknown email addresses to spammers.

I probably can't answer mails from outside providers from my account, though. You must have SPF, DKIM, and DMARC for reliable deliverability at most large providers. And I certainly shouldn't tell the world about my new account until I have anti-spam protections in place. We'll start with the Sender Policy Framework.

Sender Policy Framework (SPF)

The Sender Policy Framework (SPF) is a way for a domain to declare which hosts or IP addresses may send emails via SMTP. It does not address clients that use IMAP or submission, only the outbound MTAs.

SPF is often touted as an anti-spam measure. It isn't. It is one component of a spam assessment policy. Competent spammers are among the most reliable publishers of SPF records, gleefully declaring that any host may send mail for their domains. Emails from domains without SPF records are likely to be classified as spam, however.

In its purest form, SPF checks are applied only to the MAIL FROM statement in the envelope. The validator checks the SPF record for the domain in MAIL FROM. If the message comes from an IP allowed to send mail for that domain, the message has valid SPF. If the addresses don't match, SPF is invalid.

Some organizations also check the SPF record for the sending MTA. Your MTA's domain name and fully qualified domain name should have its own SPF record, no matter what virtual domain you use for your primary email account.

It seems like having a list of IP addresses that are allowed to send mail would be a surefire way to cut down spam, but SPF is bolted onto decades of email practice. Bounce-forwarded messages can violate SPF. Many mailing lists, especially older ones, resend messages from their users and violate strict SPF checks. Newer mailing lists often rewrite the sender's address to be the mailing list address, placing the original sender's address in a different header specifically to maintain SPF integrity. SPF is a prerequisite for DMARC (Chapter 11), so we'll start with it.

If an MTA identifies itself as a host within a domain, that hostname must have its own SPF record. The host `mail.solveamurder.org`, with IP 203.0.113.66, might be listed in the SPF record for `solveamurder.org`. If `myhostname` in `main.cf` is set to the full hostname and you're sending from the command line, the message

216

will appear to be from a sender like `root@mail.solveamurder.org`. If that's going to a recipient outside your network, you'll need an SPF record for `mail.solveamurder.org`. Messages from a virtual domain on that same host will use the configured domain name, and fall under that domain's SPF record.

SPF Mechanism

An SPF *mechanism* is a way to identify hosts that can or can't send email. The simplest mechanism is a list of IP addresses, labeled with either `ip4` or `ip6`. We'll look at more complicated mechanisms later; for now, just know that IP addresses are only one way to identify permitted senders.

The *default mechanism* tells receiving MTAs what to do with hosts that don't match everything listed before. It's the word *all*, with a qualifier to say how to treat emails from IPs not listed earlier. A leading minus sign (`-all`) means that this list is definitive, and messages that don't match this mechanism should always be rejected. A leading tilde (`~all`) means that emails that don't match this should be treated with suspicion, but can be accepted if desired. A plus sign (`+all`) means that any host can send email for the domain, which is unwise for regular sysadmins but perfect for spammers. A question mark (`?all`) means that matching hosts should not be rejected or approved on the basis of SPF.[32] If you're deploying SPF on an existing domain, you might use `?all` until you're sure you've caught all your senders.

Technically qualifiers could be added to other mechanisms, but that's rare. SPF is processed left-to-right and the first match wins, so you could use qualifiers to carve out exclusions from later mechanisms. Do it if you like, but remember that complexity causes outages.

---

32   "We don't want to use this technology, but we don't want to be penalized for not using this technology."

SPF Record Format

An SPF record is a carefully formatted TXT record. (You might see references to an `SPF` DNS record type, but it's long deprecated. Don't use it.) SPF records must be all lower case. The record uses this format:

domain. TXT "v=spf1 *mechanisms default-mechanism*"

The leading *v=spf1* indicates that this TXT record has version SPF1. There is no newer version, but protocol revisions are inevitable.

The *mechanisms* includes mechanisms that identify all hosts that can send mail directly to the Internet. Servers that send status reports or receipts or alarms to the outside world should relay outbound mail through a small number of properly configured MTAs. Only list public addresses in SPF; if your MTA is behind a NAT device, don't list the private address.

At the end, we have the default mechanism.

Here's the content of an SPF record for `ratoperatedvehicle.com`.

```
TXT "v=spf1 ip4:198.51.100.2 ip6:2001:db8::fe5 ~all"
```

This is a text (`IN TXT`) record. The quotes let us return the results as a single string. The `v=spf1` declares this to be an SPF record. This record has two mechanisms, one IPv4, one IPv6. Finally, the `~all` declares that addresses not on this list shouldn't send mail, but don't forcibly reject such messages. The soft prohibition means that messages sent to mailing lists might go through.

A large network might have multiple outbound MTAs. If you have multiple outbound MTAs on each network, and if their addresses are sufficiently close together, you can list them by netmask rather than individually.

```
TXT "v=spf1 ip4:198.51.100.24/30 ip6:2001:db8::16/125 ~all"
```

You'll sometimes see SPF records with large netmasks, like `203.0.113.0/24` or `2001:db8:bad:code::/64`. Often these records exist because the sending organization has a whole cluster of MTAs. Sometimes they exist because the organization has a network for "their servers" and the mail administrator wanted to set up SPF once and be done with the problem.

Invalid CIDR network statements make invalid SPF records. To say that your host has the IP address 203.0.113.9/24 is valid—that's your configuration on your local network. Declaring that your host's *network* is 203.0.113.9/24 is invalid. External MTAs don't care about your server's physical layout, subnet, or the size of the network your host resides on. If you have a single MTA with a single IP address, list that IP address without a netmask. Otherwise, you're saying that any host on that entire network can send mail for your domain. Spambots love those records.

If you've never worked with netmasks in this way before, remember that for SPF a netmask is shorthand for several adjacent IP addresses, allowing sites with multiple servers in multiple locations to respect the 255-character limit. Using a larger netmask than necessary means that if an intruder penetrates one of your non-MTA systems and transforms it into the Death Star of Spam, that spam will pass SPF checks. That's exactly what you *don't* want.

SPF Length

An SPF record cannot exceed 255 characters. You can create a longer record, but all SPF checks against it will fail. A record that long might seem unlikely, but if you're listing individual IPv6 addresses you can easily brush up against it. You can easily check the length of a record with a shell command.

```
$ dig txt domain +short | grep spf | wc -c
```

If your SPF record exceeds 255 characters, what can you do?

First, check for excess entries. Many small organizations consider SPF records write-only, and never verify that old entries are still necessary. You could refer to IPv6 hosts by their network rather than complete address, such as 2001:db8:5c01:fcf/64 rather than the more specific 2001:db8:5c01:fcf:5400:1ff:fe4b:e2df. Worst case, look at large mail providers such as Google or Microsoft and see how they're currently managing their SPF records. Their complicated SPF setups use more advanced mechanisms.

Advanced SPF Mechanisms

While you should use the `ip6` and `ip4` mechanisms if at all possible, larger organizations might use automated server provisioning, which means that the IP addresses of their services change with demand. They might outsource part of their services. They might have horrid architectures inherited from purchased companies. They might decide to be—ick—*clever*.[33] SPF has several sensible mechanisms to support them: `a`, `mx`, and `include`. It also has less sensible mechanisms like `ptr` and `exists`, but they're less sensible.

The `a` mechanism tells the MTA to do an address lookup on the sender's purported domain. If the DNS entry matches the email sender's IP address, the check passes.

The `mx` mechanism tells the receiving MTA to look up the MX records for the sender's domain. If one of the MX records match the sender's IP address, the SPF check passes.

Suppose that my domain `solveamurder.org`, like many small entities, uses the same MTA server for inbound and outbound mail. The web server, where the domain's A record points, can also send mail directly to the Internet. I could define an SPF record like so.

```
IN  TXT  "v=spf1 a mx ~all"
```

Whenever I renumber my web site or my MTAs, that change propagates through to my SPF records. That seems cool, except that DNS takes time to propagate. Obsolete but unexpired caches will disrupt email deliverability. It's the usual DNS headache, and amenable to the usual persnickety migration solutions.

If your domain has completely or partially outsourced mail, you can use the `include` mechanism to pull in a different domain's SPF records. The provider needs to give you the contents of the entry. Here my domain sends everything via an outside provider. These records often start with an underscore, to mark them as infrastructure.

---

33   Cleverness leads to fragility. Fragility leads to phone calls. Phone calls lead to suffering.

```
TXT  "v=spf1 include:_spf.mailspew.com ~all"
```

You can combine mechanisms.

```
TXT "v=spf1 a mx ip6:2001:db8::16/125 include:_spf.mailspew.com ~all"
```

You might also encounter SPF records that use the `ptr` or `exists` mechanisms. The `ptr` mechanism lets organizations rely on PTR records, which are easily spoofed by anyone who controls their reverse DNS. Some MTAs even ignore SPF records that include PTR entries. The `exists` mechanism lets you check to see if an A record exists for the sender's domain, which is only useful in very specific circumstances. Both of these also require DNS lookups.

SPF and Child Domains

SPF records do not cover child domains. My domain `ratoperatedvehicle.com` has an SPF record, but if I want to start sending mail as `mwl@test.ratoperatedvehicle.com`, I must create a new SPF record for the new subdomain. You need a new TXT record listing the outbound MTAs for that subdomain.

```
     TXT "v=spf1 ip4:198.51.100.2 ip6:2001:db8::fe5 ~all"
test TXT "v=spf1 ip4:203.0.113.9 ip6:2001:db8::aabb ~all"
```

Even if the subdomain uses the same outbound MTAs as the parent domain, that subdomain needs an SPF record.

SPF DNS Limits

Every mechanism other than `ip4` and `ip6` requires a separate DNS lookup. The `include` statement might require further lookups of whatever's listed in their record. It's easy to imagine a complicated SPF record would require dozens upon dozens of DNS lookups. Recursively resolving all of those could take several minutes. Once you imagine that, it's easy to imagine an autogenerated bottomless SPF record that ties up part of an MTA's resources forever. A few hundred of those and you have a denial-of-service attack. To avoid that obvious error, one SPF check will perform no more than ten DNS lookups. Some older systems refuse to do more than four lookups.

Most organizations try to hold the number of lookups as small as possible, especially when referring to outside entities. As your organization grows, you'll accumulate outside vendors that need to send email as you. Before signing a contract that involves outside mail services, check the vendor's SPF configuration and verify that it fits within your ten-lookup limit.

You might see references to *SPF flattening*, a collection of tricks for reducing DNS lookups in SPF. Today, flattening is considered poor practice.

Redirects

Maybe you have a whole bunch of domains that share an email system, and you don't want to edit the zone files every time you change anything. You can use an SPF redirect to tell clients to look elsewhere for this domain's SPF record.

```
TXT  "v=spf1 redirect=spf-zone"
```

I have many domains. I could decide to maintain their SPF records in the TXT record for `_spf.solveamurder.org`. Domains using that configuration would use this redirect.

```
TXT  "v=spf1 redirect=_spf.solveamurder.org"
```

When I re-address my MTA, editing a single zone file affects all my domains.

Viewing SPF Records

Set up SPF records for your test domains using only the `ip4` and `ip6` mechanisms. Don't use fancy includes or redirects. Once they exist, verify that you can call them up with `dig`.

```
$ dig ratoperatedvehicle.com txt
```

If the response looks right, use an outside entity to test it. Many people have put SPF checkers on the web. I like `mxtoolbox.com`, but a search engine will give you many more. You want an SPF checker that both tests validity and tells you how many DNS lookups the record requires. Your favorite search engine can offer many candidates.

SPF Alignment

Technically, SPF alignment is a DMARC concept, but we'll dig into it while SPF is fresh in your brain. *Alignment* considers how other headers in a message compare to the SPF-validated `MAIL FROM`. If the contents of `MAIL FROM` is the same as what's in the `From` header, the message is said to be in *SPF alignment*. Remember, the `MAIL FROM` address is often recorded in the `Return-Path` header. Alignment is vital for DMARC, so it's best to achieve alignment from the beginning.

Alignment can be either strict or relaxed. *Strict* alignment means that the domain in `MAIL FROM` (or `Return-Path`) exactly matches the domain in the user-visible `From` header. Consider these header snippets.

```
Return-Path: <drivers@ratoperatedvehicle.com>
...
From: "Michael W Lucas" <mwl@ratoperatedvehicle.com>
```

The email address in `Return-Path` and the user-visible `From` do not match. The domains do match, however. If this message passed SPF validation, it is in *strict SPF alignment*. If it doesn't pass, there's no alignment.

Relaxed alignment means that the domain in `MAIL FROM` is from a child of the domain in the `From` header. Look at these header snippets.

```
Return-Path: <sales@www.tiltedwindmillpress.com>
...
From: "Tilted Windmill Press" <sales@tiltedwindmillpress.com>
```

If you've looked at headers for messages from web sites, you've probably seen something like this. The host sending the message is *in* the domain, but it's not the main MTA. It's set up to look like it comes from the sales department. `www.tiltedwindmillpress.com` is in the zone `tiltedwindmillpress.com`, though. If this message passes SPF, it is in *relaxed SPF alignment*. I most often see relaxed alignment in mail from automated processes or the command line. I could set up the MTA on this host to identify itself as the main domain, but that might cause other problems.

223

With bulk mailing services, you might see headers like this.

```
Return-Path: <garbage@mwl.io>
...
From: mwl@ratoperatedvehicle.com
```

Perhaps the message passes SPF. There is no relationship between the domains in `Return-Path` and `From`, however, so this message is not aligned.

SPF and Mailing Lists

Mail gets resent. You receive a personal message at your work address and want to send it to your personal account before Human Resources gets involved. You get concert tickets for a show and forward them to an account on your phone. And, of course, Uncle Owen forwards you every daft conspiracy theory and lame joke he gets.

Mailing lists receive messages, add a couple headers, change a couple more, and send them on. Primordial mailing lists often resent messages with an unchanged `Return-Path`. This broke SPF validation. It certainly broke SPF alignment. Some mailing lists have updated their software to cope with SPF. Here are some headers from the "mailop" mailing list.

```
Return-Path: mailop-bounces@mailop.org
...
From: Michael W Lucas via mailop <mailop@mailop.org>
Reply-To: Michael W Lucas <mwl@mwl.io>
```

This mailing list accepts messages from subscribers, but sets `Return-Path` to the list address. The `From` header keeps the original sender's name, but replaces the email address with the list address. It adds the `Reply-To` header to tell people the original sender's address. This message uses the SPF records for **mailop.org**. The user-visible `From` header is in the same domain as the `Return-Path`, so it has strict SPF alignment.

Compare this with headers from a message I sent to a FreeBSD developer mailing list.

```
Return-Path: owner-freebsd-current@freebsd.org
...
From: "Michael W. Lucas" <mwl@mwl.io>
```

The `Return-Path` uses the mailing list address, so the initial SPF tests will pass. The `From` address is mine, however, so there is no SPF alignment.

I am not aware of any mailing lists that still forward messages with an unchanged `Return-Path`, but I would not be surprised to learn they still exist. Deploying DMARC will tell you if you're on any.

Validating SPF

When your MTA receives a message from an outside sender, it should attempt to validate the SPF record for the sending domain. What exactly does that mean?

An SMTP exchange identifies its origin in up to three places. There's the `EHLO` command that gives the name the source MTA identifies itself with. There's `MAIL FROM`, which identifies the sender. There's `From`, the user-visible name. SPF can validate the EHLO and the MAIL FROM addresses, although not all organizations perform both checks.

SPF validation compares the tested addresses to the policy in the domain's SPF record. SPF records express a policy, so the result can be more complicated than a simple yes or no. A validation attempt can result in a *pass*, meaning that the message's SPF is certainly valid, or it can give one of several non-valid results. You can adjust how your system reacts to SPF failures.

A *neutral* result means that your validator retrieved an SPF record for the domain, but the record is explicitly declaring that it won't declare if the source address is authorized or not. The SPF record for this domain assigns a question mark for this particular source address.

A *none* result means your DNS server can't retrieve an SPF record for this domain. Maybe the domain has no SPF record, or maybe DNS resolution has failed.

The *softfail* result means that this message probably doesn't pass. The SPF record probably ends in ~all. Messages that softfail should be treated as suspicious.

A *fail* or *hardfail* means that this message has invalid SPF. The email is coming from an IP address that policy explicitly forbids to originate that email. The SPF record probably ends in -all.

Your logs might also show *temperror*, a temporary SPF error. They're often related to DNS. When your validator gets a temporary error it should instruct your MTA to return a 400 error to the sender, telling it to try again later.

If the sender has really messed up you'll see *permerror*, a permanent error. The SPF record itself is invalid. Maybe the sending domain has multiple SPF records or requires more than ten DNS lookups to parse. Perhaps someone screwed up exiting vi(1) and the record has a :wq! in the middle of it. The variety of human failure is majestic and infinite, and the software is unable to cope.

You can configure SPF validators to accept or reject each result, as suits your policies.

Domains Without Email

Some domains don't accept incoming mail and should never send mail. Spammers forge emails using any domain that looks convenient. By providing an SPF record that says "this domain never sends mail," you're informing other MTAs that any mail from these domains is bogus and should be refused.

Here's an SPF record that says "reject all mail from this domain."

```
"v=spf1 -all"
```

Note the minus sign in front of all, rather than a tilde. This is a hard failure. Providing these records can both help others reject spam, and reduce the number of folks who complain to you about spam "from" your domain. We'll also look at DKIM and DMARC for mail-free domains later this book.

To tell the world that a domain does not accept mail, use a single null MX record. Give the MX record a priority of zero, and list a single dot as the hostname.

```
mw1.io      MX  0  .
```

You might also use a zero priority in nolisting, discussed in Chapter 15.

Rspamd and SPF

Many people have written SPF validators, but rspamd includes one and it's enabled by default. There is no standard for recording SPF validation in headers, so rspamd lists it as a symbol in `X-Spamd-Result`. Each result has its own symbol and weight value.

The R_SPF_ALLOW symbol means that the message came from an IP listed in the SPF record, and has a weight of -2. R_SPF_FAIL indicates that the message did not pass SPF checks, and has a weight of 1. Other types of failure all have a weight of zero. We'll see how to change those in Chapter 14.

Other validators often put SPF results in an `Authentication-Results` header. If you need to troubleshoot possible SPF problems, dig through the headers until you find SPF.

With MX and SPF records, you can start to tell the outside world about your domains. The moment you do, spammers will flood you. Let's get basic anti-spam protection running.

Chapter 9: Protocol Checks and Block Lists

By now you've spent time watching the mail log. If your test machines are on the public Internet, those logs show an almost constant flood of incoming connections as spammers try to relay mail through your host. Spammers are everywhere, and constant, and much of their cruddy software doesn't know it should stop trying after being rejected. The constant search for open relays can make logs unusable, and you'll quickly discover that the majority of attempted SMTP transactions are spam.

You've probably heard of SpamAssassin and rspamd and Bayesian filtering and blocklists and dozens of other anti-spam tools. Postfix can integrate with all of them. The problem is deciding which to use, and where. Heavy analysis programs like rspamd are grand, but if you run every mail you receive through them you'll need to invest in additional processors. The general rule of blocking spam is: start with the lightest and fastest tools to filter out the worst of the flood, and gradually move up to more sensitive but heavier tools.

The most effective tool for stopping the majority of spam is a DNS-based block list.

Spambot Behavior

For many years Jon Postel, one of the primordial Internet's designers and generally considered the Yoda of the early Internet community, suggested that software should be strict in what it sends but generous in what it accepts. This was so widely accepted, and Postel so respected, that it became known as *Postel's Law* or the *Robustness Principle*. When you wrote an SMTP client you should make it adhere to the standards, but your SMTP server should accept that other people would not do the same. In other words: reduce your own failings, but accept that others have failings.

Spammers' goal is to deliver the most junk in a minimum of time. Accepting the foibles of others offers spammers a whole bunch of latitude. Spambots implement a stripped-down SMTP that works on most servers. Accepting only clients that rigorously adhere to the protocol definition blocks those spambots. A trickier spambot might implement the beginning part of the protocol correctly, but try to abuse it later. You can check for those violations as well, but those tests are more intrusive and will force legitimate senders to resend their messages.

Postscreen(8) performs those tests. The non-intrusive tests are enabled by default, while intrusive tests are optional.

Postscreen

Postscreen's non-intrusive checks test incoming clients against the configured DNSBLs and verify the client's adherence to the SMTP protocol before the 220 banner. The 220 banner is the initial greeting an MTA offers clients, so these are called *pregreeting* tests. If an incoming SMTP request passes the pregreeting checks, the request is handed off to an smptd(8) process.

Like all of Postfix, postscreen is broken up into multiple smaller programs that perform specific tasks. The dnsblog(8) program performs DNSBL checks and logs the results. Postscreen outsources TLS activity to tlsproxy(8). Finally, it hands validated connections to a reconfigured smtpd(8).

Enabling Postscreen

Configure postscreen in `master.cf`. Chapter 5 discusses `master.cf` configuration, so go reread that if you need a reminder. The default configuration file includes a commented-out `postscreen` configuration.

Postscreen uses TCP port 25, so Postfix's `smtpd` can't run on that port . Disable that entry, and uncomment the following entries for `postscreen`, `smtpd`, `dnsblog`, and `tlsproxy`.

```
smtp       inet  n  -  n  -  1  postscreen
smtpd      pass  -  -  n  -  -  smtpd
dnsblog    unix  -  -  n  -  0  dnsblog
tlsproxy   unix  -  -  n  -  0  tlsproxy
```

If you have added any -o options to the default smtp entry, add them to the new smtpd entry.

Don't restart Postfix yet. You must tell dnsblog(8) which DNSBL providers to check, and how many to require. That's in the *main.cf* option postscreen_dnsbl_sites. Checking the documentation for my example providers, Spamhaus and SpamRATS gives me the zones to query.

```
postscreen_dnsbl_sites = zen.spamhaus.org
   all.spamrats.com
```

With this in place, watch your mail log and fully restart Postfix.

service postfix restart

Your log entries should switch from "relaying denied" messages to something like this.

```
mail postfix/postscreen[30254]: CONNECT from
   [198.51.100.181]:44996 to [45.76.75.68]:25
mail postfix/dnsblog[30441]: addr 198.51.100.181 listed
   by domain all.spamrats.com as 127.0.0.38
mail postfix/dnsblog[43554]: addr 198.51.100.181 listed
   by domain zen.spamhaus.org as 127.0.0.4
mail postfix/dnsblog[43554]: addr 198.51.100.181 listed
   by domain zen.spamhaus.org as 127.0.0.9
mail postfix/dnsblog[43554]: addr 198.51.100.181 listed
   by domain zen.spamhaus.org as 127.0.0.2
mail postfix/postscreen[30254]: PREGREET 11 after 0.55
   from [198.51.100.181]:44996: EHLO User\r\n
mail postfix/postscreen[30254]: DNSBL rank 2 for
   [198.51.100.181]:44996
```

The first entry shows an incoming TCP connection to postscreen. The new few lines are from dnsblog, showing the results of DNSBL checks. Each check returns one or more responses in 127.0.0.0/8, indicating that the host is on a block list. Next, `postscreen` reports that the client pregreeted, or sent commands before `postscreen` sent its initial greeting. This is a spambot.

Watching the log will probably reveal that many spambots and scanners keep pounding their fuzzy little heads against your MTA. Smarter spambots try less constantly.

Now send a message from your other test server. You'll see a log entry that your other MTA connected to smtpd and sent a message.

I'll often shunt messages from dnsblog(8) and postscreen(8) into a separate log file to keep my mail logs useful. You might point fail2ban or some other log scanner at that log file and feed spambot IP addresses to your host's packet filter, either blocking them entirely, or choking their connection down to 9600 baud to stifle the spambot's resources.[34]

Block List Weighting

After running a mail system for a while you will develop different levels of trust for the curators of different block lists. You might decide that Spamhaus is perfectly reliable, but some of the others are too aggressive. You'll also want redundancy in case one of your DNSBLs goes offline. Postfix lets you weight DNSBLs results multipliers in `postscreen_dnsbl_sites` and set scoring thresholds with `postscreen_dnsbl_threshold`.

With `postscreen_dnsbl_threshold` you set a minimum spam score needed to block a sender. Each DNSBL that declares the sender a spam source adds one point to the score. If I want two of my block list providers to agree that a sender is a spam source, I could set this to two.

```
postscreen_dnsbl_threshold = 2
```

What about varying trust in different block lists? You can multiply block lists in `postscreen_dnsbl_sites` to give them more votes. Here I give Spamhaus two votes, and leave the other two providers with one.

---

34   Tarpitting spambots remains amusing for only a few minutes, but it remains a public service *forever*.

```
postscreen_dnsbl_threshold = 2
postscreen_dnsbl_sites = zen.spamhaus.org*2
 all.spamrats.com
 dnsbl.sorbs.net
```

We need two points to block a sender. Spamhaus gets two points. If Spamhaus claims a client is not a spambot, but all the other DNSBLs agree that it's a spambot, Spamhaus gets outvoted. Otherwise, Spamhaus gets its way.

If you want to be fancy, you can fine-tune your scores based on the response code returned by the block list. The DNSWL list (`https://www.dnswl.org`) is the opposite of a block list: it attempts to list trustworthy mail servers. You could parse the response from that site and assign desirable responses a large negative multiplier. All responses from these lists resemble 127.0.0.0/8 IP addresses, so we list acceptable values in brackets.

```
postscreen_dnsbl_sites = zen.spamhaus.org*2
 ...
 list.dnswl.org=127.0.[0..255].[1..3]*-2
```

Don't get too fancy with block list weighting; if it starts to resemble a PAM chain, you're doing email wrong.

Test Response

The options `postscreen_dnsbl_action` and `postscreen_greet_action` tell Postfix how to react when a client fails a test. You can set these to `ignore`, `enforce`, or `drop`. Both default to *ignore*. Postscreen logs the violation, adds the client IP to the temporary allowlist, and permits the mail to proceed to `smtpd`. This is useful for gathering statistics, but provides no protection. Most servers should use `drop` or, if they are analyzing the incoming connections to see what fails which tests, `enforce`.

A setting of *enforce* tells postscreen to complete any other tests, but when the tests finish the connection gets dropped with a 550 "Your message is unacceptable" error. The sender and recipient get logged.

The *drop* setting is more authoritative and should be used with care. When a client fails this test the connection is immediately terminated with error 521, or "This host does not accept mail," because SMTP lacks a message code for "this host accepts mail—just not from you." The sender and recipient information might not be available yet, so logs might be minimal.

Intrusive Postscreen Tests

What makes a test intrusive?

Postscreen tests each incoming SMTP connection for basic protocol problems. All of these tests happen before SMTP's 220 greeting. If the connection passes those tests, `postscreen` hands the connection to an `smtpd` process, which offers the 220 greeting. Uncivil behavior further in the SMTP dialog is handed directly to `smtpd`. The `smtpd` process drops connections from misbehaving clients, but it does not track which hosts behaved badly. The bad client is free to try again.

Postscreen's intrusive tests retain control of SMTP sessions from new clients and check for pipelining abuses, non-SMTP commands, and bare newlines. If the client behaves, postscreen adds the client's IP address on a temporary allow list. It then gives the client a 400 error, telling the client "not now, try again later." When the same IP address shows up again before the allow list entry expires, email is immediately accepted.

These tests do not stop spam from well-behaved MTAs. When a spammer tricks a legitimate mail system into sending spam, that host is very polite and follows all the SMTP protocols as it dumps sewage into your users' inboxes. You must use resource-heavy tests to detect that spam.

Available Tests

Postfix offers three intrusive tests: pipelining, non-SMTP commands, and bare LF checks. If any of these tests are enabled, postscreen is greylisting for you.

SMTP is a back-and-forth (or *half-duplex*) protocol. It has formal rules about which participant may speak and which must listen at any stage of the transaction. This can't change without rewriting the protocol, but it's not exactly efficient. *Pipelining* is an optimization where the client sends several commands when it's allowed to speak. MTAs must declare pipelining support when initializing a session. (Chapter 3 shows this declaration.) While all modern MTAs support pipelining, legitimate clients verify that support before attempting to pipeline. Spambots do not perform that check: they assume everyone supports pipelining. Postscreen does not declare that it supports pipelining, so well-behaved clients won't try it. Anything that tries pipelining when the server doesn't declare support is either a spambot, or so badly programmed that it deserves rejection. Set `postscreen_pipelining_enable` to `yes` to enable this check.

Many MTAs still tolerate protocol errors; Postel's ghost haunts software design. But spambots are notoriously poorly programmed. They often send non-SMTP commands like CONNECT or even pure HTTP commands like GET and POST. The `postscreen_forbidden_commands` option enables this check.

Spambots are not known for robust programming. Many of them don't properly handle the difference between a bare line feed (LF) and a carriage-return with line feed (CRLF). SMTP uses CRLF. A bare line feed is a protocol violation. If you enable either of the other checks, postscreen enables this one as an aid to logging. You can explicitly enable it with `postscreen_bare_newline_enable`.

If a client fails any of these tests, postscreen disconnects the client. The client can try again. And again. And again. If you want to block these clients, configure a log watcher like fail2ban to capture IP addresses from the log and feed them to your packet filter. Some operating systems support blocklistd(8) specifically for feeding packet filters and have added that support to their Postfix packages.

Permitting Networks

The non-intrusive tests have no impact, so why would you skip them? Some legitimate networked devices have SMTP stacks programmed as badly as any spambot and cannot pass postscreen's tests. We all have those business partners that bought the least expensive SMTP server available in 2002 and haven't upgraded since.

Postscreen skips the tests for all networks listed in `postscreen_access_list`. This defaults to `permit_mynetworks`.

```
postscreen_access_list = permit_mynetworks,
    cidr:/etc/postfix/postscreen-allow.cidr
```

List network blocks in `/etc/postfix/postscreen-allow.cidr` exactly as you would other IP addresses, as discussed in Chapter 4. Use this same option to attach a postwhite allow list to Postscreen.

The Postscreen Cache

Postscreen maintains a cache of IP addresses for good and bad actors. You can control how long each type of entry is cached. By default, temporary allowlist entries are retained for seven days. Change this with `postscreen_cache_retention_time`.

DNSBL tests have their own timers. With `postscreen_dnsbl_max_ttl` and `postscreen_dnsbl_min_ttl`, you can select the maximum and minimum lengths of time Postscreen caches addresses from DNSBL checks. These timers let you override the DNSBL's time-to-live as set in DNS. These default to a minimum of sixty seconds and a maximum of one hour. (Older Postfix versions used `postscreen_dnsbl_ttl`, but that's no longer valid.)

Set how long postscreen remembers that an IP passed the pregreeting test with `postscreen_greet_ttl`. This defaults to one day.

Results from intrusive tests are cached for thirty days. You can change cache time for the various tests with `postscreen_bare_newline_ttl`, `postscreen_non_smtp_command_ttl`, and `postscreen_pipelining_ttl`.

Postfix purges the cache as dictated by
`postscreen_cache_cleanup_interval`, usually every 12 hours.

If you deploy Postfix for a small organization, someone in
Authority[tm] who fancies themselves to be "technical" will eventually
ask about the hosts on the temporary allow list. Postscreen doesn't
make this information available, but you can query the private
database for the IP list. The database format and location is defined
with `postscreen_cache_map`.

```
# postconf postscreen_cache_map
postscreen_cache_map = btree:$data_directory/postscreen_cache
```

It's in a btree file in the data directory, named *postscreen_cache*?
Fine. Where is `data_directory`?

```
# postconf data_directory
data_directory = /var/db/postfix
```

Look for file *postscreen_cache.db* there. Read it with
`postmap -s`. You must specify the database type as given in
`postscreen_cache_map`. Leave the *.db* off the filename.

```
# postmap -s btree:postscreen_cache
155.138.237.75   1699118627;1699032287;1701624227;1;
    1701624227
2001:19f0:9002:2951:5400:4ff:fe59:9971699117425;
    1699034625;1701623025;1;1701623025
40.92.19.44        1699119602;1699033262;1701625202;1;
    1701625202
...
```

Reading the database requires an exclusive lock. Postscreen might
lock this file for updates at any millisecond. On a busy server, it might
lock this file frequently. If your command hangs, either wait or hit
CTRL-C and try again. That's what happens when you try to read an
application's internal database. If you must reliably read the database:
stop Postfix, read the database, and restart Postfix.

The information after the IP address are timestamps and flags. Don't
go trying to reverse-engineer that information or relying on it in any
way. The format is internal to Postfix and can be changed at any time.

237

Skipping Greylisting

Maybe you want postscreen's intrusive tests. Maybe you want to install postgrey and do full-on greylisting. Certain companies deploy SMTP stacks that don't retry after receiving a 400 message, won't fall back to a secondary MX after receiving a 400, or try again from a different IP address. Notable among these are two behemoths of the Email Empire, Microsoft and Google. The details of coping with greylisting depend on the implementation you're using, but we'll work with postscreen's intrusive tests.

Postfix's documentation includes an example of using a faux backup MX on a single host. This is a brilliant trick that works quite well when the sending MTA immediately tries the backup MX after getting a 400 from the primary. My tests show it works great if the sender is running Sendmail or Postfix. After receiving a 400 error Gmail, and Microsoft wait for the primary MTA to recover rather than trying the backup.

While greylisting fully complies with the SMTP protocol, some other organizations' technical legalities interact poorly with it. If you greylist their email, you will never receive it. Some of us are perfectly okay with never getting emailed by anyone who uses Gmail or Office365. I, and most businesses, are not that lucky. You must maintain a no-greylisting access list.

Why would you allow the big companies to bypass postscreen's protocol tests? While Google, Microsoft, Apple and other companies in the Email Empire do send spam and their protocol stacks are by no means perfect, they don't use spammer protocol tricks so they will never trigger postscreen's protocol checks. You must use more processor-intensive checks to detect their spam, as discussed in Chapter 14. Most DNSBLs will not put these servers on their lists.

SPF allows an organization to express complicated policies. One of those policies is to list the hosts that can send mail. Some other SPF policies are not amenable to simplification into an access list. We'll abuse SPF to generate that list anyway, with postwhite and spf-tools.

Postwhite

Postwhite (`https://gi.com/stevejenkins/postwhite`) is
a shell script that reads SPF records for selected domains and
generates Postfix-compatible lists of IP addresses that are permitted
to send mail from those domains. It is built on top of spf-tools
(`https://github.com/spf-tools/spf-tools`), a collection of shell
scripts for parsing SPF records. Your Unix might not have packages for
these, but they can easily be pulled from git.

Configuring Postwhite

Postwhite has a configuration file, *postwhite.conf*. You can either
copy this to */etc* or add it as a command-line argument. Configure it
for your environment.

```
spftoolspath=/usr/local/scripts/spf-tools
postfixpath=/etc/postfix
postfixbinarypath=/usr/local/sbin
whitelist=postscreen_spf_allowlist.cidr
blacklist=postscreen_spf_blocklist.cidr
```

The `spftoolspath` option gives the directory where you installed
spf-tools. I cloned them from git, so they have their own directory.

The `postfixpath` variable is the path to the directory where
you want the finished allowlists to be installed. If you run as root,
this is probably */etc/postfix*. If you want to run `postwhite` as an
unprivileged user, set this to a directory that user can write to.

The `postfixbinarypath` option is the directory where the `postfix`
command is installed.

With `whitelist`, give the filename of the finished allow list.

The `blacklist` option is not needed by default, but if you want to
generate a list of hosts that can never mail you, set the file name here.
We'll discuss block lists later.

```
yahoo_static_hosts=/usr/local/scripts/postwhite/yahoo_static_hosts.txt
include_yahoo="no"
```

In 2015, Yahoo published a list of their outbound MTA IP addresses
on a web page. The page was taken down a year later, but the list

had been scraped and cached everywhere. In 2018 when Postwhite came out it was still possibly relevant, but it is no longer applicable. Postwhite includes the file `yahoo_static_hosts.txt` and you could set `yahoo_static_hosts` to its path for completeness, but `include_yahoo` should always be set to `no`. (Yahoo now has a new page, but Postwhite hasn't been updated.)

```
invalid_ip4=remove
simplify=no
reload_postfix=yes
```

SPF records should all be in valid subnets with valid netmasks. Postfix expects all ACLs to be in valid network blocks. SPF records like `203.0.113.50/24` demonstrate that a surprisingly large number of providers get confused between "identifying the specific hosts that can send mail" and "the IP address and netmask configured on the specific host that sends mail." The `invalid_ip4` option tells postwhite how to handle these. The default, `remove`, discards invalid records. Using `keep` includes them unchanged, which means Postfix will ignore them. The `fix` setting makes a stab at correcting them, but postwhite cannot read minds. The safe option is `remove`.

Many large organizations have overlapping SPF records, or share outbound MTAs with another business. Repeating a network block in the allow list lacks elegance. The `simplify` option tells postwhite to combine them. While I'm a fan of elegance, enabling `simplify` increases postwhite's running time from a minute or two to over fifteen minutes and the resulting allowlist was 92% the length of the unsimplified one. Increased running time might not matter during routine use, but is vital during debugging, so I leave this off.

If you want to signal Postfix to reread the allow list after updating, you can do that with the `reload_postfix` option.

```
custom_hosts="mwl.io"
```

You probably have your own domains that should never be greylisted. Add them to the domains to be included with `custom_hosts`.

Running Postwhite

Postwhite doesn't need any command-line options, unless you use an alternate configuration file. Just run it.

```
# ./postwhite
```

It will read */etc/postwhite.conf*, make temporary files, and start walking through the domain list.

If you want to use a configuration file other than */etc/postwhite.conf*, give the full path as an argument. Or, you could edit the script.

Target Domain List

Postwhite works well, but isn't very configurable. The list of domains to add to the allow list is hard-coded. I know many people who disagree with the default list, and the world has moved on—there's no need to allow irrelevant firms, like Twitter. Fortunately, that list is near the top of the script and is easily modifiable.

Block Lists

If you have spent any time on the Internet, you have a list of people and organizations you never want to hear from. You can use the `enable_blacklist` and `blacklist_hosts` options to enable generating a list of IP addresses that can never send you mail.

```
enable_blacklist=yes
blacklist_hosts="galacticempire.gov"
```

Blocking domains based on their outbound MTA can have side effects. Suppose one of your clients uses Amazon's cloud services to send mail. So do spammers. If you use IP-based blocking, both domains will be treated identically.

You'll wind up with a block list like this.

```
203.0.113.0/24    reject
2001:db8:bad:c0de::/64 reject
```

We'll see how to use this block list later this chapter.

Automating block list generation records is risky. Consider this SPF record.

```
"v=spf1 +all"
```

Any host on the Internet can send email for this domain. Spammers adore this perfectly valid SPF record. If I add a domain with this record to `blacklist_hosts`, auto-generate a block list, and feed it to Postfix, my MTA will immediately reject mail from absolutely everyone not on an earlier allow list. All block lists must be verified by a slightly paranoid human before deployment.

Once you have your allow list, add it to postscreen_access_list and restart Postfix.

Blocking Mail

If I receive another email from a particular recruiting firm offering me the magnificent opportunity of a position as an entry level help desk flunky I will violate several state laws, many national ones, and a few of the notably obscure Additional Protocols of the Geneva Convention. I would prefer to avoid spending my so-called "retirement" "savings" on a criminal defense attorney desperate enough to take my case, so prudence suggests I avoid the entire problem and block their email at the MTA level.

Blocking email is tricky. You can block by domain, but domains are cheap and forgeable. You can dig into SPF records, but they're even less expensive to alter. You can scour mail headers for items to block on, but headers are ephemeral. Still, some days it's a choice between making the attempt and accumulating legal bills.

Postfix uses the `smtpd_sender_restrictions` option to set a policy on messages this MTA will accept. Much like its mirror twin `smtpd_recipient_restrictions`, it takes other options as arguments. The settings of those options dictate which mails will be refused.

Blocking on MAIL FROM

While a spammer that has compromised a mail system often forges the sender's address, changing MAIL FROM usually requires more access than the spammer achieves. You can filter on individual email addresses, parent domains, or local accounts, using `check_sender_access`. Here I have a list of unwanted MAIL FROM components in */etc/postfix/bad-domains* and used it to build a database.

```
smtpd_sender_restrictions = check_sender_access hash:/
etc/postfix/bad-domains
```

Suppose you're sick of hearing from me. My mail email address is `mwl@mwl.io`. Consider following bad-domains entry.

```
mwl@mwl.io    REJECT
```

Any message whose MAIL FROM includes `mwl@mwl.io` will be rejected? Great! But the next day, a message from me sails straight through. The problem is, my messages don't identify themselves in MAIL FROM. Check the mail log for a *from* statement.

```
Nov 21 15:05:20 mail postfix/qmgr[88751]: 0BE4C30B4D:
   from=<mwlucas@mail.mwl.io>, size=1756, nrcpt=1
   (queue active)
```

The `from=` gives the MAIL FROM: *mwlucas@mail.mwl.io*. Reject specifically that address with a *bad-domains* entry.

```
mwlucas@mail.mwl.io      REJECT
```

This rejects my regular emails.

Unfortunately for you, I control my mail host. I can easily create new accounts. Block everything from this host by removing the account. If I bring in other hosts, you'll need to block the whole domain. Best to start there.

```
mwl.io    REJECT
```

Turns out that I'm a persistent jerk who owns many domains. Checking MAIL FROM would show that I tend to use the same username everywhere.

```
mwlucas@          REJECT
```

That should do it!

I'll probably catch on quick, though. You need something stronger.

Blocking IP Addresses

If I'm still bugging you, you could use Postwhite to parse out my SPF records as previously discussed and generate a list of the IP addresses I send mail from. The `check_sender_a_access` option lets you set a list of forbidden IP addresses. Add that to `smtpd_sender_restrictions`.

```
smtpd_sender_restrictions =
  check_sender_a_access
  cidr:/etc/postfix/postscreen_spf_blocklist.cidr,
  check_sender_access hash:/etc/postfix/bad-domains
```

No matter which of my outbound mail hosts I send from, if its IP address appears in an SPF record you have blocked it.

The catch with this is that I can decide to spin up a new VM, and acquire new IP addresses, at any time. I've even written a book about mail servers, so I (presumably) can quickly install one. Something that can dynamically react to my offenses might be more effective.

Blocking on MX or NS Records

The MX record is not a perfect measure of what hosts can send mail, but if you're not willing to receive my mail you might try adding anything in my MX records to the list of hosts forbidden to contact you. Use the `check_sender_mx_access` option for this.

```
smtpd_sender_restrictions = check_sender_mx_access
  hash:/etc/postfix/bad-mx
```

The file *bad-mx* contains a list of MTAs to forbid.

```
mail.mwl.io  REJECT
mail.michaelwlucas.com REJECT
```

Any MAIL FROM that includes a host that uses these hosts in their MX record will be rejected. If no MX record exists for the MAIL FROM host, postfix checks to see if the host's A or AAAA record matches these hosts. If there's a match, it rejects.

You could also forbid MAIL FROM hosts that use chosen nameservers for their domain. Spam operations often have standard nameservers for all their domains. Use the `check_sender_ns_access` option to point to a list of nameservers.

```
smtpd_sender_restrictions = check_sender_ns_access
    hash:/etc/postfix/bad-ns
```

List nameservers in their file exactly like MX hosts.

```
ns1.mwl.io REJECT
ns2.mwl.io REJECT
```

Much like blocking users and domains, you can block every nameserver or MTA in a domain by listing the domain.

```
mwl.io  REJECT
```

None of this is perfect, but it might reduce how often I reach your inbox.

Exceptions to REJECT

Suppose you want to allow a tiny piece of a user, domain name, or address range you've blocked. Perhaps there's one special user at my domain you are willing to accept mail from, but you want to block the rest of us. You can provide an exclusion to the list.

The trick with an exclusion in `smtpd_sender_restrictions` is that you cannot list permitted mail with OK. Tricky senders could use this to bypass other restrictions. Use DUNNO instead, declaring that this policy has no opinion if this mail should be accepted or rejected. Put the larger block first, then the narrow exceptions.

```
mwl.io  REJECT
legalcounsel@mail.mwl.io DUNNO
```

You can get now mail from my lawyer, but not me. Assuming I'm not pretending to be my lawyer, that is.

Collateral Damage

Blocking unwanted mail risks blocking wanted mail.

The Internet is not static. Perhaps you've decided that you can block all mail from amazonses.com, Amazon's mail service. That works great, until your biggest client switches to using them and doesn't inform you beforehand. Automatic generation of blocked IPs from SPF records risks blocking the entire Internet. Blocking users named `mwl@` from any domain would keep you from receiving messages from folks who aren't me. While I continuously get offers for training in South African business law, I can't categorically block all of `.za`. Deploy blocking selectively.

Escaping Block Lists

No matter how careful you are, eventually a user will behave unwisely or an intruder will break into your server and your host's IP address will wind up on one or more block lists. What do you do?

Most block lists are run by mail administrators. They experience the same problems you do, and understand you have those problems. Before they unlist your host, they want to know that the problem is fixed. Identify and resolve your problem before proceeding. Some block lists provide better feedback than others, but you can always check your logs for atypical mail patterns. Check the `postmaster@` account for bounce messages or notifications. Figure it out.

Every reputable block list has a web site with a way to request delisting, and requirements for doing so. Some even put those links in their bounce messages or the SMTP rejection message. Remember that these lists are run by people, and you have zero leverage. Explain what your problem was and how you fixed it.

If those operators discover that you haven't fixed the problem, or if you're a demanding jerk, they're perfectly capable of permanently blocking you. They are downright unkind to people who claim they've fixed a problem, but haven't.

Mail system operators are expected to be responsible citizens. It's not like being in a crowd of people you'll never see again; block list server operators *remember*.

You can now block the most egregious spambots and selected hosts. Let's consider authenticating email more strongly.

Chapter 10: DomainKeys Identified Mail

Email has no cohesive authentication system. Protocols like OpenPGP purport to authenticate people, but require a certain level of technical expertise. Submission servers authenticate users, but do not forward that authentication to other hosts—or even other parts of the local software stack—with any degree of integrity verification. IMAP servers authenticate users but, again, that authentication remains local to the host.

DomainKeys Identified Mail, or DKIM, allows MTAs to add authentication information to mail from their domains. DKIM is built on standard public key cryptography. The public key is offered in a DNS record. The MTA signs all outbound messages with the private key and adds the signature to the message headers. Where SPF validates the `MAIL FROM` and `HELO` headers, DKIM specifically addresses `From`, other headers, and the body. DKIM reduces spammers' ability to forge the sender's user-visible email address.

The Email Empire considers DKIM-signed messages more reliable than unsigned messages. If you want large providers to accept your emails, DKIM is a necessity. As long as you're deploying DKIM for outgoing messages, you might as well validate it on incoming messages.

We'll look at issues around signing messages, DKIM records, then validating messages, and finally signing our own.

Canonicalization

If you've worked with signing protocols like OpenPGP, you're familiar with digital signatures. You take a chunk of data and sign it. Any alteration to the file invalidates the signature. You might be expecting DKIM to work the same way. It can, but doesn't.

Traditional mail software has been free to rearrange messages if
the programmer thought it necessary or correct. This might include
adding or rearranging headers, substituting one kind of whitespace for
another, trimming trailing whitespace, transforming line wrapping,
and more. Any of these changes invalidate digital signatures.
Complicated mail systems might pass messages through multiple
MTAs before they reach their destination. Those systems are often
from different vendors who each interpret the standards uniquely.
Some older so-called "email firewalls" mangled messages to achieve
what they branded as "security," and a few of these systems are still in
use.

DKIM copes by one, *canonicalizing* messages before signing
them, and two, signing headers and the message body separately.
Canonicalizing a message means removing extraneous parts of the
message such as blank lines, anything in quotes in the email address as
well as the greater than and less than signs, putting all headers in lower
case, and replacing all consecutive whitespace with a single space. The
user never sees the canonicalized message; it's used strictly for signing
purposes. The rules for these transformations are very formal and
must be followed in order. Message and body canonicalization have
different rules, but they unfortunately share the names *relaxed* and
simple. Simple header canonicalization is very much not the same as
simple body canonicalization.

For header signatures, the signer gets to choose which headers
it signs. Maybe your server signs the bare minimum, the `From`
header. You might also sign `Subject`, `To`, `Message-ID`, or more.
The signer lists these characteristics in the mail. Some headers
should not be signed—every MTA that touches a message in transit
adds a `Received-by` header, so the original sender shouldn't try to
sign those. Simple header canonicalization is stricter; the headers
must be completely unchanged. Relaxed header canonicalization
converts header names to lower case, makes all headers a single line,
aggregates runs of white space into a single space, and removes any

trailing whitespace. Simple header canonicalization is unlikely to survive passing through multiple MTAs. Always use relaxed header canonicalization.

In body signatures, simple canonicalization strips trailing blank lines. Relaxed body canonicalization strips those blank lines as well as replaces any run of white space with a single space. While an MTA that transforms tabs to spaces might break a programmer, it won't break the digital signature.

The sender must describe what sort of canonicalization it used in creating the signature. Canonicalization methods are written as header method, a slash, then body method. If you want relaxed canonicalization for your headers, but simple canonicalization for the body, that would be written *relaxed/simple*. Both methods of simple canonicalization are fragile and should almost always be avoided. Most of us should always use relaxed/relaxed. You can't control what daftness remote MTAs might perpetrate.

Always specify both sorts of canonicalization. If you put only a single word, it applies to the header method. The body method will default to simple. You probably don't want that.

DKIM Records

The DNS record is the public face of your DKIM implementation. Like SPF records, a DKIM record is a specially formatted TXT record.

```
selector._domainkey.domainname  TXT  "v=DKIM1;
  k=algorithm;" "p=publickey"
```

The *selector* is a fancy word for "key name." A domain can have multiple keys. Each DKIM signature identifies the name of the key the signature was created with. The DKIM validator extracts that name and checks the sending domain's DNS for a public key of that name. The selector is an arbitrary text string. Many tutorials suggest using the word *default*, but that selector declares that you deployed DKIM and never rotated the key.[35] Others suggest using a date string, or a

---

35   Even if you wholeheartedly agree with the arguments against regularly rotating keys, there is no reason to inform everyone of that fact.

string that includes a date, but some folks don't want to provide that information to the public. Much like server names, what you choose for a selector doesn't really matter. Selectors also allow multiple hosts to sign email for your domain.

The `_domainkey` declares that this is a DKIM record.

A DKIM record goes under your domain name, just like an A or MX record.

What remains is a key-value store. Surround the record value in parentheses, and separate the components with semicolons.

The first tag, `v`, is the DKIM version. DKIM is at version 1 today so you don't have to explicitly declare it, but one day they'll issue version two and you'll wish you had declared it. The version must appear first.

The `k` tag gives the key algorithm and encoding. The default is *rsa*, which declares that the key in this record is an RSA public key with SHA256 hashing, in ASN.1 format, encoded in DER and further encoded in base64. While standards permit other algorithms such as EdDSA, large providers haven't deployed validation support.

The `p` value is the actual public key. This is usually a base64 string, using an encoding defined by the `k` value. Key generators provide both a `k` and a `p`, and you must include both without changes. The key is very long, and must go on a single line. You might have to break it into 255-byte chunks with quotes, but most key generators do that for you.

DKIM supports other fields, such as `n` for notes. DNS limits record size, however, so such usage must be tightly limited. Keep any notes outside of the record itself. If nothing else, record when you deployed each selector and what it's for.

DKIM records do not apply to child domains. The DKIM record used to sign mail from `mwl@ratoperatedvehicle.com` does not apply to `mwl@mail.ratoperatedvehicle.com`, even though they're the same host. Each child domain must have its own DKIM record.

With this, we can now understand what the validator does.

DKIM Signatures

A DKIM signer adds a DKIM-Signature header to the message. These headers look complicated, but become approachable when you break them down. Much like a DKIM DNS record, the DKIM-Signature header consists of several key-value pairs. The DNS record and the header use the same key names whenever possible. Here's a signature for mail from my domain.

```
DKIM-Signature: v=1; a=rsa-sha256; c=relaxed/simple;
 d=mwl.io; s=mwl; t=1702932921;
 bh=PHvggxbkGSIzdlkBmP+jU+86V9altffxu//x/ntKa4g=;
 h=Date:From:To:Subject;
 b=WvWODED5cYETtcPLmrMCHDTNBx5OzvRqvMba+X9Ws7QSMt70hK
    O28kWhmuDu2ZW5jATUhu5Cw4JObcdJO
    YlwowqOKRul79pLVeMxz3JBkUySoxT
    +asaLD4V88LxdkzyUsF
...
```

If you go look at a signed message from Google or Microsoft, you'll see a few more keys.

The v field is the DKIM version.

The a field is the public key algorithm. RSA-SHA256 is the default and the most commonly supported algorithm.

Canonicalization appears in c. This message uses relaxed/simple, indicating that the headers can be tweaked but the message body itself must not be touched.

The signing server's domain appears in d. The DKIM validator will check this domain for a DKIM record. This domain is mwl.io. If the user-visible From header matches the domain in the d value, the message is said to be in *DKIM alignment*.

The selector appears in s. The selector in this message is mwl. Combined with the domain name, this tells the validator to check DNS for a public key in the DKIM TXT record at mwl._domainkey.mwl.io.

The t field timestamps signature creation, in epoch time.

The bh field gives the hash of the canonicalized message body. This message uses relaxed/simple canonicalization, meaning that the body cannot be transformed in any way other than trimming trailing blank lines. If the body is long enough that the signer only computed the signature for the first few thousand bytes, the number of bytes appears in l.

The h field lists the headers included in this signature.

The last field, b, gives the complete digital signature.

You might also see x, or the signature's expiration date in epochal time. The default is not to expire, but some organizations declare that signatures are only good for a week. "Expiration" doesn't mean that the message becomes inauthentic while sitting unread in your inbox, but rather that the sender expects the destination MTA to receive and validate the message before this date. Expiration is not a defense against replay attacks.

The i key indicates if some other entity signed the message for the sender, and if so, who.

The q (DKIM key retrieval method) and z (copied headers) keys are valid, but rarely used.

You will occasionally see other keys in a signature. They are experimental values that mail providers use to test DKIM improvements.

DKIM Validation and Failures

When a validator checks a message, it looks at the headers included in the DKIM signature (the h field). It canonicalizes those headers and computes their hash. If the hash matches that in the digital signature, the message has valid DKIM. If not, the message fails DKIM. If the validator can gather all the information it needs to try to validate the signature but the signature is invalid, it's a permanent failure. If the validator has trouble gathering everything—say, if DNS queries for the DKIM record time out, the failure is temporary.

With successful validation, rspamd assigns the R_DKIM_ALLOW symbol.

An invalid signature is assigned the R_DKIM_REJECT symbol with a weight of 1. It might also get R_DKIM_TEMPFAIL or R_DKIM_PERMFAIL.

If a message entirely lacks DKIM, it is assigned R_DKIM_NA.

Many validators use an `Authentication-Results` header, much like SPF. Some validators combine SPF and DKIM results in a single header.

```
Authentication-Results: mail.ratoperatedvehicle.com;
 dkim=pass (2048-bit key; unprotected) header.d=mwl.io
 header.i=@mwl.io header.b=WvWODED5
```

These list the host performing the authentication, the result of the validation attempt, and some of the headers tested.

DKIM Alignment

DKIM *alignment* measures the relationship between the domain in the DKIM record and the domain in the `From` header. As with SPF alignment, DKIM alignment is a DMARC concept that makes sense to discuss here. Also like SPF alignment, DKIM alignment can be *strict* (exact match) or *relaxed* (child of domain). Consider this snippet of headers.

```
DKIM-Signature: v=1; d=ratoperatedvehicle.com;
...
From: mwl@ratoperatedvehicle.com
```

The domain in the signature's d tag exactly matches the domain in the `From` header. This message meets *strict DKIM alignment*. Compare that with a snippet from another email.

```
DKIM-Signature: v=1; d=tiltedwindmillpress.com;
...
From: sales@www.tiltedwindmillpress.com
```

255

The `From` header declares that the host
`www.tiltedwindmillpress.com` sent this message. The signature's
`d` tag says this is for that domain, but not that host. This message
achieves *relaxed DKIM alignment.*

Mailing lists present problems for DKIM alignment. They receive
messages, alter the headers, add footers, and resend them. All this
exceeds the transformations permitted by canonicalization. If the
mailing list forwards the original DKIM signature, it will not validate.
Most mailing lists add their own DKIM signatures to messages sent to
their lists. Many of them preserve the sender's original `From` header,
however. The signature has the mailing list's domain, but the `From`
address is in a wholly different domain, so the message cannot have
either sort of DKIM alignment. Many mailing lists preserve previous
signatures with DMARC Authenticated Receive Chain (Chapter 11).

Now that we can validate signatures, let's sign our own mail.

Signing Outbound Mail

Rspamd's `dkim_signing` module will sign outbound mail for you.
It can store and configure DKIM keys in a few different ways. You
can use commercial key storage, or stuff keys into Redis. We'll use
OpenDKIM-compatible key configuration to offer an easy migration
path to OpenDKIM or to interoperate with standalone mail senders
signing with OpenDKIM, as we'll discuss in Chapter 15.

To sign mail you must create keys, publish those keys, build a key
table and a signing table to tell rspamd where to find those keys, and
attach rspamd's milter to the Postfix submission service.

Key Creation

Each domain needs its own keypair, and a domain might have multiple
keys, so get organized from the beginning. I recommend creating
a directory for storing keys and a subdirectory for each domain.
Within those directories, name the files for a given keypair after the
key's selector. (Remember, a *selector* is just a fancy word for "name.")
We're using OpenDKIM-style configuration for broad compatibility,
so we'll put the keys in the OpenDKIM locations: `/var/db/opendkim`

on FreeBSD and `/etc/dkimkeys` on Debian. Create the directory and make **rspamd** the owner. Within that directory, create a subdirectory for one of the domains you want to sign.

Rspamd protects you from horrid OpenSSL commands by providing a less horrid rspamadm(1) subcommand that calls OpenSSL for you: `dkim_keygen`.

```
# rspamadm dkim_keygen -s 'selector' -d domain \
 -b 2048 -k selector.private > selector.txt
```

The `-s` option sets the selector, and `-d` the domain. With `-b` you set the bits in the key. The default, 1024, is now considered weak. The `-k` option lets you give a file to put the private key in. The command normally outputs this key's DNS record, but we all know that will scroll out of view before you need it, so write that to a file as well. Here, I create a key with the selector `wookie` for the domain **ratoperatedvehicle.com.**

```
# rspamadm dkim_keygen -s 'wookie' \
 -d ratoperatedvehicle.com -b 2048 \
 -k wookie.private > wookie.txt
```

The file `wookie.private` contains the private key.

In `wookie.txt` you'll find the DKIM record you need to add to your domain's DNS record. It's two lines, wrapped.

Publishing DKIM Keys

The DKIM record format is persnickety and fragile. Never try to create those records by hand. The key creation command provides that record in the exact format you need. Use it. The file will be in the key directory, named after the selector and ending in `.txt`. I created the key `wookie` for **ratoperatedvehicle.com**, so I need `/etc/dkimkeys/ratoperatedvehicle.com/wookie.txt`.

```
wookie._domainkey  IN   TXT      ( "v=DKIM1; k=rsa; "
  "p=MIGfMA0GCSqGSIb3DQEB..." )
```

It's on two lines. Just like with many SOA records, use parentheses to contain them on one line. The second line is very long. The key might be broken into pieces to fit within TXT record limits. Copy this entry into your zone and reload the zone. Then double-check that your nameserver has actually published it.

```
$ dig wookie._domainkey.ratoperatedvehicle.com txt @localhost
```

If your key is in DNS, proceed.

Key Table

An OpenDKIM-style key table is a file that maps files to DNS entries and selectors. I put it in */etc/mail/dkim.keytable* unless an OS package manager declares otherwise.

Every key in use needs a key table entry. Each entry contains four values on a single line: the DNS entry for the key (including the selector), the domain, the selector on its own, and the file containing the associated private key. There's a space after the DNS entry, but the rest are all colon-delimited.

```
DNS domain:selector:keyfile
```

Here's the entry for the key we just created for `ratoperatedvehicle.com`. (It's wrapped in your book for physical reasons, but in the file it's a single line.)

```
wookie._domainkey.ratoperatedvehicle.com
  ratoperatedvehicle.com:wookie:/
  etc/dkimkeys/ratoperatedvehicle.com/wookie.private
```

This entry uses the selector *wookie* for the DKIM key for `ratoperatedvehicle.com`. It specifies the domain `ratoperatedvehicle.com`, then uses a colon to indicate the path to the private key.

If you have multiple domains, or multiple keys for one domain, list each key on its own line.

```
wookie._domainkey.ratoperatedvehicle.com
  ratoperatedvehicle.com:wookie:
  /etc/dkimkeys/ratoperatedvehicle.com/wookie.private
fuzzball._domainkey.ratoperatedvehicle.com
  ratoperatedvehicle.com:swamp:
  /etc/dkimkeys/ratoperatedvehicle.com/swamp.private
zamwessel._domainkey.immortalclay.com
  immortalclay.com:zamwessel:
  /etc/dkimkeys/immortalclay.com/zamwessel.private
```

You can use a percent sign (%) in certain places to substitute for the apparent domain name, but that leads to confusion. You can also put the DER-encoded private key directly in this file, rather than pointing to the key file, but that gets very long very quickly. Stick with key files and full domain names.

Hash marks (#) indicate comments. If you leave no other comments, record the key creation date and the host the key is used for. When you need to perform a key rollover or audit, that information will be precious.

Signing table

The signing table tells rspamd which sender email addresses should be signed with which key. I put it in */etc/mail/dkim.signingtable* unless a package manage has other ideas. OpenDKIM format requires that each domain rspamd signs has a signing table entry. Each entry is a single line, matching email accounts to a DKIM record. Use an asterisk to indicate "all users at this domain." Here, I match all users two of my domains to their keys.

```
*@ratoperatedvehicle.com
  wookie._domainkey.ratoperatedvehicle.com
*@immortalclay.com zamwessel._domainkey.immortalclay.com
```

Email from all users at each domain will be signed by the assigned key. Yes, you could have specific keys for specific users but one, get the basics working first and two, why?

dkim_signing

Now tell the module dkim_signing to use those tables. The main configuration is in `/etc/rspamd/modules.d/dkim_signing.conf`. You'll see references to enabling the module by specifying the `path` variable, but we're not using that method. Create `/etc/rspamd/local.d/dkim_signing.conf` and set `signing_table` and `key_table`.

```
signing_table = "/etc/mail/dkim.signingtable";
key_table = "/etc/mail/dkim.keytable";
```

Reload rspamd.

Attaching Postfix to Rspamd

We already connected Postfix to rspamd for messages arriving from external MTAs, but that's separate from messages from authenticated users via the submission service. Rspamd treats authenticated messages the same as it does mail from local addresses, and disables checks like greylisting and SPF. Find the submission entry in `/etc/postfix/master.cf` and add the milter option.

```
smtpds inet n - n - - smtpd
  -o syslog_name=postfix-submission
  -o smtpd_tls_wrappermode=yes
  …
  -o smtpd_milters=inet:localhost:11332
```

Restart Postfix and test.

Testing Signing

Like everything else, test your signatures before you rely on them. Verify that both of your test hosts are running rspamd, and send mail from your host with DKIM keys to the other. The receiving MTA should add the R_DKIM _ALLOW symbol. If it doesn't, find the R_ DKIM symbol it did add and see what's missing. Check the Postfix and rspamd error logs.

Multiple DKIM selectors

An organization might have dozens or thousands of MTAs, often controlled by different entities. Sharing DKIM keys between all of these is impractical. The only sensible way to handle these is to allow each MTA to have its own DKIM keys.

That's fine.

My main MTA has a DKIM key. So does my mailing list provider. All of their keys are identified with different selectors. External MTAs don't care how many DKIM keys my domain has; they only care if they can find the particular DKIM key they're looking for. That's why we use selectors.

What if one of your MTAs doesn't sign at all? External MTAs will treat its messages with all the respect due unsigned messages. DMARC lets you instruct external MTAs to reject unsigned mails, but that's your choice.

Key Lifetime and Rotation

Public key encryption gets broken. The more valuable your organization, the more people try to break your keys. Breaking keys takes time. The standard way to avoid intruders brute-forcing public keys is to periodically rotate them. But should *you* rotate *your* keys?

Modern DKIM uses 2048-bit keys. With current mathematical understanding, they are not brute-force breakable before the expected heat death of the universe. Modern cryptographic algorithms don't fall to brute force, however. Mathematicians nibble at them, discovering weak point after weak point until, eventually, someone figures out how to break them in a reasonable time. Computer speed might not be accelerating the way it did a couple decades ago, but processing power is far more accessible than ever. Every year, any definition of "reasonable time" encompasses more and more processing power.

Will your key be broken? Probably not.

Is your organization a target for intruders? Do you handle money, battle station plans, or personally identifiable information? Are legal stormtroopers likely to loom over your world and blast it into a billion shreds? If so, rotating your key every year or so is a respectable item on the list of things you do to convince auditors that you're taking sensible precautions. Create a new key, add it to DNS, let it propagate, switch your mail system to use it, and remove the old key from DNS.

Now that your domain provides DKIM and SPF records, you can establish DMARC.

Chapter 11: DMARC

One of the joys of long-lived open standards is that anyone can implement them. That's also a giant problem. Programs might be intermittently abandoned, resurrected, reincarnated, forked or reimplemented without a name change, taken over by a company intent on privatizing the standard, or thrown down a garbage chute. Occasionally, they're carefully maintained for decades by people who care.

Somewhere on the Internet, every variant of every one of these programs is deployed in production. SPF validators work, mostly. DKIM validators? Same, except when they don't. The problem comes when these programs cause someone to reject your mail. Maybe they'll bounce it back to you. Maybe they'll fling it into a spam folder or silently discard it.

And you have no way to know.

Domain-based Message Authentication, Reporting, and Conformance, or *DMARC*, provides a way for you to tell external MTAs your expectations for your messages, and for those MTAs to provide feedback when your messages do not meet those expectations. It's defined in RFC 7489. DMARC addresses SPF and DKIM alignment, which is not the same as valid SPF or DKIM. A host might be sending mail for your domain from an IP address listed in your SPF record, but its bad headers make it misaligned (Chapter 7). An email could have a valid DKIM signature, but if the user-visible `From` header is wrong, it fails DKIM alignment (Chapter 9). A DMARC policy claims nothing about SPF or DKIM validity, only about the alignment.

DMARC lets you offer guidance to external MTAs on how you want them to treat your nonconformant messages and where to send aggregated reports of DMARC failures. The mail operator can look at the report, identify which alignment checks the messages fail, what host sent the message, and decide what action to take.

By nature, sysadmins want their systems to conform to the highest possible standards. Our web servers are secure (whatever that means). Our passwords include mixed-case letters, numbers, symbols, and the Imperial March. We intend to sign everything with DKIM, and we publish SPF records that contain every host that might possibly send mail. In this mindset, anything without perfect alignment is obviously forged and should be unilaterally discarded. Anyone who's worked in computing more than a week understands that we'll miss something, though. Some critical system sends mail from its own hostname rather than the domain, or there's that weird system that sends mail only when the Galactic Senate starts its decennial session. DMARC deliberately allows a soft deployment. You can publish fierce policies that require strict alignment of SPF and/or DKIM, but ask that failures be reported to you rather than discarded. Use the failure reports to find and fix deployment gaps. Eventually the failure reports will stop coming and you update your policy to ask others to quarantine or even reject noncompliant mails.

That's the theory, at least. Practice is a little different.

DMARC Components

A DMARC record describes tests you want performed, a policy for handling test failures, report recipients, and the types of reports you want.

DMARC tells external MTAs how to evaluate DKIM and SPF alignment. A domain can declare that messages should have simple or relaxed SPF or DKIM alignment. If you don't declare a policy, the default is that both are relaxed.

The DMARC policy tells the receiving MTA how to treat messages that don't meet the requested SPF and DKIM alignment levels. A policy can request that the mail be quarantined (probably as spam), rejected, or processed normally. You must explicitly declare your policy.

Reporting is key to DMARC. You must define an email address to receive aggregated reports. You can define another address to receive detailed, per-message forensic reports. Not all recipients send failure reports, let alone forensic reports, but you must provide a recipient in case they do.

Define all these with a DMARC record.

DMARC Records

Like every other email-adjacent protocol, DMARC records are a collection of key-value statements distributed via DNS TXT records. Some of the tags are mandatory, while others were created for later expansion and can be ignored for now. DMARC records apply to child domains, so the DMARC record for `ratoperatedvehicle.com` gets applied to `mail.ratoperatedvehicle.com` unless you create a different record. DMARC records appear in their zone at `_dmarc` and look like this.

```
_dmarc.mwl.io.  TXT  "v=DMARC1; p=none; rua=mailto:dmarc@mwl.io;"
```

DMARC records have a few mandatory tags, and several optional ones.

Mandatory DMARC Tags

Here's a minimal DMARC record containing only the mandatory tags.

```
v=DMARC1; p=none; rua=mailto:dmarc@ratoperatedvehicle.com;
```

The `v` tag gives the DMARC version. It should always be set to `DMARC1`, as version 2 does not yet exist.

The `p` tag is the policy, and tells remote MTAs how to handle messages that fail SPF and DMARC alignment tests. A policy of *none* tells the recipient to process the message the way they normally would, and is often called "report-only mode." A DMARC deployment on an existing domain should always start in report-only mode. A *quarantine* policy tells the recipient to sequester the email, probably in the spam pit. The *reject* policy tells recipients to reject the message during the SMTP transaction.

The `rua` (*reporting URI: aggregate*) tag defines where external MTAs should send failure reports. The account must exist and must accept mail. While email is the only method currently supported, people are working on other methods. For future-proofing, each address must start with the `mailto:` keyword. Separate multiple addresses with commas.

Once you have a basic policy, you might add additional tags.

Forensic Reports

Normal DMARC reports identify when a message fails the DKIM or SPF alignment policy declared in your DMARC record. We'll look at one of those reports later, but you might want detailed reports on specific messages that don't pass your DMARC policy. These forensic reports are a stripped-down copy of the email that failed. They contain SPF and DKIM headers, the MTA that sent the message, and the sender. Forensic reports are a great way to find misconfigured hosts on your network. They're also a great way to get flooded with non-actionable information about every spam message that tries to forge your domain.

Your policy must define which sorts of failures you want to know about and a recipient for those reports. Use the `ruf` (*reporting URI: forensic*) tag for the email address people should send forensic reports to.

The `fo` tag tells external MTAs what sorts of failure reports you want. The default, `0`, declares you want reports only when both SPF and DKIM fail to pass alignment. To get a report when either SPF or DKIM fail, set `fo` to `1`. To specifically look at failed DKIM messages, use a `d`. Use `s` to get reports on all failed SPF tests. You can list multiple values by separating them with semicolons. Here, I ask for forensic reports at **forensic@ratoperatedvehicle.com**, and request reports 0 and 1.

```
v=DMARC1; p=none; rua=mailto:dmarc@ratoperatedvehicle;
    ruf=mailto:forensic@ratoperatedvehicle.com; fo=0;1;
```

Forensic reports are a public service, but many organizations do not send them. If someone forges your domain on millions of spam messages, you would receive tens of thousands of forensic reports. If someone uses the Death Star of Spam and forges millions of messages from you to Gmail, can your tiny MTA cope with Google forwarding details on every forged message to you? Probably not.

Alignment

DMARC accepts relaxed SPF and DKIM alignment. Perhaps your email system is pristine, and you want to enforce strict alignment for one or both. Use the `aspf` tag to set SPF alignment, and `adkim` to set DKIM alignment. A value of `r` means relaxed alignment, while `s` indicates strict. Relaxed alignment is the default, and does not need to be declared.

```
v=DMARC1; p=none; rua=mailto:dmarc@ratoperatedvehicle;
  aspf=s; adkim=s;
```

The example above tells external MTAs to require strict alignment. Requiring strict alignment for either SPF or DKIM is almost always a poor decision.

Other Tags

The remaining tags offer options for deployment speed and report intervals.

The `pct` tag tells external MTAs what percent of your domain's messages should be filtered. If you switch your policy from `none` to `quarantine`, but set `pct` to `1`, external MTAs should put one percent of DMARC-violating messages in the spam folder. This permits a slow rollout of DMARC enforcement.

You can use `ri` (report interval) to ask external MTAs to send violation reports at certain intervals, but many MTAs ignore this in favor of their own settings. Set this to a number of seconds. Anything less than 3600 (one hour) or greater than 86400 (one day) is especially likely to be ignored.

While the standard defines other tags, they have only one legitimate value and declaring them changes nothing.

What's Wrong With DMARC

DMARC works great in a world where individual entities send messages to individual entities. Everything goes wrong when you forward messages.

Clients can forward messages as attachments without trouble. The forwarded messages are wrapped in a new message with proper SPF and DKIM headers. Bounce-style forwarding, where a client resends a message through its local MTA with the original headers, breaks both SPF and DKIM. Bounced messages will almost certainly violate DMARC policies. A quarantine or refuse policy means that the external MTA will block the message or consign it to the spam folder.

Chapters 7 and 9 discussed the problems with alignment and mailing lists. If your domain deploys a report-only policy, sending messages to a mailing list will generate a DMARC failure report from every MTA that receives the message. Some mailing lists have tens of thousands of subscribers.

Suppose I send a message to a list with fifty thousand subscribers. My message gets new headers and is forwarded to all fifty thousand people. If a tenth of them send DMARC failure reports, I will receive five thousand reports. Worse, these reports will be *non-actionable*. I can do nothing about how the mailing list works. And I'll get that every time I post to the list.

DMARC advocates want mailing lists to change how they send messages. Many mailing lists have done so. Others have not. Changing mailing lists to comply with DMARC often means degrading the user's experience or violating user expectations, especially on long-lived lists. I am on several mailing lists that are over thirty years old, operated by different organizations, and have hundreds of thousands of subscribers. Many of those lists send messages with a `From` header that uses the original sender's name and email address, breaking alignment. The subscribers use mail clients scattered across the entire history of the Internet. Changing headers on these lists would impact every subscriber. Some of those subscribers are software that parses and analyzes the messages. Some mailing lists are hosted on software that hasn't been updated in decades. Changing the behavior of the world's email systems is like using a canoe paddle to steer an iceberg. Even if all the mailing list software and client configurations could be updated, some mailing list operators want nothing to do with DMARC and actively advocate against it.

I'm not going to say if DMARC is the "right" solution or not. Some organizations, including much of the Email Empire, check to see if incoming messages are from domain with a DMARC record and use the results as part of their spam scoring system.

You must have a DMARC record. What you *do* with that DMARC record is negotiable.

DMARC Authenticated Received Chain

When you send a message to a mailing list, the mailing list software can validate the message's DKIM signature. It could even validate alignment and comply with the DMARC policy. The mailing list cannot forward the DKIM signature in a verifiable manner, however. Subscribing MTAs have to trust the mailing list software.

The *DMARC Authenticated Received Chain*, or ARC, specifically supports mailing lists. ARC lets a mailing list declare "The DKIM signature on this message was fine when I got it," signing that declaration with its own signature. If the receiving MTA accepts that signature, it does not send DMARC failure reports for messages received via that list.

The problem with ARC is that it has no mechanism for distributing trust. Each MTA operator must decide which mailing lists it trusts. Those decisions are driven by convenience and awareness. If I know that many folks on my server subscribe to the Debian or FreeBSD mailing lists, I'll probably trust those senders. If I don't know, I won't. If I take the time to review the DMARC reports I send, I might notice others who I should probably trust. Many MTA operators set up their

DMARC system before ARC and haven't updated their systems, so they send reports regardless of ARC.

Running a mailing list is beyond the scope of this book. You don't need to deploy ARC. You only need to recognize that it exists. The headers `ARC-Message-Signature`, `ARC-Authentication-Results`, and `ARC-Seal` all relate to ARC.

The upshot is: even with ARC, any time any of your users sends a message to one of these mailing lists, you will receive non-actionable "failure" reports.

DMARC and the Small Mail Server

If you don't publish DMARC records, spam detection systems evaluating your messages will say, "I find your lack of DMARC disturbing." That increases the odds of your messages plunging into the spam folder. But what should you do about reporting, mailing lists, and so on?

If you are running a mail system truly for yourself and you don't use mailing lists, or if you know none of your users will ever sign up for mailing lists, you could safely deploy aggressive DMARC policies. Start in reporting mode with a "none" policy, and increase strictness when the reports you receive say you can.

If you use mailing lists regularly, you'll still need a simple DMARC record. Search the initial reports for weirdness, and chase down any unexpected senders on your systems. Once you confirm everything works as expected, check them maybe monthly and get on with your mailing lists.

The other question is: should you send failure reports? Failure reports are intended as a public service. Will reports from you serve the public? The Email Empire's DMARC reports will outweigh anything you might send. Sending DMARC reports will increase the amount of email your server sends, and the amount of undeliverable mail you cope with. If a domain you correspond with frequently provides a reporting address maintained by the Email Empire, and you send a lot of failure reports, the odds of the Empire marking your server as a spammer increase. If your goal, like mine, is for your MTA to coexist peacefully on the Internet without being crushed by forces you can't control, do not send DMARC reports. Deploy a simple DMARC record like this and get on with your life.

```
_dmarc.example.com.  TXT  "v=DMARC1; p=none;
  rua=mailto:dmarc@example.com;"
```

Use one of the many online DMARC record testers to verify the world understands your record. Many will complain about your "none" policy. Ignore that.

If you want to send DMARC reports, investigate OpenDMARC (`http://www.trusteddomain.org/opendmarc/`).

Receiving Reports for Other Domains

I operate several domain names. While many have SPF records publicly declaring an oath of email silence, a few do send messages. I want all the DMARC reports for all my domains to come to a central mailbox. You can't just point your reporting address anywhere, however. If your DMARC record lists a reporting address in a domain other than itself, that domain must declare in DNS that it agrees to receive your reports. The record looks like this.

```
domain._report._dmarc  TXT "v=DMARC1"
```

This record declares that this domain accepts failure reports for this domain in DMARC version 1.

All the DMARC reports for my tiny empire go to `dmarc@ratoperatedvehicle.com`. The DNS for `ratoperatedvehicle.com` needs an entry for each domain, like this one for solveamurder.org.

```
solveamurder.org._report._dmarc  TXT     "v=DMARC1"
```

If you skip this, advanced spam systems will declare your DMARC record invalid.

Processing Reports

DMARC reports are strictly formatted XML. Reading unfamiliar XML by eye is annoying. You could use a tool like dmarc-cat to make individual reports easily parsable, but DMARC reports are most useful when aggregated together. As you'd expect, many people have written DMARC parsers. Many are intended for large operations, and require tools like Grafana or Splunk or the entirety of AWS.

Dmarcts-report-parser from Techsneeze is a reasonable selection for small servers. It reads messages from an IMAP mailbox and feeds them to a MariaDB database. It has a companion PHP script, dmarcts-report-viewer, which reads the database and presents the results on a web page.

We'll get reports into the database, then get the data back out.

dmarcts-report-parser

Find dmarcts-report-parser at
`https://github.com/techsneeze/dmarcts-report-parser`.
The parser is a Perl script meant to run on a schedule, via cron(8) or similar. It uses a configuration file and a database. Most Unixes offer a package. Before doing anything, create the database and create a dedicated account to own the database.

```
$ mysql -u root -p
> create database whinging;
> create user 'c3p0'@'localhost'
  identified by 'HeadBackwards!';
> grant all privileges on whinging.*
  to 'c3p0'@'localhost';
> flush privileges;
```

Also gather the information for your DMARC report account. Save yourself pain and verify that the username and password are correct before setting up the parser.

Configuring dmarcts-report-parser

Configure the parser in `/etc/dmarcts-report-parser.conf`. It starts with core behavior settings.

```
$debug = 0;
$delete_reports = 0;
```

The parser only produces output if there's a serious problem. If the parser does not work as expected, set `debug` to `1` to get verbose output. You can also enable debugging on the command line for interactive testing.

The parser can delete reports after reading them, leave them in the inbox, or move them to a folder. Once you know the parser works and data is going into the database, you might want to delete the emails by setting `delete_reports` to `1`. For now, leave them in place.

Now we have the database settings.

```
$dbtype = 'mysql';
$dbname = 'whinging';
$dbuser = 'c3p0';
$dbpass = 'HeadBackwards!';
$dbhost = 'localhost';
$dbport = '3306';
```

Enter the database name, username, and password. The default database type, host, and port should be fine unless you tampered with your database server.

We then have account login information. Your mail system provides IMAP over TLS, so use that.

```
$imapserver      = 'localhost';
$imapuser        = 'dmarc@ratoperatedvehicle.com';
$imappass        = 'ExposeMyFlaws';
$imapport        = '993';
$imapssl         = '1';
$imaptls         = '0';
$tlsverify       = '1';
$imapignoreerror = '0';
```

The IMAP server, user, and password should come straight from the DMARC report account. The system set up in this book only accepts IMAP connections over TLS, so set `imapport` to 993.

The `imapssl` and `imaptls` options are confusingly named. The `imapssl` option means "does this host use a TLS-dedicated port?" Our server does, so set this to 1. The `imaptls` option enables opportunistic TLS, or switch an unencrypted connection to TLS midstream. Our Dovecot configuration doesn't enable that, so leave it off.

The `tlsverify` option tells the parser to verify the server certificate.

Finally, the `imapignoreerror` option is a workaround for a specific Microsoft Exchange 2007 bug. Don't enable it.

We then tell the parser where to find new reports, where to store processed reports, and how to manage unparsable reports.

```
$imapreadfolder   = 'Inbox';
$imapmovefolder = 'processed';
$imapmovefoldererr = 'Inbox.notProcessed';
$maxsize_xml = 50000;
$delete_failed = 0;
```

The `imapreadfolder` tells the parser where to find incoming reports.

Setting `imapmovefolder` tells the parser to move processed reports to another folder.

DMARC reports come from all over the world and are sent by many different software systems. The parser might choke on some of them. Your DMARC report address is public, so it might attract spam. If you set `imapmovefoldererr`, messages the parser can't add to the database will be saved in a separate folder. Similarly, the `maxsize_xml` option lets you set the maximum report size in bytes. You can increase the maximum size, if your database will accept it. Verify it works before changing it!

If you want to delete unparsable reports, set `delete_failed` to 1.

The parser should be ready to receive mail now.

Testing dmarcts-report-parser

Run the parser at the command line to verify it works. Use the -i flag to tell it to use IMAP. It normally runs silently, so add the --info flag to get some output.

```
$ dmarcts-report-parser.pl -i --info
dmarcts-report-parser.pl: Adding missing table
  <rptrecord> to the database.
dmarcts-report-parser.pl: Adding missing table
  <report> to the database.
dmarcts-report-parser.pl: Processed 0 emails.
```

This is good, and boring. The parser connected to the database and added missing tables. It connected to the message store and found zero emails, but at least the email connection works.

If you don't see something like this and you want detailed output, enable debugging with -d.

Now the hard part: this account has not yet received any DMARC reports. When you do receive reports, run it again.

```
$ dmarcts-report-parser.pl -i --info
dmarcts-report-parser.pl: Processed 3 emails.
```

You might check your database to verify the reports were entered. At that point, you can schedule dmarcts-report-parser -i to run daily. Once you have data, you can set up the report viewer.

dmarcts-report-viewer

Find dmarcts-report-viewer at
`https://github.com/techsneeze/dmarcts-report-viewer`.
Unlike dmarcts-report-parser, dmarcts-report-viewer is rarely
packaged.[36] You might need to pull it from git.

```
# cd /var/www
# git clone https://github.com/techsneeze/dmarcts-report-viewer.git
```

Go into the dmarcts-report-viewer directory.

Configuring dmarcts-report-viewer

The viewer contains more stuff than the parser, because web sites need
to be pretty. The only file you need to worry about is the configuration
file *dmarcts-report-viewer-config.php.sample*. Copy that to plain
dmarcts-report-viewer-config.php and make your changes there. The
viewer uses the same configuration options as the parser, in exactly the
same way.

```
$dbtype="mysql";
$dbhost="localhost";
$dbname="whinging";
$dbuser="c3p0";
$dbpass="HeadBackwards!";
$dbport="3306";
```

That's it. Note the complete absence of any authentication settings.
The viewer has no authentication system. Run it only on a private
network, or add a password at the web server. On the other hand, the
viewer does not permit altering the data and letting other sysadmins
see your failures would make them feel better about their own.

Configure your web server to show the directory. Here's an example
for Apache.

---

36   Who cares what the data says, so long as you have it?

```
<Directory "/var/www/dmarcts-report-viewer/">
 Require all granted
</Directory>
Alias /dmarc /var/www/dmarcts-report-viewer
```

Restart your web server.

Viewing Reports

Point your web browser at the *dmarcts-report-viewer.php* script. You might add a redirect somewhere to point calls to that directory at the script. You'll get a page showing the most recent reports, with options to select different months and report sources and different criteria.

If the report doesn't show up, debug it as you would any PHP application.

Use the reports to identify which hosts are sending mail with bad alignment, or hosts that are sending mail on their own rather than through your MTA. Once you've solved those problems, you can decide what to do with further reports.

Going Live

Now that you have DKIM, SPF, and DMARC, you can realistically send test mails into the Email Empire. You have an account somewhere in there. Send yourself a mail. Verify that this MTA can validate your SPF and DKIM, and that it recognizes your DMARC. See if it sends a DMARC report, or if they accept your mail as-is. If the Empire sees that you have these standards configured from the first moment that become aware of you, they won't immediately block you. They might sort you into their spam folder. Don't immediately send your new address to all your contacts, though. Start sending mail slowly. Let the Empire get used to your server. Start slow.

Now let's talk about the big problem with receiving mail: reading and sorting it.

Chapter 12: Webmail

Mail clients like Thunderbird and mutt are useful, but asking the flight attendant to scan your boarding pass off your laptop screen is a great way to get an assigned seat in Ewok Class. A web-based client that you can access from any device is useful. Many people have never used a proper actual mail client, and only know how to use web-based email. If you're providing email service, you'll need webmail.

We'll use Roundcube (`https://roundcube.net/`), a database-backed PHP application. It's well-maintained, flexible, and offers modules to add functionality like LDAP integration and calendars. Roundcube is good for small sites, but for larger environments it also supports caching engines like Redis and memcached. Even a small install uses a database for user accounts, address books, and so on. It supports the industry-standard Sieve mail filtering protocol discussed in the next chapter.

Installing Roundcube

Most operating systems offer a perfectly serviceable Roundcube package. Use it. It should install the PHP code in one directory, a documentation directory elsewhere, and set certain directories to be writable by the web server. The documentation includes an INSTALL file discussing how to set up a MariaDB database, with commands something like this.

```
$ mysql -u root -p
> CREATE DATABASE ewoksarecanon CHARACTER SET utf8mb4
  COLLATE utf8mb4_unicode_ci;
> CREATE USER 'onlyThreeFilms'@'localhost' IDENTIFIED
  BY 'NeverTellMeTheOdds';
> GRANT ALL PRIVILEGES ON ewoksarecanon.*
  TO onlyThreeFilms@localhost;
> quit
```

279

The database password is not only for the application: it is the Roundcube GUI's administrative password. Use a password you can reliably type best out of three.

Once you have a database, configure the web server to support the application. Roundcube provides a `.htaccess` file for rewriting URLs and protecting sensitive files. Many web servers have disabled `.htaccess`-based configuration. You can either enable `.htaccess`, or copy the settings in the provided `.htaccess` directly into an Apache web server configuration. Integrating the settings into your web server configuration is undeniably more correct.

Browse to the URL you've configured. Roundcube isn't configured yet so you'll get a customized Roundcube error message, but it'll tell you that the web server sees Roundcube.

Configuring Roundcube

Roundcube uses a configuration file, but rather than building it from scratch they provide a convenient installer to create the initial file for you. Unlike many convenient installers, it usually works. Point your web browser at Roundcube's `installer` subdirectory and you'll get a page listing all of Roundcube's dependencies. Check for missing shared libraries and PHP modules. Operating system packages are great, but not all packagers pull in all dependencies and not all environments need all dependencies. Roundcube lists PHP's LDAP module as a dependency, but if you're not using LDAP don't install it. PHP's ImageMagick module is also a dependency, one that drags with it all sorts of shared libraries and programs and Ghostscript and Cups and probably blueprints for a secret battle station. Users expect their webmail client to support pictures, though, so install it. You'll also see errors for databases you're not using. If Roundcube sees it has MariaDB/MySQL support, you're fine.

When you click "Next," you'll get a list of Roundcube options. The first section contains basic interface details, like `product_name` and `support_url`, used to compose web pages. Others are optional, like integration with Google's spellcheck service.[37]

The next section discusses logging. By default, Roundcube logs to a file inside the application directory. In production I recommend using syslog so you can manage Roundcube logs exactly like any other application. For your first setup, use Roundcube's native file logging.

Then we have the database setup. Enter the database name, username, and password.

Below that are the IMAP settings and SMTP settings. That gets tricky. Roundcube uses the option `ssl` to mean "TCP port requires TLS," which is how we've configured IMAP on port 993. The option `tls` means "use opportunistic TLS," like mail submission on port 587 uses. Roundcube will attempt to verify the X.509 server certificate using the given hostname, and refuse to connect if it can't. While you're probably running Roundcube on the same host as the MTA, your certificate doesn't include the hostname `localhost`. Use the actual host name.

In my install, IMAP should be set to use `ssl://mail.ratoperatedvehicle.com:993`. The SMTP server should be set to `ssl://mail.ratoperatedvehicle.com:465`.

If your Roundcube will only support one domain, you can add a default domain. The listed mailboxes match those used by most mail clients, including Thunderbird and Outlook, so don't change them unless you want to create extra folders.

The installer offers a choice of display settings, but on your first Roundcube install you have no idea how the default settings will annoy you. Leave them alone until you experience actual annoyance.

At the very end, the installer lets you select plugins. The next chapter needs *managesieve*. You might also find *markasjunk* useful when we get to spam filtering. If you expect trouble, you might want *debug_logger*. The *password* plugin lets users change their own passwords. You probably want that.

37   I wouldn't go to the trouble of setting up my own mail system only to send every keystroke every user types straight to the Email Empire, but we can't all be proper rebels.

At the bottom of the page, you'll see a *Create Config* button. Click it. The installer will present you with the contents of a configuration file. The web server doesn't have permission to write the actual configuration file.[38] Either copy the contents into a blank `config.inc.php` in the application directory with your text editor, or hit the "save to /tmp" button and then copy it to the application directory. This basic configuration should suffice to get Roundcube running. Once you've installed the configuration file, hit *Continue*.

The installer's third page verifies your settings work and gives you a chance to test SMTP and IMAP. If everything works, and your tests are successful, you're done. Fixing errors is the line between "the installer is easy" and "just edit the config file." This page reads the installed configuration file, so you can reload the page to test configuration changes. The file `defaults.inc.php` lists all of Roundcube's configuration options and their default settings. Most of these are useful only for special circumstances, large environments, or supporting obsolete software.

Setup Debugging

Roundcube defaults to logging to files in the web site's `log` directory. Logs are especially useful during debugging. Roundcube has a general problem log, `logs/error.log`, but supports separate logging for SQL, IMAP, and SMTP transactions, as well as LDAP. If part of your configuration fails, start by verifying that you set your IMAP to `ssl` on port 993 and SMTP to `ssl` on port 465. Then enable debugging for the database, IMAP, or SMTP as needed.

```
$config['sql_debug'] = true;
$config['imap_debug'] = true;
$config['smtp_debug'] = true;
```

---

38   Unless you screwed up.

Setting these writes all transactions to `sql.log`, `imap.log`, and `smtp.log`. Retest the configuration on the installer page, and the test output will get logged to the file. It's the same sort of output you'd get if you connected to the service with OpenSSL or mysql(1). These logs can grow quite large, though, so don't leave them enabled.

Roundcube has other debugging options, such as for HTTP sessions and Redis integration. Check `defaults.inc.php` for details.

Final Setup

Once the installer stops complaining, configure long-term logging and disable the installer.

Presumably you'll be using Roundcube for a while. The logs will grow. Arrange log management before placing any application in production. You can either rotate the logs in the Roundcube log directory, or have Roundcube feed its logs to syslog. Log management is the purpose of syslog, so use it. Don't dump Roundcube logs into the mail log, though. That's like putting your web server log in the mail log. Assign Roundcube its own facility. Here's how you would do that in traditional syslogd(8) or the rsyslogd(8) "basic" format.

```
local1.*    /var/log/roundcube/roundcube.log
```

Restart syslogd and test your configuration with logger(1).

```
$ logger -p local1.debug "roundcube syslog config test"
```

That message appearing in the log means your logging works. Now tell Roundcube to use syslogd.

```
$config['log_driver'] = syslog;
$config['syslog_facility'] = LOG_LOCAL1;
```

Test this by returning to the installer page and testing IMAP or SMTP. Debugging output should appear in the log file. Once you know Roundcube logging works, comment out the debug logging.

Last, disable the installer. You can delete the `installer` folder and all its contents, but that might make scheduled package integrity checks complain every time they run. Some packaging systems even restore altered files. Disable the installer in `config.inc.php`.

```
$config['enable_installer'] = false;
```

The browser session you've been working in will have a cache of the installer page and a valid session cookie, but new browser sessions won't be able to access it.

Point your web browser at the Roundcube directory. It will ask you for your username and password. The web interface resembles every other webmail interface. We will use Roundcube's ManageSieve feature to build server-side mail filters in the next chapter.

Roundcube has many more built-in features and add-on plugins, and could fill a book on its own.[39] They have a well-maintained wiki, a community forum, and an active bug tracker. If you need more features, look. They probably exist.

The Password Plugin

While you've configured the core of Roundcube, it's also a convenient place for users to change their passwords. Start by enabling the password plugin in `config.inc.php`. Roundcube ignores unenabled plugins.

Find the plugin in the subdirectory `plugins/password`. Copy the plugin's `config.inc.php.dist` file to `config.inc.php` and make all your changes to that file. Do not edit `config.inc.php.dist` unless you want to lose your changes at the next upgrade. The plugin includes support for several password backends, including LDAP. While you won't find explicitly labeled PostfixAdmin support, the SQL driver suffices.

First, set `password_driver` to use the SQL driver.

```
$config['password_driver'] = 'sql';
```

The plugin can evaluate the quality of new passwords by setting `password_minimum_score` on a range from 0 to 5. 0 allows people

---

39   A book written by someone else.

to change their password to *password*, while 5 requires extremely complex passwords. For common users, I set this to 1.

```
$config['password_minimum_score'] = 1;
```

Tell the plugin where to find the database using the password_db_dsn option. The database connection string should be identical to Roundcube's configured Data Source Name (DSN). This is a wholly different DSN than Delivery Status Notifications, and the Roundcube configuration wizard figured it out for you. Copy the value of Roundcube's db_dsnw setting into the plugin's password_db_dsn.

Use password_algorithm to tell the password plugin what hashing method our passwords use. We're using Blowfish.

```
$config['password_algorithm'] = 'blowfish-crypt';
```

Now the tricky part: set password_query to a database query that updates user passwords. The DSN lets the plugin connect to the correct database with the necessary privilege, but the query must include the database name anyway. A query to change a PostfixAdmin password looks like this.

```
update database.mailbox set password=password,
  modified=NOW() where username = user
```

The plugin offers the convenient %P macro for the new password and %u for the username, and the database name never changes. Our test database is named *slurry*. That gives us this config.inc.php setting.

```
$config['password_query'] = 'update slurry.mailbox
  set password=%P, modified=NOW() where username = %u';
```

The plugin is now ready. Watch the log for errors and test it.

Upgrading Roundcube

One final note before you deploy Roundcube. The package was simple to install. New versions are not quite as simple. Every new Roundcube release includes an UPGRADING document with specific instructions on how to seamlessly move your plugins and database to the newer release. Follow it meticulously. I can't provide details, because upgrades vary.

We can now look at server-side mail filtering.

Chapter 13: Filtering with Sieve

If you're running your own mail system you probably get a substantial amount of mail. Some clients filter for you. Thunderbird, for example, lets you define rules so that when you connect to the server, it rearranges new mail into folders. IMAP lets clients connect from any number of machines, however, and maintaining identical rules on your phone, tablet, and desktop is annoying. The best place to filter mail is when the Local Delivery Agent sends it into the Message Store.

Sieve is a server-side mail filtering language defined in RFC 5228 and documented at `http://sieve.info`. Sieve can sort received mailing list messages into their own folders, divert spam, send vacation replies, and more. Sieve is a powerful filtering language, and while not as complex as a full programming language it does require skill. You write Sieve rules and upload them to the mail system, which compiles and applies them. A separate protocol, ManageSieve, lets clients add, edit, and remove Sieve rules. ManageSieve clients might be integrated into mail clients or standalone. You can even use ManageSieve with `openssl s_client`. Sieve supports many complex features for specific use cases. We will focus on the common cases of sorting mail into folders based on headers and addresses.

Using Sieve requires installing a Sieve engine and integrating it with your Local Delivery Agent, enabling a ManageSieve server, and offering users a client. Dovecot supports Sieve and ManageSieve via Pigeonhole (`https://pigeonhole.dovecot.org/`). Roundcube includes a ManageSieve client. Once you have these, you can write Sieve rules.

Configuring Pigeonhole

Almost every Unix that has a Dovecot package also offers Pigeonhole. Once installed, configure Pigeonhole in `dovecot.conf`. Start by adding *sieve* to Dovecot's `protocols` list.

```
protocols = lmtp imap sieve
```

Now configure the Sieve protocol.

```
protocol sieve {
  managesieve_max_line_length = 65536
  managesieve_implementation_string = dovecot
    ssl = yes
}
```

The `managesieve_max_line_length` option tells Dovecot what limits to set on Sieve scripts. A user who writes a Sieve script with a single line longer than 65536 characters needs to take some time off to consider their poor life choices.

ManageSieve servers often support implementation-specific extensions. Tell ManageSieve clients that they're talking to Dovecot so they can use the correct extensions. Pigeonhole uses extensions for features like vacation replies and processing duplicates. You can investigate those once you have a functional basic system.

We're passing authentication strings around, so set `ssl` to `yes` to require STARTTLS

With the sieve protocol enabled, we can connect the ManageSieve service to the network. TCP port 4190 is the standard.

```
service managesieve-login {
  inet_listener sieve {
      port = 4190
  }
}
```

Now configure where Pigeonhole stores Sieve rules.

```
plugin {
  sieve = file:~/sieve;active=~/.dovecot.sieve
  sieve_default = /usr/local/etc/dovecot/sieve/default.sieve
  sieve_before = /usr/local/etc/dovecot/sieve/allusers.sieve
}
```

The `sieve` option tells Pigeonhole where to look for the text files containing the user's Sieve rules. The tilde (~) represents the user's home directory. If this file does not exist, the user is not using Sieve. This shows two values. The `~/sieve` setting means that all of the users' scripts are stored in their `sieve` directory. Of those rules, one script file is *active*. The file `~/.dovecot.sieve` is a symlink to the active script. Changing filter rules requires only changing a symlink. To disable the user's filtering rules, remove the symlink.

The `sieve_default` defines default Sieve rules. Pigeonhole uses the default rules only when the user has no personal Sieve rules.

The `sieve_before` option lets you set Sieve rules that Pigeonhole applies to all users before processing either the default or personal rules. This is where you would put spam and virus quarantine rules that apply to all users. We'll discuss that.

Finally, tell LMTP to use Sieve.

```
protocol lmtp {
  mail_plugins = sieve
}
```

Reload Dovecot. Verify that `dovecot` is listening on port 4190, and that log shows that sieve is enabled. You can now connect with a client.

ManageSieve Clients

The Sieve web site lists many ManageSieve clients for Unix, MacOS, and Windows. There's a client for Emacs, so you can manage your rules on any modern platform and most forgotten ones.[40] You can spend your free time exploring clients but for now, we'll use the Roundcube client. Log into your test account via Roundcube and go to Settings -> Filters. The *Actions* button will let you edit the default Roundcube filter, or add a new filter and edit it. Either way, you'll get a panel with a text editor. Write your rules in the text editor and save them. You can have multiple sets of rules, but only one can be active at a time. Use the *Action* button to enable or disable rule sets.

No matter which client you wind up using, the basics of Sieve rules apply.

---

40   Plan 9: a more elegant operating system, from a more civilized age.

Using Sieve

Sieve is a modular language for writing mail filtering rules. It supports simple if-then decision-making, header checks, and sorting mail into folders. It cannot access syscalls or run arbitrary commands, however, to make it safe to use on complicated email systems.

Rule sets are a key part of Sieve. You might have one set of rules for working hours and another for off hours. Only one rule set can be active at a time. Rule sets are kept in the user's `sieve` directory. Pigeonhole place all rule sets in files named after the rule set, with a `.sieve` extension. The currently active rules are identified by a `.dovecot.sieve` symlink in the user's home director.

Sieve is a compiled language. When Dovecot delivers a message to a user, it checks the user's home directory to see if `.dovecot.sieve` exists. If that file exists, it compares the file's modification date to the timestamp on the compiled rules file (`.dovecot.svbin`). If the text file is newer than the compiled rules, or if there are no compiled rules, Pigeonhole compiles the rules and uses them to sort the new mail. If there is no `.dovecot.sieve` file, Dovecot dumps all incoming mail into the user's inbox.

Do not edit Sieve rules files in place. Yes, you have shell access and could call up the file in a text editor. Experienced sysadmins save their work frequently. A half-edited rules file that doesn't compile will generate errors, but a half-edited rules file that's missing vital features is worse. Edit your rules in a client or a separate file, and swap the file into place. If you want to manage Sieve rules via the command line, say for automation, investigate doveadm-sieve(1).

Sieve Rulesets

Sieve rulesets have two parts: the capabilities statement and rules written to use those capabilities.

Sieve itself contains only basic logic. Everything a user might want to filter on is supported via *capabilities*. File a message into a folder? That's a capability. Create a new mailbox? Another capability. Your rules must start with a list of the capabilities your rules need. Capabilities are sometimes called *extensions*, although the word "extensions" is also used to describe new features added to the language. IANA maintains a central catalog of Sieve capabilities in their "Sieve Extensions" document (`https://www.iana.org/assignments/sieve-extensions/sieve-extensions.xhtml`). Here are some common capabilities, however.

envelope—test based on envelope information
fileinto—store messages in a mailbox other than Inbox
mailbox—test mailbox existence, and create nonexistent mailboxes
reject—bounce message back to sender

Here I declare that this ruleset uses the `fileinto` and `mailbox` capabilities.

```
require ["fileinto", "mailbox"];
```

If you write rules that use capabilities not listed in the `require` statement, those rules will not compile.

After this, we have actual rules. Sieve lets you build complicated rules that handle innumerable edge cases, but most of us will never use them. Pigeonhole includes several example Sieve rule sets, and you should review them if interested. The Sieve web site includes the language's formal definition. I will discuss common uses.

Mailing Lists

My most common use for server-side filtering is mailing lists. I subscribe to quite a few lists, and I want each mailing list sorted into its own folder. Best practice calls for mailing lists to add a `List-Id` header to every message they send, identifying the list. You can use this header to sort those messages into a folder.

```
if header :contains "List-Id" "freebsd-arch.freebsd.org"
{
  fileinto :create "arch";
}
```

The first line declares that we're looking at the message headers. The `:contains` gives the kind of test we're performing. All Sieve tests and options begin with a colon. We're testing the header `List-Id` for the content `freebsd-arch.freebsd.org`. These checks are case-insensitive. If this header exists and contains that string, the test is successful and Sieve carries out the instructions in the braces.

The second line, inside the braces, uses the `fileinto` capability to send the message to the folder *arch*. The `:create` option tells Sieve to create the folder if it does not exist.

Colons are reserved for Sieve instructions. Never include the colon in header names. A test for the header `List-Id:` will always fail, because of the colon.

You might encounter documentation that says all folders should be children of the inbox, like as *INBOX.arch*. That's part of Cyrus IMAP, and not relevant to Dovecot.

Addresses

You might want to put email from certain people in their own folders. Perhaps you want all the mail from your mom to go into a folder. Or, maybe there's some annoying twit you never want to hear from.

```
if address :is "from" "mwl@mwl.io" {
  fileinto :create "Trash";
}
```

The `address` keyword declares we're inspecting addresses. We want an exact match, so we use `:is`. This rule tests the email's `from` against `mwl@mwl.io`. If the test is successful—that is, if they match—we use `fileinto` to send the message to the *Trash* folder.[41]

Sieve supports more fine-grained address matching with the `:localpart`, `:domain`, and `:all` arguments. The `:localpart` argument matches everything to the left of the @ sign, while `:domain` matches everything on the right. Suppose you figure out that I have a whole bunch of domains, but I use the username `mwl` at all of them.

```
if address :is :localpart "from" "mwl" {
  fileinto "Trash";
}
```

Meanwhile, Amazon keeps sending you mail. You need the receipts and order confirmations, but don't need them cluttering your inbox. They use many different email addresses, so you want to fling everything from that domain into its own folder.

```
if address :is :domain "from" "amazon.com" {
  fileinto :create "Bezos";
}
```

You can also turn this around. Suppose you have email from another account forwarded to your main account. You want those emails to go into their own folder. Test the *to* domain rather than the *from*.

```
if address :is :domain "to" "immortalclay.com" {
  fileinto :create "marketing";
}
```

By comparing sender and recipient addresses as well as header fields, you can sort email anywhere you like.

---

41   You're better off refusing my mail in Postfix rather than user-by-user.

Subject

Certain topics make the most well-intentioned person consider joining the bad guys. You might want to filter messages based on subject. Do this with a rule similar to the one for mailing lists, but test the Subject header instead. Here I test for any subject field containing "nagios."

```
if header :contains "subject" "nagios"
{
  fileinto :create "mewling";
}
```

I can't automatically delete these messages, because management occasionally asks if I'm getting them. I must manually enter the folder and delete them all.

Rejecting

Suppose sending someone's email into the Trash isn't enough. You want them to *know* that you're rejecting them. Sieve has a `reject` capability. Match the address, then use the `reject` action with a quoted message.

```
require ["reject"];
if address :is "from" "mwl@mwl.io" {
  reject "I told you to go away";
}
```

This generates a new email with your message, attaches the original message, and sends it back to the sender. The new mail comes from your domain's `postmaster@` account, not your individual account, so it looks official.

Never use `reject` for spam. Sieve filtering happens after Postfix has accepted the mail. The source address of most spam is either forged to a nonexistent account, forged to a real account the spammer doesn't own, or a throwaway account. If your rules `reject` a thousand spams, that's a thousand messages your MTA sends. If the spam source is forged, Postfix will spend days trying to deliver all those undeliverable messages. If the spam source is a disposable account, your server will dump those thousand messages on another provider. If the spam source is a forged real account, you're dumping the mail on an innocent bystander. The first makes more work for the sysadmin. The last two increase the chances of a block list maintainer adding your server to their list.

Rejecting Harder

You're sure you don't want that message? You don't even want it in the trash? Use `discard` instead of `fileinto`.

```
if address :is "from" "mwl@immortalclay.com" {
  discard;
}
```

Be sure. The user will get no notice of this message.

Implicit Keep

Sieve assumes that you want your email. Every ruleset ends with an *implicit keep*. If Sieve has not otherwise filtered, folded, or mangled an email, it goes into the user's inbox.

If mail you think should be filtered starts appearing in your inbox, the sender changed something in how they send mail.

Debugging and Testing Rules

If you set `mail_debug` to *yes* in *dovecot.conf*, Pigeonhole will log where it sends messages. That's great for the sysadmin, but average users will learn that their Sieve rules broke when messages go to their inbox rather than a folder. If a Sieve script won't compile, Pigeonhole logs "Failed to compile script" messages that include the location of the user's Sieve debug log. Look at that log for Sieve compiler errors.

```
test: line 11: error: unexpected character(s)
  starting with '.'.
```

As you can see, Sieve adheres to the time-honored compiler tradition of not telling you anything helpful. All this truly says is that you goofed on or before line 11.

The best way to debug Sieve rules is before installing them on the server. You can find online Sieve rule validators. The libsieve-php project includes a Sieve validator you can install on your own web site. You can use the Sieve compiler sievec(1) at the command line, however.

 # sievec test.sieve

This will create either a *test.svbin* binary, or a compiler error. If you want an explicit declaration that the compilation worked, add the -D flag for debugging output.

 # sievec -D test.sieve
```
sievec(mwlucas): Debug: sieve:
 Pigeonhole version 0.5.21 (f6cd4b8e) initializing
…
sievec(mwlucas): Debug: sieve:
 Script `test' from /usr/home/mwlucas/test.sieve
 successfully compiled
```

Compiling Sieve rules is only half the problem. How do you know the rules work the way you want? Use sieve-test(1). The Maildir format saves all messages as separate files. Copy a message you want to filter to a convenient place. Copy your Sieve ruleset there also. As an unprivileged user, run:

$ sieve-test *ruleset message*

The sieve-test command compiles the ruleset and runs the message through the filter. Here I try my test rules to see where Sieve would put a message originally sent to one of my mailing lists.

```
$ sieve-test testrules.sieve testmails/freebsd-arch
...
Performed actions:

 * store message in folder: f-arch

Implicit keep:

 (none)

sieve-test(mwlucas): Info: final result: success
```

This command is for debugging, so it prints a few lines of internal details. The "Performed Actions" line shows what the filter does with the message. This message would be routed into the *f-arch* folder. The "Implicit Keep" section tells us if the message went to the user's inbox.

I store one copy of each kind of message I want to filter in a folder. Whenever I need to change my Sieve rules, I edit the local copy and test the changes against those messages. If it works, I upload the modified ruleset via ManageSieve.

Server-Wide Rules

Sometimes you want to apply filtering rules to all your users. You might want to send certain mail to the spam folder, or route mail from the CEO into the trash. Use the `sieve_before` option in the plugin section of `dovecot.conf` to set a script that affects everyone. Dovecot must have permission to write the compiled rules to the filter directory.

```
plugin {
  sieve = file:~/sieve;active=~/.dovecot.sieve
  sieve_default = /usr/local/etc/dovecot/sieve/default.sieve
  sieve_before = /usr/local/etc/dovecot/sieve/allusers.sieve
}
```

If you want to run multiple filters, add ordering to the `sieve_before` option.

```
plugin {
  …
  sieve_before1 = /usr/local/etc/dovecot/sieve/viruses.sieve
  sieve_before2 = /usr/local/etc/dovecot/sieve/spam.sieve
  sieve_before3 = /usr/local/etc/dovecot/sieve/hr.sieve

}
```

You could also set `sieve_before` to a directory. Files in that directory ending in `.sieve` will be complied and executed in name order.

Dovecot also supports a `sieve_after` option. Filters in `sieve_after` run after the user's scripts, and only affect messages that the user's filters send to their inbox via implicit keep. You can have multiple `sieve_after` filters or use a directory, exactly like `sieve_before`.

Just like Dovecot, Pigeonhole has many more features than what's discussed here. The sysadmin can create a collection of Sieve scripts for their user to include in their own rules. Users can set up rules to handle automated responses and vacation messages. You can add those as you wish.

Let's go on to spam detection.

Chapter 14: Managing Rspamd

We installed a basic rspamd configuration in Chapter 7, then used it for SPF and DKIM validation.

Spam and Sieve

The `X-Spam` header gives us an easy target for filtering. This is a prime use for a `sieve_before` rule as discussed at the end of Chapter 12, letting you apply a filter before anyone's personal filters have to kick in.

Add a new Sieve filter in *dovecot.conf*.

```
plugin {
  sieve = file:~/sieve;active=~/.dovecot.sieve
  sieve_before = /etc/dovecot/sieve/spam.sieve
}
```

Now all we need is a Sieve rule that searches for that header.

```
require ["fileinto", "mailbox"];

if header :contains "X-Spam" "Yes" {
  fileinto :create "spam";
}
```

Be sure to specify `:create`, so if a user deletes their spam folder Dovecot will recreate it.

Dovecot and Sieve will now file everything with the `X-Spam` header set to "yes" in the spam folder. By adjusting the `add_header` action threshold in */etc/rspamd/local.d/actions.conf*, you can increase or decrease sensitivity.

Allow Listing

We all have legitimate correspondents with terrible mail systems. One of my business partners has an MTA that envies the technological sophistication of the primordial Novell Netware mail gateway. I have no idea how anyone else accepts their messages, but I must. Rspamd has an allow listing system that lets you reweight messages from select correspondents. Rspamd still tests on messages from listed domains, but the allow list assigns an additional weight for those messages. The trick is to assign weights that allow the message to overcome the symbols they normally carry, while leaving room to detect forged messages.

The allow list works on checks of SPF, DKIM, and/or DMARC. Anyone sending mail to the wider internet today must have at least one of these. Check the headers of a message to see what they provide, and double-check DNS to be sure it's still present.

The allow list rules in */etc/rspamd/modules.d/whitelist.conf* define symbols for valid and invalid SPF, DKIM, DKIM with SPF, and DMARC. Let's consider the DMARC list.

```
"WHITELIST_DMARC" = {
  valid_dmarc = true;
      domains = [
          "https://maps.rspamd.com/rspamd/dmarc_whitelist_new.inc.zst",
          "$LOCAL_CONFDIR/local.d/maps.d/dmarc_whitelist.inc.local",
          "${DBDIR}/dmarc_whitelist.inc.local",
          "fallback+file://${CONFDIR}/maps.d/dmarc_whitelist.inc"
      ];
  score = -7.0;
  inverse_symbol = "BLACKLIST_DMARC";
```

This rule requires valid DMARC, and applies to a map of enumerated domains. Remember, a map aggregates multiple data sources into a single list. This map pulls a current list from the rspamd.com web site, a local file, and the web server's data directory. The last map entry is a fallback list. Messages that come from these domains and have valid DMARC have a weight of -7. Messages from these domains that fail DMARC validation are assigned the symbol BLACKLIST_DMARC. A check of `/etc/rspamd/scores.d/whitelist_group.conf` shows that symbol has a weight of 6.

The map contains a list of domains that have been verified to have solid DMARC policies. Email from these domains should always have valid DMARC. Looking at the fallback list reveals financial institutions, social media companies, and ecommerce firms. This allow list declares that messages from these entities can be trusted if the message's DMARC validates.

The net effect is that messages that are actually from these big banks get low scores and should pass through rspamd unscathed, even if their MTA is otherwise uncivil. Messages that pretend to be from your bank, or any other bank that's on the list, are heavily weighted and should sink like bricks.

You almost certainly have organizations you want to put on the allow list that do not appear on the default list. Take a look at the messages those organizations send you. Do they have valid SPF and/or DKIM? Each of those symbols has their own maps with local allow lists. If you like the domain's DMARC policy, you could add them to that list.

My tiny credit union has a solid DMARC policy, so I want to add them to the allow list. As per the map above, I create `/etc/rspamd/local.d/maps.d/dmarc_whitelist.inc.local` and list their domain name on its own line.

My business partner's horrid MTA only uses SPF. I check the WHITELIST_SPF definition and add its domain to `dmarc_whitelist.inc.local`.

Overriding Symbol Scores

Symbol scores are assigned in `/etc/rspamd/scores.d`. Each symbol is in a group, and each group has its own file. Find your symbol. If your symbol isn't in a file, search the web interface for the symbol. You'll see the group. Check the scores directory for a file named after that group, and customize it with a `local.d` entry.

I often receive spam addressed to many recipients. Earlier I encountered the RCPT_COUNT_ONE symbol, which led me to the symbol RCPT_COUNT_GT_50 for messages addressed to more than fifty recipients. This symbol has a value of zero. I get almost no messages with over fifty recipients, and almost all of those are spam. I want to give it a weight of 2, saying this characteristic is quite spammy. The web interface says that this symbol is in the "headers" group. Checking `/etc/rspamd/scores.d` reveals the file `headers_group.conf` full of entries like this, assigning a weight and a description.

```
symbols = {
  "FORGED_SENDER" {
     weight = 0.3;
     description = "Sender is forged (different From:
        header and smtp MAIL FROM: addresses)";
  }
  …
```

There is no entry for RCPT_COUNT_GT_50, so we must create one in a local file. Create `/etc/rspamd/local.d/headers_group.conf` with this text.

```
symbols = {
  "RCPT_COUNT_GT_50" {
     weight = 2;
     description = "50+ recipients, custom weight";
  }
}
```

I assign the weight of 2, and add a description saying that this is a custom weight because, again, I will need the reminder.

Reload rspamd to make the change take effect.

Math versus Spam

Spam is not math, but spam follows patterns and patterns are math. Your ham also follows patterns. Spammers change their patterns to try to evade detection. Ham also changes, but more slowly. The first type of analysis applied to spam detection was Bayesian statistics, but other sorts of statistical analysis have joined it. Mathematical spam detection is often called Bayesian no matter what algorithms are used, but rspamd calls the entire class of techniques *statistics*. Rspamd runs a bunch of statistics on each message and comes up with the odds that the message is spam, then converts those odds into a weight.

Before you can use statistics, you must analyze a bunch of known ham and known spam. This process is often called *learning*, although there's no actual thought or education involved. Rspamd calculates the characteristics and patterns of your ham and spam, and two hundred pieces of each is enough to start.

No statistics are perfect. They require constant updating as patterns change. They're useful enough that statistics support is part of rspamd's core, rather than in a module. Rspamd's statistics support starts with training the system, then updating that teaching.

Use rspamc(1) to analyze your ham and spam. Here I've gone to my main mail directory, where each IMAP folder is a directory. In Dovecot, the folder's `cur` subdirectory contains messages that have been read, while `new` holds unopened messages. I don't always open my spam, so let's learn from both. Use the `learn_spam` argument.

```
# rspamc learn_spam .spam/new/
# rspamc learn_spam .spam/cur/
```

Check that it accepted those messages with rspamc's `stat` option. You can read it all, or grep out the statistics information.

```
$ rspamc stat | grep Statfile
Statfile: BAYES_SPAM type: redis; length: 0; free
blocks: 0; total blocks: 0; free: 0.00%; learned: 227;
   users: 1; languages: 0
Statfile: BAYES_HAM type: redis; length: 0;
   free blocks: 0; total blocks: 0; free: 0.00%;
   learned: 0; users: 0; languages: 0
```

It processed my 227 spam messages. It knows nothing of ham, however. Feed it ham from your inbox and a couple select folders.

```
# rspamc learn_ham cur/
# rspamc learn_ham .bobafett/cur/
# rspamc learn_ham .auntberu/cur/
```

This provided roughly the same amount of ham as I had spam. Rspamd immediately starts using that information. Checking the headers of the next message I receive shows:

```
...
BAYES_HAM(-0.03)[55.20%];
...
```

Statistical analysis declares this message is 55.2% likely to be ham. It was an automated message from my web server. The next message shows more decisiveness.

```
...
BAYES_HAM(-3.00)[99.99%];
...
```

As you add more spam and ham to the statistical training data, rspamd will grow more accurate. You don't want return to the command line to process individual messages, however. The learning process should happen transparently, through your email client.

Ongoing Spam Training

When spam makes it to your inbox or legit messages fall into your spam folder, check the symbols. Perhaps you need to weight something more heavily. Perhaps someone broke their DMARC, DKIM, or SPF. No amount of Bayesian analysis will outweigh forged addresses and bad SMTP stacks.

But maybe the statistical analysis is wrong and needs correcting. Adding more spam won't fine-tune a Bayesian classifier. Most of it will be stuff it's already seen. Only correcting false positives and false negatives improves the model. When a spam message winds up in your inbox, saving it to the spam folder should tell rspamd to learn from the message. When a legitimate message is mistakenly filed as spam, moving it to another folder should trigger rspamd studying it as ham. You update rspamd's understanding of spam by saving messages in different folders. Arrange this through Pigeonhole's IMAPsieve and extprograms modules.

IMAPSieve and Extprograms

Sieve was designed for use during delivery from the MTA, and is normally called by LMTP or the LDA. IMAP is separate from both. Pigeonhole's *IMAPsieve* plugin adds Sieve to IMAP. We'll add a rule that says "learn messages moved to the spam folder as spam" and another that says "learn messages moved out of the spam folder as ham."

The *extprograms* extension lets Sieve scripts call external programs. The module has three sub-privileges: vnd.dovecot.pipe, vnd.dovecot.filter, and vnd.dovecot.execute. Each must be separately enabled.

These extensions default to only working for scripts written by the system administrator. Users can use their own scripts only if you specifically configure that access. History has repeatedly demonstrated that badly written shell scripts that process arbitrary email inflict suffering, so we won't cover that configuration.

Enabling Sieve Modules

We have not previously needed to configure the IMAP protocol itself—we've told the IMAP daemon what port to listen on, but not the innards of the protocol. Create a new dovecot.conf section for the IMAP protocol and enable imap_sieve with the `mail_plugins` option. This enables the IMAPSieve extensions within the IMAP protocol.

```
protocol imap {
  mail_plugins = imap_sieve
}
```

You must also inform Sieve that it'll be supporting IMAPSieve. Do so in the *dovecot.conf* plugin section, right next to the sieve, sieve_before, and sieve_after settings. Also use the sieve_global_extensions option to enable the sieve_extprograms module's vnd.dovecot.pipe extension.

```
plugin {
  …
  sieve_plugins = sieve_imapsieve sieve_extprograms
  sieve_global_extensions = +vnd.dovecot.pipe
  sieve_pipe_bin_dir = /etc/dovecot/bin
}
```

If you want to allow regular users to execute shell scripts by moving messages from one IMAP folder to another you could use sieve_extensions instead, but that's not generally recommended.

Here, I tell dovecot that if an IMAPSieve script uses vnd.dovecot.pipe, it should look for external commands in */etc/dovecot/bin*. My systems all have defined locations for storing add-on scripts, but I don't want to give Sieve access to the system-wide */usr/local/bin* or */usr/local/scripts*. This directory certainly shouldn't be in your $PATH. Filters called by receiving or filing arbitrary emails should be able to access a minuscule set of commands.

Reload Dovecot to make these modules available to sievec(1).

Training Scripts

You need shell scripts to teach rspamd about new spam and ham, and Sieve filters to steer refiled messages to those scripts. Let's start with the rspamd scripts. Create the directory */etc/dovecot/bin* to store the scripts. Here's a spam learning script, rspamd-learn-spam.sh.

```
#!/bin/sh
exec /usr/local/bin/rspamc learn_spam
```

This accepts a spam message on standard input, and tells rspamd to learn it. Make the script executable. Test it by saving a spam message to a file and feeding it to the script.

```
# cat /tmp/spam1 | ./rspamd-learn-spam.sh
Results for file: stdin (0.0345 seconds)
success = true;
filename = "stdin";
scan_time = 0.034474;
```

You might get a warning that the message has already been learned. That's fine; your script called rspamc. Once that works, create a similar rspamd-learn-ham.sh.

```
#!/bin/sh
exec /usr/local/bin/rspamc learn_ham
```

Test it with a legitimate message. Rspamd might also reject learning from this message, but its output confirms that it saw the message.

We need a directory for IMAPSieve scripts. Where most Sieve scripts are compiled by **dovecot**, these scripts will be compiled by the IMAP user, **vmail**. The **vmail** user must have permission to write the compiled files. I'm using */vhosts/sieve*, owned by **vmail**. I make the actual script files owned by **root**: **vmail** because sieve should compile them, not alter them. Here's *learn-spam.sieve*.

```
require ["vnd.dovecot.pipe", "copy", "imapsieve"];
pipe :copy "rspamd-learn-spam.sh";
```

This filter is built on the vnd.dovecot.pipe extension, the copy feature, and imapsieve. It accepts input from a pipe, and sends that input to the script rspamd-learn-spam.sh. Compile the filter.

```
# sievec learn-spam.sieve
```

If you get a compilation error, dovecot is not configured to support all the modules and extensions. If it compiles, you can create the ham-learning filter. It is exactly the same as the spam-learning filter, except it calls the script to learn new ham.

```
require ["vnd.dovecot.pipe", "copy", "imapsieve"];
pipe :copy "rspamd-learn-ham.sh";
```

The script must be executable by the **vmail** user.

Do learn-spam.sh and learn-ham.sh need to be scripts? No, you could insert commands directly in the configuration. When things go wrong, however, I often need debugging or logger(1) statements. That's easier to do in scripts.

Testing Ongoing Learning

We must verify that messages moved to the spam folder trigger rspamd's analysis and learning. Rspamd will learn each type of message exactly once. Many spam messages are sufficiently similar that rspamd can't learn anything more from them. When a user triggers learning by moving messages to the spam folder, we need to verify that the configuration worked and learning happened. We need some spam to move to the spam folder, and some ham to move out of the spam folder.

We'll need to save spam to the spam folder to trigger the search. You already have a bunch of spam, but it's probably in your spam folder. You can't move spam from your spam into your spam; that doesn't work. Move all your spam to another folder with a name like "sample spam." You can now move those messages one at a time to see if the IMAPSieve script catches, if the rspamc command fires, and if the redis database grows.

Now that your spam folder is empty, copy some legitimate mail into it. We'll use that to correct misfiled ham.

Finally, wipe rspamd's knowledge of your spam. Connect to the Bayes redis instance and erase it with flushall.

```
Redis bayes.sock> flushall
OK
```

Verify that rspamd has forgotten everything with rspamc stat. The statistics are only updated every sixty seconds, so you might need to wait for them to update.

```
$ rspamc stat | grep BAYES
Statfile: BAYES_SPAM type: redis; length: 0; free
blocks: 0; total blocks: 0; free: 0.00%; learned: 0;
  users: 0; languages: 0
Statfile: BAYES_HAM type: redis; length: 0;
  free blocks: 0; total blocks: 0; free: 0.00%;
  learned: 0; users: 0; languages: 0
```

The statistical engine knows nothing, and will learn from anything we send it.

Now tell Dovecot to send refiled messages to our filters.

Configuring IMAPSieve

IMAPSieve rules go in the `plugin` section of *dovecot.conf*, right by the rest of the sieve configuration. Here's our first set of rules.

```
imapsieve_mailbox1_name = spam
imapsieve_mailbox1_causes = COPY
imapsieve_mailbox1_before = file:/vhosts/sieve/learn-spam.sieve
```

The leading `imapsieve` labels this an IMAPSieve rule. The term `mailbox1` marks a single rule. Subsequent rules will be labeled `mailbox2`, `mailbox3`, and so on. Everything beginning with `imapsieve_mailbox1` is a single set of rules.

The `name` qualifier gives the destination folder. We're looking at the `spam` folder.

An IMAP session has environment variables that a script can pull in. Per the standard, IMAPSieve sessions must set `$imap.cause` to one of FLAG, APPEND, or COPY. We're copying a message to the folder, so use `imapsieve_mailbox1_causes` to set it to COPY. An IMAPSieve script could read this variable—and many more—from the environment.

Finally, `imapsieve_mailbox1_before` identifies the IMAPSieve filter that should be run before any IMAPSieve user scripts. Point this at your spam-learning Sieve filter.

The "learn misfiled ham is spam" script is similar.

```
imapsieve_mailbox2_name = *
imapsieve_mailbox2_from = spam
imapsieve_mailbox2_causes = COPY
imapsieve_mailbox2_before = file:/vhosts/sieve/learn-ham.sieve
```

The name qualifier is a wildcard. This rule applies if you're saving messages to any folder. The `from` is a new qualifier, declaring that this rule only applies if you're moving messages from the spam folder. The rest of the rule calls the ham-learning filter.

You should be ready. Let's test it.

Testing IMAPSieve with Rspamd

Verify that you have test spam saved in a place that isn't your spam folder, and that your spam folder contains legitimate email. Erase rspamd's Bayes redis and verify with `rspamc stat` that rspamd has forgotten all its training. Enable `mail_debug` in *dovecot.conf* so that any errors appear.

In one terminal window, run `tail -f` on the mail log. In another, `tail -f` the rspamd log. Any errors or activity will appear in one of these.

Go to your mail client. Move one of your non-spam messages from the spam folder to another folder. If Dovecot is misconfigured or your sieve filter is buggy or your ham-learning shell script crashes, you'll get errors in the mail log. If Dovecot successfully hands the message to rspamd, the rspamd log will show entries about the Bayes classifier. If you wait a moment, `rspamc stat` should show that it learned about some ham.

Go to your folder of training spam and save one of it to the spam folder. Watch the logs. If rspamd logs the analysis, you now have corrective training. If it doesn't, read the error messages and fix the problems.

Rspamd Greylisting

Rspamd greylists by default, but in a slightly different way than postscreen. Chapter 8 discusses the advantages and disadvantages of greylisting. Greylisting might not be the top cause of arguments between mail operators, but it's certainly in the top five. You don't have to participate in those arguments, but you do need to decide where you stand.

If you don't want to greylist, disable the module in `/etc/rspamd/local.d/greylist.conf`.

You could greylist in both postscreen and rspamd, or in only one. The two programs do not share information so unknown MTAs trying to send you a message that happens to resemble spam would be delayed once by postscreen, once by rspamd, and finally get through on the third attempt. Postscreen's intrusive protocol checks are far lighter than rspamd analysis, but ignore message contents. Which should you use? That depends entirely upon the spam you receive and how you feel about delays.

Rspamd automatically greylists messages if their spam score equals or exceeds the `greylist` action. Messages with a lower spam score are not delayed. Rspamd will not accept messages from an unknown MTA sending a message that resembles spam for five minutes. If that MTA tries again after the five minutes, rspamd accepts the message and adds the host to the allow list. Allow list entries expire after one day, forcing the sending MTA to reverify its spammy messages.

Rspamd greylists based on network blocks, as dictated by the module's `ip4_mask` and `ip6_mask` settings. Redelivery attempts from organizations like Gmail will come from a different address but often in the same network, so rspamd considers a second attempt from any host in the same /64 IPv6 network or /19 IPv4 network adequate.

Postscreen greylisting is based on adherence to the SMTP protocol. It makes sense to allow list the Email Empire's MTAs; SMTP protocol checks will never trigger on spam from Microsoft. While the big email networks send a lot of spam, they also send many legitimate messages.

Do you want to delay those messages because of one suspicious message? Maybe. That's your choice.

Tell rspamd where to find your allow list with the `whitelisted_ip` option. We created an allow list for large providers in Chapter 8, and it works just as well for rspamd.

```
whitelisted_ip = /etc/postfix/postscreen_spf_allowlist.cidr
```

You can control how soon the greylisting module will accept mail from a network with the `timeout` setting, and how long it retains those entries with the `expire` setting. Increasing the time before you'll accept the message gives DNSBL contributors time to identify a spam source and add it to their feed. Here I set those to ten minutes and one week, respectively.

```
expire = 1w;
timeout = 10m;
```

If you want to be kind to MTA operators who have to troubleshoot messages, you might include a meaningful human-readable message with the delay notice, rather than the default "Try again later." Set custom text with `message`. The `report_time` option tells rspamd to add the amount of time remaining to that message.

```
message = "Greylisting suspicious message; try again in ";
report_time=yes;
```

With this, you're ready to start increasing rspamd's sensitivity.

Rspamd Slow Rollout

We first set up rspamd in a watch-only mode, using impossibly high `action` scores. Now that it's computing scores and doing statistical analysis, you can adjust the sensitivity.

Start by examining the `X-Spamd-Result` header on both the legitimate messages you receive and spam you get. Is there a trend in point values? Is there an obvious numerical score where you can declare "everything over this is spam, everything below it is ham?" If so, try that. If not, make your best guess. Error on the high side. In */etc/rspamd/local.d/actions.conf*, set `add_header` to that value.

```
add_header = 8
```

Rspamd will start adding the x-Spam: Yes header to messages it finds suspicious.

Add a global Sieve rule to file messages containing that header in the spam folder. Here's an */etc/dovecot/sieve/spam.sieve*.

```
require ["fileinto", "mailbox"];

if header :contains "X-Spam" "Yes" {
 fileinto :create "spam";
 }
```

Tell Dovecot to apply that filter before any other filters with a *dovecot.conf* entry like this.

```
sieve_before = /etc/dovecot/sieve/spam.sieve
```

Wait for a day or two, and see which messages go to the spam folder, and which go to your inbox. If your email address is brand new, your slow start will be extremely slow. Adjust the add_header threshold until you're comfortable with what gets routed where and you only need occasionally retrain the statistics engine.

Also consider the scores of what's in your spam folder. Is there a score where you're comfortable saying "anything above this is absolutely spam and should never even reach the spam folder?" Set the reject action to that value. Again, error on the high side.

Messages with a score above the greylist value but below the reject value will be greylisted. Consider the messages with that score. Did it make sense to delay them? If so, keep greylisting. Do you want more aggressive greylisting? Lower greylist. If your address is busy, you'll settle on suitable values within a few days. If not, don't worry. Send some messages out into the world and the spammers will find you soon enough.

Once you have rspamd tuned as you wish, it mostly runs itself. You can explore additional modules to cope with specific problems you have, or adjust settings as your email evolves. When the time comes to upgrade, carefully read the release notes. You might need to change settings to take advantage of new features or run scripts to update your stored data. Be warned, though, that every optional rspamd module you discover and enable will interact with all the modules already running. Keep your rspamd install as simple and as close to the defaults as possible.

Now let's consider some edges of email.

Chapter 15: Technical Edges

This book contains what everyone must know, not every topic everyone must know. Be careful when looking at ideas that aren't commonly used. Tools like challenge-response authentication for email might be convenient for you, but it creates backscatter and gets your system added to DNSBLs. Email is not a place to be clever. Email is a place to be boring.

Given that, here are a few common technical matters that many of you will need or find useful.

Slow Transport

Sometimes you legitimately need to contact two hundred people with mail run by Microsoft or Google, but suddenly spewing lots of email is a leading indicator of possible spambot infection. I mail people in the Email Empire every day, but one at a time. When I finish writing this book, however, I'll have to notify my magnificent sponsors via email. About a third of my sponsors have email addresses backed by Gmail or Microsoft. If I suddenly drop dozens of messages on both of them, the Empire will perk up and take a good hard look at my host. Avoiding notice is the best defense, so fly casual.

Postfix normally sends email as fast as the system supports it, but you can deliberately throttle how quickly it sends to select sites. Perhaps sending identical messages to thirty recipients simultaneously will awaken Gmail's spam guardians, but those same messages one at a time, several seconds or even a minute apart, will pass unnoticed. Email is not a real-time protocol, so those messages can wait a few minutes or even an hour. Postfix controls delivery speed through the queue manager and transport maps.

The *transport map* tells Postfix how to deliver messages to destinations. We haven't needed it so far because almost everybody's MTA speaks SMTP. If messages for a particular destination needed to go via UUCP, carrier pigeon, or smuggled inside a robot, you'd use a transport map to configure the destination and the delivery program.

The queue manager qmgr(8) is the service that handles all of Postfix's various queues, including the outbound message queue. It schedules delivery reattempts, and moves mail between queues. We'll define a transport that says "call the queue manager with super-restrictive settings," then build a map that attaches destination domains to that transport.

The queue manager is the most complicated part of Postfix. Its default settings evolved after many years of real-world testing and evaluation. Do not play with it lightly. Attempts to "optimize" it for "better performance," whatever that means, are almost always ill-advised.

A Trickle Transport

Define transports in `/etc/postfix/master.cf`. We discuss `master.cf` in Chapter 3. Here's an example of a deliberately throttled outgoing SMTP transport named *trickle*.

```
trickle    unix - - n - - smtp
  -o syslog_name=postfix-trickle
  -o trickle_destination_concurrency_limit=1
  -o trickle_destination_rate_delay=1m
  -o trickle_destination_recipient_limit=5
  -o trickle_destination_concurrency_failed_cohort_limit=10
  -o smtp_tls_security_level=encrypt
```

The `trickle` transport listens on a Unix socket. It is an unprivileged public service, and not chrooted. It runs as many processes as it needs and is not called on a schedule. Finally, it runs the smtp(8) command with the given options.

The first option, `syslog_name`, tells Postfix how to log messages from this transport. Using a separate name in the system log helps troubleshooting, and verifies that a particular message left our server via this transport.

The following options all have names beginning with `trickle` to attach the option to the transport. They are documented in the manual using the word "transport" rather than the transport name. For example, `trickle_destination_concurrency_limit` is documented as `transport_destination_concurrency_limit`.

The option `trickle_destination_concurrency_limit` sets how many deliveries Postfix will make in parallel to a single domain. I've set this to 1, so Postfix will attempt to deliver one message at a time to each domain. If I send a message to a bunch of folks at Gmail, and a bunch of folks at Microsoft, this setting breaks delivering those messages up into two separate streams.

With `trickle_destination_rate_delay`, I've set the amount of time Postfix will wait between attempts to deliver to a single domain. If you don't specify a time unit, seconds is the default. Here, I've set it to one minute. Combined with the concurrency limit, we'll mail one message at a time and wait one minute per message per domain.

The `trickle_destination_recipient_limit` sets the number of recipients at a domain in one transaction. Perhaps I've copied fifty people at Gmail on this message, but the recipient limit of 5 means the message will go at most to five recipients at once.

Control error tolerance with `trickle_destination_concurrency_failed_cohort_limit`. If Postfix has this many consecutive failed delivery attempts to a domain, it places the destination domain on a temporary "dead domain" list and will try later.

Finally, I'm also adding a requirement for TLS on this connection. Any company so large that they insist I slow down is certainly using TLS.

The Transport Table

Use the transport table, `/etc/postfix/transport`, to route domains to particular transports. It's a common key-value table, with the domain on the left and the transport on the right.

```
gmail.com        trickle:
```

Every time you update the transport table, update the hash file.

```
# postmap transport
```

Now that you have the trickle transport and a map that can tell Postfix which domains to trickle, add a `main.cf` entry to inform Postfix that they exist.

```
transport_maps = hash:/etc/postfix/transport
```

Restart Postfix and send a test mail to a trickled destination. The mail log should show a message using your custom log name.

```
Feb 12 15:42:20 mail postfix-trickle/smtp[98708]: 9A1AEA578: to=…
```

You have made your email system crawl enough that even the Email Empire will accept it. Congratulations. I guess.

Send-Only Servers

I've configured more than one application that is supposed to inform users whenever their account is updated, a deposit is made, or a new warrant is issued. These applications often use incomplete SMTP implementations that don't comply with current standards, don't understand TLS, or lack documentation and debugging alike. Rather than fight with such clients, it's often easier to install Postfix on the server and tell the application to send mail via the local host or sendmail(8).

You can either have such a server send everything directly to its destination, or have it relay though a smart host. Having the host send its own messages to the world is a simpler Postfix configuration, but requires editing your SPF and DKIM DNS records. Using a smart host is a slightly complicated Postfix configuration and adds a dependency on your MTA for outbound mail, but leaves your DNS unchanged. You have a selection of annoyances!

Both configurations share some `main.cf` settings, however. Send-only servers only accept connections from the local host, so bind Postfix to `localhost`.

```
inet_interfaces = 127.0.0.1
```

You will probably have a few local aliases to route messages to `root`, `www`, and so on to a person who's supposed to read them. Activate the aliases file.

```
alias_maps = hash:/etc/aliases
```

All other configuration depends on how you want the system to work.

Postfix as an SMTP Client

You can configure your MTA to accept messages from known hosts, sign them, and send them on to the world. This has the advantage of reducing the number of SPF records and DKIM keys you must support, but makes those hosts dependent on your MTA for sending mail.

On the MTA, verify that you have DKIM keys for all domains that will relay messages through your server. The client address must be listed in `mynetworks`. For rspamd, list those same source addresses in `local_addrs` in `/etc/rspamd/local.d/options.inc`. Restart rspamd and Postfix.

On the client, set `inet_interfaces` and `alias_maps` as per earlier this chapter. Also set `relayhost` to point at your MTA.

```
inet_interfaces = 127.0.0.1
alias_maps = hash:/etc/aliases
relayhost = mail.ratoperatedvehicle.com
```

Restart the client's Postfix.

You should now be able to send mail from the client machine to the world, relaying through the MTA. The MTA should add a DKIM signature. As usual, test it and see what happens. When you have a problem, read your logs carefully.

Direct Senders

Having your web server send mail directly to the Internet is easy to set up in Postfix but requires configuring a DKIM signer and editing your SPF and DKIM records. Here, I'm configuring my host `www.ratoperatedvehicle.com` to send mail directly to external MTAs. This host is not listed in an MX record, so replies will go to the actual MTA.

Senders need a DKIM signer. Rspamd is overkill for a host that doesn't receive mail. I recommend OpenDKIM. Almost every Unix has an OpenDKIM package. While it supports features like database backends and using a specific signing key for specific users, those features are also overkill for a tiny server. Investigate these features if you need to support hundreds of domains.

Configuring the OpenDKIM Milter

Install OpenDKIM from your operating system's packages. Some operating systems, like Debian, assume that you'll run OpenDKIM in milter mode and create an unprivileged user and socket directory for you. Others, like FreeBSD, assume you will not and leave you to create the socket directory and an unprivileged `opendkim` user and group to own them. Add `postfix` to the `opendkim` group so it can access the run directory and the socket.

Configure OpenDKIM in `/etc/mail/opendkim.conf`. Hash marks indicate comments, but you don't need equal signs to assign values to variables.

OpenDKIM uses the `mode` setting to determine if it's validating messages, or validating and signing. A `s` indicates signing, while `v` means validating.

```
Mode    s
```

The `Socket` setting tells OpenDKIM where to put the milter socket. OpenDKIM can listen to the network, but unless you have so much mail load that you need a dedicated host for DKIM processing, use a local socket. Similarly, `PidFile` tells the milter where to record its PID.

```
Socket local:/var/run/opendkim/opendkim.sock
PidFile /var/run/opendkim/opendkim.pid
```

Define the unprivileged user and the umask that user will use when starting the milter. A umask of 007 means that the user `opendkim` and others in the group can use the socket, but others cannot.

```
UserID   opendkim
UMask    007
```

Permissions with OpenDKIM can be tricky. Some OpenDKIM packages will not sign messages if the `opendkim` group has any users other than `opendkim`. The `postfix` user needs access to the milter socket, however. The solution is to make the socket directory owned by the user `root` and the group `postfix`. This way, the milter socket gets created with that ownership and Postfix can call the milter.

We must also tell OpenDKIM where to find the key and signing tables. The signing table has wildcards, so identify it as using regular expressions with the `refile` keyword.

```
KeyTable /etc/mail/opendkim.keytable
SigningTable    refile:/etc/mail/opendkim.signingtable
```

With this, you can configure the milter process to start on boot. Check your mail log to be sure it starts correctly and continues to run.

DKIM Key Generation

DKIM keys need the same handling as any public/private keys. The secret private key must be protected. While the public key will be shared with the world via DNS, you don't need to place the key file in a publicly accessible directory. Create a directory to own these keys, and make it inaccessible to anyone but `root` and `opendkim`. I'm using */var/db/opendkim*.

```
# install -d -m 0750 -o opendkim \
  -g opendkim /var/db/opendkim
```

For clarity, I recommend giving each domain you sign its own key directory. All directories must be owned by `opendkim`. If you have a permissions error on a new key, check if `root` owns a directory or file.

In the domain directory, use opendkim-genkey(8) to create a keypair. It needs two pieces of information, the selector and the domain name. Again, the selector is just a name. You can use any text string. The selector appears in the signature, so do *try* to avoid obscenities. Use a different selector for each domain. Use −d to give the domain name, and −s to give your chosen selector. The -b flag lets you set the number of bits. 2048 is the current recommendation. Here I'm adding −v for verbose output.

```
# opendkim-genkey -d ratoperatedvehicle.com \
  -s wookie -b 2048 -v
opendkim-genkey: generating private key
opendkim-genkey: private key written to wookie.private
opendkim-genkey: extracting public key
opendkim-genkey: DNS TXT record written to wookie.txt
```

You'll get two files, *wookie.txt* and *wookie.private*. The *wookie.private* file is the private key, while *wookie.txt* is the DKIM DNS record that includes the properly encoded public key.

If you don't have per-domain directories, give these files names that include the selector and the domain name. When the time comes to rotate DKIM keys, though, you'll wish you had used one directory per domain.

Create a key table and a signing table, exactly like we did with rspamd in Chapter 10. This connects your keys to domains. Now update your DKIM and SPF records and configure Postfix.

Configuring Postfix

Mail from this host should not show up as coming from the hostname. I want it to appear as the plain domain, so that replies to go my actual MTA listed in the MX record. In `main.cf`, set `myhostname` and `mydomain` to the desired domain. Also lock Postfix to the loopback interface and set up any aliases.

```
inet_interfaces = 127.0.0.1
alias_maps = hash:/etc/aliases
myhostname = ratoperatedvehicle.com
mydomain = ratoperatedvehicle.com
```

Local applications might submit mail via SMTP on port 25. They might submit mail via sendmail(8). Permit both paths by enabling the DKIM milter on both.

```
smtpd_milters=unix:/var/run/opendkim/opendkim.sock
non_smtpd_milters=unix:/var/run/opendkim/opendkim.sock
```

Run `tail -f /var/log/maillog` to watch for problems, and restart Postfix. It should restart cleanly, but many problems don't show up until Postfix attempts to process an email. Keep the log open and have your host send an email.

If OpenDKIM behaves in ways you don't expect, such as not signing messages for domains with keys, enable detailed logging with the milter's `-l` option. If that logging doesn't explain what you're seeing, enable the *Why?!* log with `-W`. This log explains what decisions OpenDKIM made, at the cost of much larger logs. You can also enable full logging with `opendkim.conf` options.

```
Syslog yes
LogResults yes
LogWhy yes
```

Is it better to have your servers send directly, or relay everything through your MTA? That depends on your environment, connectivity, and requirements. Make your best guess and live with it.[42]

---

42   Rule of System Administration #63: "If a decision appears to be correct, you just don't know how it's wrong. Yet."

323

Nolisting

Spambots all choose shortcuts. Postscreen catches many of them. Greylisting plays against others. A popular shortcut many spambots choose is to ignore backup MX records. These spambots attempt to contact the target's primary MX, but if that fails they proceed to the next victim.

Remember, the SMTP protocol originated when "high availability" meant buying expensive machines and "virtualization" meant hosting more than one domain on a machine. When hardware failed, it might remain offline for several days before the thirty-ton replacement got shipped in on an 18-wheel tractor-trailer from a couple states away. Legitimate MTAs *had* to communicate with the backup MX.

If most spammers ignore the backup MX, but legitimate senders respect it… what if you turn off the MTA listed in your primary MX? What if it doesn't even run an MTA? Legitimate senders fall back to the backup, and optimized spammers give up. That's the idea behind *nolisting*.

Consider these MX records.

```
ratoperatedvehicle.com  MX  10 www.ratoperatedvehicle.com.
ratoperatedvehicle.com  MX  20 mail.ratoperatedvehicle.com.
```

The primary MX is a web server, while the backup is an MTA? A human would look at these and say "wow, that's kind of weird, but okay." The trick here is, the web server does *not* accept connections on port 25. In case someone misconfigures an MTA on that host, it has a packet filter to block all connections on port 25. If the organization's monitoring system ever detects port 25 open, it alarms.

Spambots give up immediately. Legitimate MTAs immediately open a connection to the backup MX and deliver their message. It imposes less load on external MTAs than greylisting.

Nolisting requires technical competence. The primary MX must be on a real host with a real IP address that you control, and you must be able to *guarantee* that it will never accept SMTP connections. You can't list private addresses, `localhost`, or anything clever like that. Mismanagement means bouncing and losing email.

Nolisting is less controversial than greylisting, but only because it's less well known. Some people swear it's their best anti-spam defense. Others declare it useless. Will it work for you? That depends entirely on the types of spambots you attract.

Certificate Validation with MTA-STS

Server-to-server SMTP historically accepts self-signed certificates. Yes, everything the user sees has a nice pretty security seal, but everything the user can't see is built out of scrapyard detritus bound together with decaying tape and kindergarten paste.[43] Globally valid certificates are a growing minority, but still a minority. You cannot validate certificate authenticity without being told it is safe to do so. DANE is one way to make that declaration. *Mail Transfer Agent Strict Transport Security* (MTA-STS) is another.

Use MTA-STS to inform compliant external MTAs that your MTA has a globally valid X.509 certificate and that they should both verify its validity and use it. A companion protocol, *TLS Reporting* (TLS-RPT), lets external MTAs tell you about problems with your MTA's TLS and/or DANE configuration. MTA-STS requires a web server with either a valid certificate or valid DANE.

Why have both MTA-STS and DANE? DANE is a decades-old community effort that grew into a standard, and exists separately from certificate authorities. MTA-STS was created by Google, Microsoft, and Verizon, and requires certificate authorities. DANE is far more widespread, but MTA-STS raises the difficulty of man-in-the-middle attacks against the big carriers.

When an MTA that supports MTA-STS connects to domain's SMTP server, it first checks for an `_mta-sts` TXT record in the zone. If that record exists and is correctly formatted, the MTA then looks for a policy file at a standard location on the domain's web site. That policy file tells the MTA what sort of TLS enforcement the recipient

---

43   This is the guiding principle of Internet architecture.

domain expects. If the MTA can comply, it sends the message. If the MTA cannot comply, it uses TLS-RPT to inform the remote server that there's a problem. Performing a man-in-the-middle attack against a site protected by MTA-STS requires multiple fraudulent X.509 certificates, and intercepting traffic to multiple hosts using two different protocols.

Do you need MTA-STS today? That depends on your environment. If you're running email for yourself and a few friends or a small organization, perhaps not. If you want to transmit confidential information, you should use a protocol other than SMTP. You can't control what messages other folks will choose to send you, however, and if they're likely to send their medical history or passwords or even *I hid the stolen plans in the stubby droid*, perhaps you should use MTA-TLS to reduce the risk.

Providing MTA-STS

Setting up MTA-STS for your domain tells external MTAs to use proper DNS when mailing you. It requires setting up a channel for receiving reports, a policy file on a web site, and a DNS record. The DNS record is easiest, but once it's there, outsiders will start poking for the other two, so do it last.

If you have multiple domains using a single MTA, start with the domain that the MTA is in. All of my domains list `mail.ratoperatedvehicle.com` as their MX, so I'll do that first.

Receiving Reports via TLS-RPT

Just because your TLS looks fine to you, doesn't mean that it works for everyone else. MTA-STS is one of those rare cases where if the Email Empire sees a problem, they'll tell you about it. Before configuring MTA-STS, set up TLS-RPT so outsiders can report problems.

You can receive reports via HTTPS or email. People who run large email systems probably want to set up web-based reporting dashboards, but there's no freely available version of such. Use email. TLS failure reports are specifically permitted to ignore SMTP TLS errors, even if that means they're sent via 2000s-style slipshod TLS or even unencrypted. You can't fix problems you don't know about, after all. You might also use a reporting address outside your domain that presumably still has working TLS.

Declare the recipient address with a TLS-RPT DNS record.

```
_smtp._tls.domain  TXT  "v=TLSRPTv1;rua=reportaddress"
```

The `_smtp._tls` record is the standard for a TLS-RPT record within a domain. It's a text record. The value always starts with the version number; TLS-RPT records that start with anything except `v=TLSRPTv1` are ignored. After that, use `rua=` to give the email address errors should be reported to. Here's a complete record for my domain `mwl.io`.

```
_smtp._tls.mwl.io.  TXT  "v=TLSRPTv1;rua=mailto:mwl@mwl.io"
```

Reloading the zone tells the world where to inform me of my mistakes. Now let's write a policy.

The MTA-STS Policy

A policy file declares how you expect your MTA's current TLS configuration to work and how strictly that policy should be enforced. It must be available via HTTPS on the host `mta-sts` within your domain at `.well-known/mta-sts.txt`. If I want to activate MTA-STS on my domain `ratoperatedvehicle.com`, I must put the policy at `https://mta-sts.ratoperatedvehicle.com/.well-known/mta-sts.txt`. Poke at providers like Gmail and Microsoft to see their policies.

The most critical part of a policy is the *mode*, telling external MTAs how to use the policy. A mode of *testing* means that you don't yet trust your TLS configuration and that you want external MTAs to deliver messages from you but report any errors. The *enforce* mode means that you want external MTAs to refuse to deliver messages if they get a TLS error from your system and to report that error. The last mode, *none*, means that this policy is being abandoned—probably because you're rearchitecting everything. Every policy should start in testing mode, and only move to enforcing mode after a few problem-free weeks.

Simple ones require four fields: the version, the mode, a list of mx statements, and `max_age`.

The policy *version* is always `STSv1`, because no other version exists.

The *mode* is one of `enforce`, `testing`, or `none`. Always start with `testing`.

```
version: STSv1
mode: testing
```

List the MTAs this policy applies to. My domain `ratoperatedvehicle.com` has a primary incoming MTA of `mail.ratoperatedvehicle.com`, but suppose I also have a backup MTA at `mail.solveamurder.org` and possibly one in the `mwl.io` domain. List each separately in an mx statement. Use an asterisk to say "any host in this domain." A domain's mx list should include every entry in the zone's MX DNS records.

```
mx: mail.ratoperatedvehicle.com
mx: mail.solveamurder.org
mx: *.mwl.io
```

Finally, the `max_age` gives how long in seconds external MTAs should cache this policy. According to the standard, once your policy is `enforcing` external MTAs should be able to cache this policy for weeks. While you're testing, you might want to set it lower. Many sites reject times under 86000 seconds, however. The maximum `max_age` is one year, but a production policy of one to two weeks is considered appropriate.

```
max_age: 86400
```

MTA-STS cache policies as `max_age` dictates. Policies are discovered via DNS records, which are independently cached with their own expiration times. When troubleshooting, you must allow plenty of time for old DNS entries and old policies to expire from client caches.

Make this policy available at the standard URL, and you're ready to tell the world.

The MTA-STS DNS Record

Now that you have a reporting address and a policy, you can ask people to respect them. The MTA-STS record looks like this.

```
_mta-sts.domain   IN TXT  "v=STSv1; id=string;"
```

The `_mta-sts` record tells external MTAs that a policy exists at the standard-defined location and that they should respect it. The version, given by `v`, is always `STSv1` and must appear first. If anything else appears first, the record is rejected. Finally, the `id` is a text string that identifies this particular policy. When an external MTA caches a policy, it records the identifier. If the identifier doesn't change, the external MTA knows that the policy hasn't changed. When you change your policy, you must update the identifier. I assign my identifiers the same way I do the zone's serial number, by using the date and an increment. Here's the record for **ratoperatedvehicle.com**.

```
_mta-sts        TXT     "v=STSv1; id=2024022901;"
```

With this record live, external hosts that support MTA-STS will start paying better attention to your X.509 certificate.

Proving a negative is difficult. I strongly recommend using external TLS-RPT and MTA-STS checkers, like the one at **mxtoolbox.com**, to verify that your record and policy parse and are valid. Now let's see how you can check for MTA-STS and TLS-RPT on other hosts.

Reading Reports

Once your MTA-STS record is available in DNS, outside MTA-STS validators will query your policy. Every day, external MTA-STS validators that mail your system will send a summary report to the address in your TLS-RPT record. The message will have a subject declaring a Report Domain, a Submitter, and a Report-ID.

```
Subject: Report Domain: ratoperatedvehicle.com
Submitter: google.com
Report-ID: <2024.03.06T00.00.00Z+ratoperatedvehicle.com@google.com>
```

The report will be attached as a JSON file (possibly compressed) with a specified filename format.

source!policy-domain!start-time!end-time!unique-ID.json

The *source* is the domain sending the report. The *policy domain* is the domain the report covers. Start and end times are epochal dates. The optional *unique identifier* is an alphanumerical code used to differentiate reports. A report file from Microsoft about my domain mwl.io, for 4 March 2024, has a filename like *microsoft.com!mwl.io!1 709596800!1709683199!133542271517543541.json*. Microsoft uses long unique IDs, while Google uses something like 001.

Unfortunately, there is not yet an open-source report aggregator. You must use jq(1) or your favorite JSON transformer to make it easily readable.

```
$ jq . /tmp/microsoft.com\!mwl.io\!1709596800…
```

The report opens with basic information identifying the organization.

```
{
  "organization-name": "Microsoft Corporation",
  "date-range": {
    "start-datetime": "2024-03-05T00:00:00Z",
    "end-datetime": "2024-03-05T23:59:59Z"
  },
  "contact-info": "tlsrpt-noreply@microsoft.com",
  "report-id": "133542271517543541+mwl.io",
```

The report includes its cached version of your MTA-STS policy. This is important if you've changed your policy recently.

```
"policies": [
  {
  "policy": {
    "policy-type": "sts",
    "policy-string": [
    "version: STSv1",
    "mode: testing",
```

```
    "mx: mail.ratoperatedvehicle.com",
    "mx: www.mw1.io",
    "max_age: 86400"
  ],
  "policy-domain": "mw1.io"
},
```

Finally we have the summary of results.

```
"summary": {
  "total-successful-session-count": 6,
  "total-failure-session-count": 0
  }
```

In enforcing mode, failed sessions indicate messages that the sender would not transmit because it could not validate your X.509 certificate. That's bounced mail. In testing mode, those messages are delivered anyway. Taken as a whole, this means Microsoft is fine with me requesting that they validate my server's certificate.

On the same day, Google sent a report that included this tidbit.

```
...
"policy": {
  "policy-type": "no-policy-found",
  "policy-domain": "mw1.io"
...
```

A policy type of *no-policy-found*? Microsoft found my policy, various online validators found my policy, why not Google? The error is misleading. They found the policy, but rejected it. Figuring out why they rejected it required carefully reading their MTA-STS requirements page and comparing it to my policy.[44]

Once all your daily reports indicate regular routine validation of your MTA's X.509 certificate, you can change the policy to `enforcing`.

---

44   And this, folks, is how I learned that many sites reject policies with a maximum age under 86000 seconds.

Validating MTA-STS

MTA-STS and DANE occupy a similar space in the email ecosystem, and Postfix can only validate one of them for each destination. DANE is far more widespread, so the Postfix developers recommend validating DANE by default and only steering select destinations known to use MTA-STS to it.

Start by installing and testing postfix-mta-sts-resolver, then telling Postfix to use it.

postfix-mta-sts-resolver

The postfix-mta-sts-resolver package includes `mta-sts-daemon` which checks, validates, and caches MTA-STS policies. It's written in Python and configured in YAML. By default, the daemon listens on `localhost` port 8461. You can change that in the configuration file, `/etc/mta-sts-daemon.yml`. While you can tweak the configuration to support data in sqlite or Redis, the default configuration is perfectly fine for these small uses.

The included `mta-sts-query` utility asks `mta-sts-daemon` to retrieve the MTA-STS policy for a domain. Use it to check to see if a domain has configured not only a _mta-sts DNS record, but a parsable policy.

```
$ mta-sts-query solveamurder.org
(<STSFetchResult.NONE: 0>, None)
```

This domain has no MTA-STS, but as you might expect Microsoft's hosted Outlook does.

```
$ mta-sts-query outlook.com
(<STSFetchResult.VALID: 1>, ('20190225000000Z',
  {'mx': ['*.olc.protection.outlook.com'], 'version':
  'STSv1', 'mode': 'enforce', 'max_age': 604800}))
```

This is a Python object-dump. It's almost, but not quite, JSON. You can see that we got a list of valid MTAs that receive mail to this domain, and that the policy is being enforced. Postfix will do its own MX record lookup, but if an MTA isn't listed in the MTA-STS policy Postfix won't use it.

Now we can instruct Postfix to use MTA-STS rather than DANE.

Connect Postfix to MTA-STS Resolver

Postfix supports a *TLS policy map* to set how it should connect to external MTAs, through the option `smtp_tls_policy_map`. It's much like the transport policy map used to throttle outbound mail demonstrated earlier this chapter.

In `/etc/postfix/master.cf`, create a service that uses the resolver.

```
mta-sts     unix - - n - - smtp
 -o syslog_name=postfix-mta-sts
 -o smtp_tls_security_level=secure
 -o smtp_tls_policy_maps=socketmap:inet:127.0.0.1:8461:postfix
```

This transport is named *mta-sts*, and looks like our regular outbound SMTP service with a few extra options.

The `syslog_name` option gives the transport its own name in the log, so we easily verify which emails use it and can readily track down problems.

By setting `smtp_tls_security_level` to *secure*, we're telling Postfix to fully validate the external MTA's X.509 certificate.

Integrate mta-sts-daemon into this transport with `smtp_tls_policy_maps`. The `socketmap` keyword tells Postfix this is a socket, not a file. It's a network socket, on **localhost** port 8461. Postfix will identify itself by the name *postfix*.

Now go to the transport map, `/etc/postfix/transport`, and direct recipient domains to that transport.

```
outlook.com  mta-sts:
```

Run `postmap /etc/postfix/transport`. Restart Postfix. Send a test message. The log should show the email using that transport. If you have TLS logging enabled, you'll also get a note that the X.509 certificate was validated.

What about destinations that you want to use MTA-STS for, but also send slowly? If everyone you trickle mail to also supports MTA-STS, add the `smtp_tls_security_level` and `smtp_tls_policy_maps` to that transport. Otherwise, create a new transport that combines the two.

You're now validating MTA-STS, but what about reporting? The primary entities that use the protocol are the large providers. They have their own monitoring systems, and not only are they uninterested in daily TLS-RPT messages, they'd probably classify them as spam. They're the Email Empire. TLS (and every other protocol) works the way they declare they work, and you are by definition wrong. That's why there's no open-source MTA-STS reporting implementation.

Postfix and Dovecot have far more features than could be covered in a book this size, but you now have a solid knowledge base to build on. Both projects have thorough documentation, and will guide you through adding other features you might need.

Good luck.

Afterword: Living Independent

The huge mail providers can crush you at any time. The best ways to survive running your own email is to start slow, obey their rules, and send messages that people want to receive.

If you stand up a new mail system and immediately start spewing messages across the Internet, you will look suspicious. The key to successfully launching a new mail system is to launch it slowly. Start by sending a few messages to people you know. Let the Email Empire acclimate to your existence. If you've followed along in this book, you've already sent a handful of emails from your new server to big provider accounts that you control, to demonstrate that you have DMARC, DKIM, and SPF. It's a start. Begin doing your routine correspondence through your new server. If you're in any doubt, trickle emails to big providers. If you're migrating from one IP address to another, have your old MTA relay a part of its mail load through your new server. Once the big carriers and your peers accept that you're following best practices, demonstrate that you'll keep following those practices.

If you want to learn more about email, I strongly recommend the Mail Operators' List (`https://www.mailop.org`). The mailing list archive is a treasure hoard of experience.

If you want to maintain deliverability to the big providers, you must send messages that people want to read. Maybe you're writing to interesting people to see if they want to be guests on your podcast, but if the recipients keep throwing your messages into the spam bucket, the big providers will eventually decide that they don't want to accept your email. Your messages might be sincere, and technologically verifiable as authentic, but if people keep saying they're spam the big carriers will treat you as such.

And always remember: in email, citizenship is *everything*. The modern Internet was built by companies, but companies run by people who believed in connection and cooperation. People worked together so that we could inexpensively share messages across the world in minutes. *We* built this. *We* turned SMTP into a protocol that tied communities together. There's no reason to give it all to giant companies.

Whatever you do, never surrender the protocols. Run your own mail server.

Sponsors

These lovely folks supported me through writing this book. I am sincerely touched by their support, especially when the book took longer than expected. My gratitude to you all.

If you'd like to sponsor a book, you can sign up for my sponsor announcement mailing list at https://mwl.io/. I only send mail to that list when I open a new sponsorship, and a reminder right before I close one.

My print sponsors were, in date order: Rogier Krieger, Lucas Raab, Craig Maloney, Bob Eager, Paul Anthony Stanton, Carsten Strotmann, Philip Jocks, Bernard Lezaire, Reinis Martinsons, Timothy Olsen, Darryn Nicol, Chris Dunbar, Amolith, Patrick Mahan, Jeremy Self, Xavier Belanger, William Allaire, David Hansen, Niall Navin, Carl Rigney, tanamar corporation, Henrik Kramselund, Nicholas Brenckle, Patrick Bucher, Sean McBride, James Brown, Eric LeBlanc, John W. O'Brien, Jonathon Fletcher, Russell Folk, Bob Proulx, Ilias Vrachnis, Jet Spear, Paul Gatling, David Maxwell, Ray Percival, Murray Bollinger, Bruno Beaufils, Jens Grassel, Chris Wojtyna, Brooks Davis, Trix Farrar, Matti Anja, Jeff Frasca, Chris Horton, Ed Nicholson, Daniel Clemeth Bjerkeland, Neil Roza, Manuel Solis Aguero, Ed Silva, Maurice Kaag, Jeremy Bryant, Daniel Uber, Joseph Brothers, Annie Herrmann, 4censord, Bernd Kohler, Cameron Katri, Andrew Cornwall, Jacob S. Gordon, Nick Doyle, Florian Limberger, Brad Heightman, Finn Häse, Stephan Lohse, Scott Blaydes, Seth Hanford, Daniel Parriott, Lutz Weber, Bob Beck, Clark Shishido, Jon Thorson, Shawn O'Shea, Florent Charton, Mark Moellering, Stephen Kellat, Mohammad Noureldin, Anthony Carpenter, Lucas Raab, Jim Pingle, William Allaire, Darren VanBuren, Joseph Holsten, Michael Bryant, Marek Krzywdziński, Joachim Ernst, Georg Kilzer, Luis Viant, Roman Obukhivskyi, Uwe Trenkner, Cal Ledsham, Patrizia Kaye, and Dave Cottlehuber.

Index